W9-BKK-344

BIBLICAL LITERACY

BIBLICAL LITERACY

The Essential Bible Stories

Everyone Needs to Know

TIMOTHY BEAL

HarperOne
An Imprint of HarperCollinsPublishers

HarperOne

HarperCollins books may be purchased for educational, business, or sales promotional use. For information please write: Special Markets Department, HarperCollins Publishers, 10 East 53rd Street, New York, NY 10022.

HarperCollins Web site: http://www.harpercollins.com

HarperCollins®, 🏭®, and HarperOne™
are trademarks of HarperCollins Publishers

FIRST EDITION
Designed by Level C

Library of Congress Cataloging-in-Publication Data is available upon request.

ISBN 978–0–06–171862–5

09 10 11 12 13 RRD (H) 10 9 8 7 6 5 4 3 2 1

For Clover Reuter Beal

Contents

How to Read the Bible Like President Obama—or Bob Dylan

When Frederick Douglass's master discovered that his wife, Mistress Sophie, was teaching this eight-year-old slave to read the Bible, he sternly forbade her to do so again. "If he learns to read the Bible it will ever unfit him to be a slave," he said, and in no time "he'll be running away with himself." This, the renowned abolitionist Douglass later reflected, was the first antislavery lecture he had ever heard, and it inspired him to do anything he could to read more of the Bible. He recalls zealously gathering scattered pages of it from the gutters of Baltimore streets, carefully washing, drying, and collating them to read in secret. He had begun to realize what Master Hugh (and no doubt Mistress Sophie) knew—that there was power, indeed subversive, revolutionary power, in reading and interpreting the Bible for oneself, and that the institution of slavery in fact depended on controlling biblical literacy—who can read the Bible when and how. Many years later he wrote, "Let the reader reflect upon the fact, that, in this Christian country, men and women are hiding from professors of religion, in barns, in the woods and fields, in order to learn to read the *Holy Bible*." Hiding, that is, from those who claim authority to say what it means, to control its interpretation. The Bible can look dangerously different when you read it on your own.

LEAVES IN THE GUTTER

Not many of us today can imagine ourselves sifting through gutter garbage for a handful of filthy loose leaves from a discarded Bible. Most of us would avert our eyes and keep walking. There are, after all, plenty of brand-new Bibles available free to anyone who wants one. The Gideons hand them out by the hundreds of millions per year, and just about any church you happen into will be happy to comp you one.

But I think the reasons for our lack of biblical interest go a little deeper. For one, many have come to think that the Bible is irrelevant to contemporary culture. What could this ancient collection of stories, poems, and laws, written thousands of years ago in foreign tongues in faraway lands, possibly have to offer us today? Leave it in the pew, where it belongs. I've learned over fifteen years as a professor of biblical literature that its cultural relevance outside religion no longer goes without saying. In fact, its irrelevance is usually presumed.

In class the other day, we were discussing the current financial fiasco, asking where the prophetic voices were, those who had the courage to address the ugliest dimensions of the matter (such as the injustice of predatory lending that so many banks were practicing), even when speaking out might make them unpopular and their words unpublishable. I asked my students to take a look at the second chapter of the prophet Micah for a potential model.

"Where do we find that?" someone asked.

"In a Bible," I suggested.

Another followed up, "Do you actually think we just have Bibles sitting around our dorms?"

Others nodded, amazed that I seemed to be imagining that a Bible would be anywhere near any of them or that they would deem it remotely relevant to their lives, in or out of the classroom. They had a point. How foolishly presumptuous of me. The cultural relevance of the Bible is not a given. Many, maybe most, would say that ours is a postbiblical age.

Which makes rediscovery all the more exciting and surprising. Take Micah, for example. The relevance of this ancient prophet's unmeasured, passionate words to our current crisis is downright uncanny. He paints a picture of the financial movers and shakers of his time lying in bed at night dreaming up schemes to take advantage of the poor and weak and then waking up in the morning to carry them out, "because it is in their power." Because they can get away with it. Sound familiar? Read on:

They covet fields, and seize them;
    houses, and take them away;
they oppress householder and house,

> people and their inheritance. . . .
> "Do not preach"—thus they preach—
> "one should not preach of such things;
> disgrace will not overtake us." (2:2, 6)

Micah was railing against the financiers of ancient Israel over twenty-five hundred years ago, but his words ring ominously true today. More than that, a passage like this makes us ask broader, deeper questions about our society. Where are the prophetic voices today? How do we make space for them, even when they make us squirm? Why do we so often prefer comfort to truth, even at our own peril?

The Bible is far from culturally irrelevant. Indeed, I would argue that you can't be culturally literate without being at least basically familiar with biblical literature. Biblical literacy is a prerequisite for cultural literacy. The Bible is quoted, referenced, and alluded to by thousands of great writers, orators, composers, and artists in tens of thousands of classic cultural works. The vast majority of English authors over the centuries have presumed that their readers were biblically literate. One would be hard-pressed to find a reading list in any introductory high-school or college English literature course that doesn't include multiple biblical references. In works from Beowulf and Chaucer to Milton and Shakespeare, to Jane Austen and Bram Stoker, to Toni Morrison and Neil Gaiman, the Bible continues to resonate deeply—for those, that is, who have eyes to see and ears to hear it.

The same holds true for art and music. How much depth and complexity do we miss when beholding Rembrandt's *The Blinding of Samson* or listening to blues legend Blind Willie Johnson's "If I Had My Way I'd Tear the Building Down" without knowing the biblical story of Samson? What is lost when we hear the sublime word paintings of Haydn's *Creation* oratorio without knowing what words he's painting?

So too in everyday speech and popular culture. How many times have you heard someone say something's just a "drop in the bucket" (Isaiah 40:15) or that so-and-so is "the apple of my eye" (Deuteronomy 32:10) or "a man after his own heart" (1 Samuel 13:14)? Or that there's a "season for everything" (Ecclesiastes 3:1), a time to "eat, drink, and be merry" (Luke 12:19) and, we hope, soon a time to "turn swords into plowshares" (Isaiah 2:4) in this world of "wars and rumors of wars" (Matthew 24:6)? "Out of the mouths of babes" (Psalm 8:2), as they say. Or maybe you're watching Sunday night television and Marge Simpson sidles up to Homer and says, "I could be the Rachel to your Jacob" (Genesis 29), while Bart calls his grandfather Methuselah (Genesis 5:27). One newspaper editorialist declares that the United States is "reaping the whirlwind" (Hosea 8:7) of past foreign policy decisions in the Middle East, while another says that "the writing is on the wall" (Daniel 5). The Band sings about "forbidden fruit" (Genesis 3), while Bob Marley laments, "How long shall they kill our prophets?" (Matthew 23:37). Grandpa complains about abuses by the "powers that be" (Romans 13:1), while Grandma counters that it's just "sour grapes" (Ezekiel 18:2) because he voted for the other guy.

At the same time, the biblical idiom shapes our social and political lives, just as it has for centuries. The narrative of liberation from bondage in the book of Exodus and the prophetic calls for justice against oppressive regimes course between the lines of the Declaration of Independence of the United States and reverberate in the rhetoric of civil rights movements. It's impossible to understand either side of the conflict over slavery, for example, without understanding the ways each interpreted the Bible. Biblical interpretation has also been a site of struggle for women's rights. As activist Angelina Emily Grimké put it, "My Dictionary is the Bible; my standard authors, prophets and apostles." No accident that she and her sister were teachers and mentors of Elizabeth Cady Stanton, leader of the suffragist movement and editor of *The Woman's Bible,* a series of commentaries on each of the books of the Bible by women writers and scholars.

The compelling power of Martin Luther King Jr.'s famous letter from Birmingham City Jail to moderate white pastors is at least half missed when we don't recognize that it was modeled on letters from the apostle Paul to his own sometime opponents within the early Jesus movement. In fact, all of King's speeches and writings are steeped in the evocative imagery and prophetic pathos of the Bible. When, at a crescendo in his "I Have a Dream" speech, he declared that we must not be satisfied until "justice rolls down like waters, and righteousness like a mighty stream," he was channeling the prophet Amos (5:24). Many assume that those are King's own words. And they are, insofar as he made them his own. Yet when we know the prophetic tradition that stands behind them, we begin to fathom the deeper and wider biblical pool of imagination in which King found vision and inspiration.

Biblical literature continues to find its way into local, national, and international politics today. Political underdogs pump themselves up by describing themselves as David, the apple of God's eye, facing off against the ungodly Philistine giant Goliath. Adam and Eve are summoned to courtrooms and cited in op-ed columns as witnesses in arguments both for and against gay marriage and civil unions. Tensions between Israel and Palestine are framed by biblical stories about the Israelite conquest of the Promised Land and its indigenous inhabitants, the Canaanites. And more than a few Americans believe that it's no coincidence that Iraq is located in the former land of Babylon, that great empire that destroyed the First Temple in Jerusalem and, in the book of Revelation, represents the diabolical force of evil in the world. All that is to say that our cultural, social, and political imaginations are fueled by biblical stories, songs, and prophetic visions, so much so that one cannot be culturally literate without being biblically literate.

FINDING INSPIRATION

For some, perhaps, the motivation to *avoid* cultural illiteracy is reason enough to spend some time becoming biblically literate. Who wants to look dumb at a dinner party or between acts at a Shakespearean play? But I believe there's a deeper, more positive reason to get to know the Bible— it is *inspiring*. I mean that in the broadest sense and without any necessary reference to the Third Person of the Trinity. The Bible engenders creative thought and action. It generates new meanings, new ways of seeing ourselves and our world. Maybe that's why Ronald Reagan said that if he were shipwrecked on a desert island and could have only one book to read for the rest of his life, he'd choose the Bible. It is the kind of literature you keep reading and rereading in relation to new situations.

That is why Bob Marley could see the Jamaican struggle for liberation, political and spiritual, as a new Exodus from a new Pharaoh. And why Ozzy Osborne in the early Black Sabbath song "Warpigs" sounds so much like the biblical prophet Jeremiah. And why the San Diego punk band Drive Like Jehu named themselves after an upstart biblical king about whom it was reported, "It looks like the driving of Jehu son of Nimshi; for he drives like a maniac" (2 Kings 9:20). It's also why Leonard Cohen could turn his retelling of the story of Abraham's near sacrifice of his son Isaac (Genesis 22) into an antiwar song. And why Bob Dylan could retell the same story, out on Highway 61, in a completely different way that is both funny and chilling:

> Well, God said to Abraham, "Kill me a son."
> Abe says, "Man, you must be puttin' me on."
> God say, "No." Abe say, "What?"
> God said, "You can do what you want, Abe, but
> the next time you see me comin' you better run."
> Well, Abe says, "Where do you want this killin' done?"
> God says, "Out on Highway 61."

Highway 61 is a place where refugees of the welfare system go to die, where crooks sell defective goods, where promoters turn the next world war into a spectator event—and where fathers are driven to sacrifice their children in order to save their own hides.

The stories and poetry of the Bible are alive, plastic, adaptive. They invite, and even sometimes provoke, creative rereadings and remakings on new horizons of meaning. If there's anything that's clear from two millennia of biblical interpretation, it's that its stories are not reducible to obvious points or simple moral lessons. They have evoked many very different interpretations. Indeed, that's what has given them such amazing staying power.

Frederick Douglass understood this. So did his debate partner Abraham Lincoln. And so does today's most acclaimed orator, Barack Obama. Indeed, his openness to the power of biblical language to inspire and move allowed him to do something truly remarkable in his 2009 inaugural address. I'm not talking about how he hoped it up one more time and got us all believing in him. I'm talking about how he was able to suggest, ever so subtly, that what can guide us through tough times and get us beyond political partisanship might be, of all things, love. Yes, love. Not exactly a common theme in presidential speeches. Did you hear it? It was easy enough to miss. "We remain a young nation," he declared, "but in the words of Scripture, the time has come to set aside childish things." That is a quotation from chapter 13 of Paul's first New Testament letter to the community in Corinth, a community that was suffering from tensions and divisions. Paul called them to overcome their childish partisanship through *love*. Love, Paul says, is "patient and kind," never "envious or boastful or arrogant or rude. It does not insist on its own way; it is not irritable or resentful; it does not rejoice in wrongdoing, but rejoices in the truth. It bears all things, believes all things, hopes all things, endures all things." He concludes, "Faith, hope, and love abide, these three; and the greatest of these is love." It would probably have been weird for President Obama to talk explicitly about love, but the biblical idiom allowed him to say it between the lines.

Later in the ceremony, in her inaugural poem, "Praise Song for the Day," Elizabeth Alexander alluded to the very same biblical passage, this time speaking more openly about love's greatness. She wondered, "What if the mightiest word is love?" In the lines that follow, the poem describes what kind of love she means in words that are her own and yet reminiscent of Paul's own writing on love. It is a love that reaches well beyond marriage, family, and even nation; a "love that casts a widening pool of light, with no need to pre-empt grievance." With this perhaps mightiest of all words still echoing, she declared,

> In today's sharp sparkle, this winter air,
> any thing can be made, any sentence begun.

And begun in the biblical pool of imagination.

AND HOW

Let's say you're convinced. You agree that the Bible is anything but culturally irrelevant. You agree that you need to get to know it better. More important, you want to. Whether you're religious, irreligious, or antireligious, you can see that it might even be inspiring. The trouble is that you're not sure where to start and how to proceed. That's perfectly understandable. Biblical literacy is about not only *what*, but also *how*. And to many readers the Bible seems inaccessible. They feel unauthorized to read and interpret biblical literature for themselves. Somehow they've come to see the Bible as a book "closed" to them and "open" to other, more biblically devout people who hold the keys to understanding it.

If you feel that way, take heart. Ask yourself where that feeling came from. Is it not the same feeling that Frederick Douglass himself inherited and had to overcome? Like him, you have begun to see that there's power in reading the Bible for yourself. That's why others want to control it, as Master Hugh well understood. And so did Douglass's fellow slaves who snuck a Bible out into the woods to read it on their own, away from professors of religion.

Reading the Bible is not about getting it right. It's about making meaning from it. It's up to you. I truly believe that the main reason most people haven't read the Bible is that they are worried that they'll read it wrongly. They'll raise a taboo question or interpret it in some heretical way, maybe without even knowing it. But there is no right way to read and interpret the Bible, as biblically inspired poets from Bob Dylan to Elizabeth Alexander can attest. And there's no experience necessary. In fact, I often find that the students who come into my classes without ever having cracked open a Bible before are the ones who raise some of the most interesting questions about it and have the most fascinating insights into it.

With that in mind, I see my role in this book as guide rather than interpreter. I want to welcome you into the fascinating world of biblical literature, equip you with the basic information you need to explore it for yourself, and encourage you to trust your own good instincts and insights. What is important here is not to gain a certain orthodox understanding of these texts, but simply to get into them, to see whatever you see from your own unique perspective, and to have fun.

PART 1

The Hebrew Bible

Introduction

The Hebrew Bible, also known as the Old Testament, is both strange and familiar. In a lot of ways, it could hardly be stranger. It comes to us from a distant time, well over two millennia ago, and from a distant place, the ancient Near East. Its original language, ancient Hebrew, is as foreign to most of us as Chinese. It's not part of the Indo-European language family. In fact, it was no one's lingua franca for nearly two thousand years, until it was reinvented as modern Hebrew in the late nineteenth century. If the Hebrew Bible were "all Greek to me," it'd be way less strange. It is the most non-Western member of the Western canon of great literature.

Even in translation, the contents of the Hebrew Bible often ring very strangely in our ears. Its main characters often seem, at least on first read, disturbingly amoral, some downright pathological. Fratricide, polygamy, drunkenness, incest, rape, and child sacrifice are just a small sampling of what you can find in the first twenty or so pages. The biblical God too is disconcertingly unpredictable, a figure of great pathos who can swing from profound compassion to passionate rage in a few lines. Greek philosophical terms like "omnipotent," "omnipresent," and "omniscient" make no sense here. And where else in your typical library or bookstore can you find detailed directions for how to ritually slaughter, drain, dress out, and burn a bull?

Even the way the Hebrew Bible tells its stories seems weird to us. It's nothing like our most familiar story form, the novel. The biggest difference is its economy of words. It offers precious little description of people, places, and things. Verbs are rarely modified with adverbs. Figurative language is almost never used. Perhaps most significant, windows into the thoughts and feelings of characters in the stories are extremely few and far between. And the narrator almost never passes judgment on them. Action is decisive, dialogue is terse, motives are seldom explicit, and any possible moral of the story is left in question. All that is to say the Hebrew Bible is strange, like nothing else we read.

But it's also, at the same time, entirely familiar—indeed, the most familiar of all Western literature. After all, it makes up almost 80 percent of the Christian Bible, which is, hands down, the literary bestseller of all time. It was the first major book of modern print culture, and more copies of it have been published in more editions than any other. It was the primary textbook for learning how to read and write for centuries. It's everywhere.

Although the way it tells stories seems strange to us novel readers and movie watchers, the stories themselves are not. Their themes of love, lust, faith, murder, betrayal, fear, and hope continue to speak to us today. Indeed, their characters are unrivaled in popularity: Adam and Eve in the Garden of Eden, Cain and Abel, Noah during the flood, Abraham and Sarah and Hagar, Isaac and Ishmael, Joseph wearing his coat of many colors, Moses leading the Exodus, Ruth, King David and Bathsheba, King Solomon and the Queen of Sheba, Elijah, Jezebel, Esther, Job, Daniel in the lions' den, Jonah in the whale, and on and on. Few stories are more familiar, even today.

As you find your way into these fascinating stories, try to be open to *both* their strangeness and their familiarity. On the one hand, make room for the unusual, unexpected, and even bizarre. Look to be surprised. Allow yourself to respond sometimes with an honest "huh, what?" On the other hand, seek out points of connection with the stories and their characters. In what ways do they reflect ideas and experiences that you can relate to? Remember the dictum of the Roman playwright Terrence: "I am human, so nothing human is alien to me."

Three more words of advice before you begin. First, remember that the Hebrew Bible didn't drop down from the sky in the form we now have it. This isn't the place to explore its literary history from its earliest beginnings more than three thousand years ago to its latest translations and publications in modern English. Still, we need to keep in mind that the story of its development is long and complicated, involving countless hands over thousands of years, right up to this day. The Bible's pasts are always present, even if only between the lines and even if we are not fully aware of them.

Second, keep in mind that the Bible is not a book. Granted, your typical Bible sure does look like a book. And granted, "the Bible" literally means "the Book." But it's not a book in the way we usually think of books. We think of a book as having a beginning, middle, and end. You start on the first page and finish on the last. Not so with the Hebrew Bible, which is not a single narrative, but a diverse collection of stories, poetry, and other writings that don't all come together into a single, book-length story. We also think of a book as having a single author and point of view. Not so the Hebrew Bible. It is, rather, a collection of many different writings reflecting a wide range of points of view and social contexts. Add to that the fact that there are more than thirty very different English translations available today in more editions than Moses could shake his rod at, and you get the picture. It's not a book.

Finally, mind the gaps. Hebrew biblical stories are so economical, so condensed, that they leave many gaps. What's left unsaid is as significant as what's said. This is by design. It's part of the literary craft. The Hebrew Bible tells its stories not so much to make a point, pass a judgment, or teach a moral as to provoke your imagination. What was she thinking? What was he feeling? What did he look like? What motivated her to do that? As you read, pay attention to what the story does *not* show or say. What remains hidden? What questions are you left with? These are your entry points into the fascinating worlds behind these stories.

Torah

"LET THERE BE LIGHT"

Words are powerful; they shape our world and make it meaningful. Here, in the first words of Genesis, the first book of the Torah, the world is literally spoken into being: "Let there be light." The Hebrew is even more direct: *yehi 'or,* "it's light." And there was light. And so it begins, a world of words whose meanings are as rich as they are open to interpretation.

The world that emerges in this story is one of order and symmetry, beauty and goodness. The work of creation crescendos with humankind, male and female, made in the divine image. Not surprising, then, that this story is the cornerstone for proponents of "intelligent design" in the ongoing evolution-versus-creationism debates. Others read it as poetic rather than scientific truth, a parable of the human situation—a position supported by the fact that a second, different creation story follows this one. That the humans are given almost godlike dominion over the rest of creation has also encouraged certain environmental policies that see the earth as a resource: a "gift" or "bounty" whose benefits we are obliged to use maximally.

As you read, pay attention to the repetition of words and phrases. These help construct a symmetry that builds throughout the story. Also note those places where patterns of repetition are interrupted. What do they signal?

GENESIS 1:1–2:4

In the beginning when God created the heavens and the earth, the earth was a formless void and darkness covered the face of the deep, while a wind from God swept over the face of the waters. Then God said, "Let there be light"; and there was light. And God saw that the light was good; and God separated the light from the darkness. God called the light Day, and the darkness he called Night. And there was evening and there was morning, the first day.

And God said, "Let there be a dome in the midst of the waters, and let it separate the waters from the waters." So God made the dome and separated the waters that were under the dome from the waters that were above the dome. And it was so. God called the dome Sky. And there was evening and there was morning, the second day.

One of the most celebrated examples of composer Franz Joseph Haydn's use of "word painting" is in his *Creation* oratorio (1798). Out of the sotto voce of its opening representation of primordial, unformed chaos, the first moment of creation, "and there was light," bursts forth in a fortissimo C-major chord.

And God said, "Let the waters under the sky be gathered together into one place, and let the dry land appear." And it was so. God called the dry land Earth, and the waters that were gathered together he called Seas. And God saw that it was good. Then God said, "Let the earth put forth vegetation: plants yielding seed, and fruit trees of every kind on earth that bear fruit with the seed in it." And it was so. The earth brought forth vegetation: plants yielding seed of every kind, and trees of every kind bearing fruit with the seed in it. And God saw that it was good. And there was evening and there was morning, the third day.

And God said, "Let there be lights in the dome of the sky to separate the day from the night; and let them be for signs and for seasons and for days and years, and let them be lights in the dome of the sky to give light upon the earth." And it was so. God made the two great lights—the greater light to rule the day and the lesser light to rule the night—and the stars. God set them in the dome of the sky to give light upon the earth, to rule over the day and over the night, and to separate the light from the darkness. And God saw that it was good. And there was evening and there was morning, the fourth day.

And God said, "Let the waters bring forth swarms of living creatures, and let birds fly above the earth across the dome of the sky." So God created the great sea monsters and every living creature that moves, of every kind, with which the waters swarm, and every winged bird of every kind. And God saw that it was good. God blessed them, saying, "Be fruitful and multiply and fill the waters in the seas, and let birds multiply on the earth." And there was evening and there was morning, the fifth day.

And God said, "Let the earth bring forth living creatures of every kind: cattle and creeping things and wild animals of the earth of every kind." And it was so. God made the wild animals of the earth of every kind, and the cattle of every kind, and everything that creeps upon the ground of every kind. And God saw that it was good.

Then God said, "Let us make humankind in our image, according to our likeness; and let them have dominion over the fish of the sea, and over the birds of the air, and over the cattle, and over all the wild animals of the earth, and over every creeping thing that creeps upon the earth."

The First Seven Days in the First Creation Story

1. Light from darkness (day and night)
2. Domes (heavens above and watery underworld below)
3. Earth and seas
4. Sun, moon, and stars
5. Birds and sea creatures
6. Animals and humans
7. God rests (the first Sabbath)

So God created humankind in his image,
in the image of God he created them;
male and female he created them.

God blessed them, and God said to them, "Be fruitful and multiply, and fill the earth and subdue it; and have dominion over the fish of the sea and over the birds of the air and over every living thing that moves upon the earth." God said, "See, I have given you every plant yielding seed that is upon the face of all the earth, and every tree with seed in its fruit; you shall have them for food. And to every beast of the earth, and to every bird of the air, and to everything that creeps on the earth, everything that has the breath of life, I have given every green plant for food." And it was so. God saw everything that he had made, and indeed, it was very good. And there was evening and there was morning, the sixth day.

Thus the heavens and the earth were finished, and all their multitude. And on the seventh day God finished the work that he had done, and he rested on the seventh day from all the work that he had done. So God blessed the seventh day and hallowed it, because on it God rested from all the work that he had done in creation.

These are the generations of the heavens and the earth when they were created.

"FLESH OF MY FLESH"

Where does desire come from? Where love? Here, in the second creation story, it seems to emerge from recognizing the other in oneself and oneself in the other. We begin with the creation of a single human being, formed from the earth (*ha'adam*, "the human," from *ha'adamah*, "the earth") and animated into a living being by divine breath. Later the human is divided into two individuals, male and female. Thus the first relationship is one of otherness and sameness, identity and difference.

As the Bible's first couple, Adam and Eve are no strangers to modern courtroom debates over same-sex unions. "God made Adam and Eve, not Adam and Steve," some say, while others question how appropriate this text is to the argument. Would this mean, for example, that remaining unmarried would also be against God's intended natural order for humanity?

The image of the human as divinely inspired dirt suggests that the relation of people to their environment is one of intimate connection rather than dominion. Not surprisingly, those environmental positions that emphasize interdependence start with this creation story rather than the first.

As you read, notice how different this mode of storytelling is from the previous one. Pay attention to the dynamics of likeness and difference, intimacy and distance in the relationships between the story's three main characters.

GENESIS 2:4-25

In the day that the LORD God made the earth and the heavens, when no plant of the field was yet in the earth and no herb of the field had yet sprung up—for the LORD God had not caused it to rain upon the earth, and there was no one to till the ground; but a stream would rise from the earth, and water the whole face of the ground—then the LORD God formed man from the dust of the ground, and breathed into his nostrils the breath of life; and the man became a living being. And the LORD God planted a garden in Eden, in the east; and there he put the man whom he had formed. Out of the ground the LORD God made to grow every tree that is pleasant to the sight and good for food, the tree of life also in the midst of the garden, and the tree of the knowledge of good and evil.

A river flows out of Eden to water the garden, and from there it divides and becomes four branches. The name of the first is Pishon; it is the one that flows around the whole land of Havilah, where there is gold; and the gold of that land is good; bdellium and onyx stone are there. The name of the second river is Gihon; it is the one that flows around the whole land of Cush. The name of the third river is Tigris, which flows east of Assyria. And the fourth river is the Euphrates.

The LORD God took the man and put him in the garden of Eden to till it and keep it. And the LORD God commanded the man, "You may freely eat of every tree of the garden; but of the tree of the knowledge of good and evil you shall not eat, for in the day that you eat of it you shall die."

In Plato's *Symposium,* Aristophanes offers a somewhat similar story of the birth of desire. Human beings, he recounts, were originally whole and complete in themselves. Then Zeus cut these "circle people" in half. Love, then, is the desire to find one's other half and thereby become complete again. In the Bible, the Song of Songs may be read as a "return to the garden," as the two lovers express their desire to be made whole through each other.

Then the LORD God said, "It is not good that the man should be alone; I will make him a helper as his partner." So out of the ground the LORD God formed every animal of the field and every bird of the air, and brought them to the man to see what he would call them; and whatever the man called every living creature, that was its name. The man gave names to all cattle, and to the birds of the air, and to every animal of the field; but for the man there was not found a helper as his partner. So the LORD God caused a deep sleep to fall upon the man, and he slept; then he took one of his ribs and closed up its place with flesh. And the rib that the LORD God had taken from the man he made into a woman and brought her to the man. Then the man said,

> "This at last is bone of my bones
>   and flesh of my flesh;
> this one shall be called Woman,
>   for out of Man this one was taken."

Therefore a man leaves his father and his mother and clings to his wife, and they become one flesh. And the man and his wife were both naked, and were not ashamed.

FORBIDDEN FRUIT

Naked and not ashamed. That's where we just left Adam and Eve. But shame soon enters the story. So do clothes. So does wisdom. And so does a one-way ticket out of paradise. Would we have it any other way?

Throughout Western culture, this story has generated mixed judgments about Eve. Many have seen her decision to eat from the Tree of Knowledge as the original sin. Others see it as the original act of curiosity, the desire to know. To the former, she is the cause of "the Fall," encouraging many men since to blame women for all their woes. To the latter, she is the mother of wisdom.

Still others wonder if we're reading altogether too much into it. Maybe it's simply a just-so story that explains why childbirth hurts, why we have to work to eat, and why we fear snakes. And, of course, why we wear clothes.

Some questions worth asking while you read: Does the serpent (never called Satan) lie? Where is Adam during Eve's conversation with the serpent? Why doesn't Adam protest when Eve offers him the fruit? Why did God put the tree there in the first place?

GENESIS 3:1–24

Now the serpent was more crafty than any other wild animal that the LORD God had made. He said to the woman, "Did God say, 'You shall not eat from any tree in the garden'?" The woman said to the serpent, "We may eat of the fruit of the trees in the garden; but God said, 'You shall not eat of the fruit of the tree that is in the middle of the garden, nor shall you touch it, or you shall die.'" But the serpent said to the woman, "You will not die; for God knows that when you eat of it your eyes will be opened, and you will be like God, knowing good and evil." So when the woman saw that the tree was good for food, and that it was a delight to the eyes, and that the tree was to be desired to make one wise, she took of its fruit and ate; and she also gave some to her husband, who was with her, and he ate. Then the eyes of both were opened, and they

> If the first woman God ever made was strong enough to turn the world upside down all alone, these women together ought to be able to turn back, and get it right side up again!
>
> —Sojourner Truth

knew that they were naked; and they sewed fig leaves together and made loincloths for themselves.

They heard the sound of the LORD God walking in the garden at the time of the evening breeze, and the man and his wife hid themselves from the presence of the LORD God among the trees of the garden. But the LORD God called to the man, and said to him, "Where are you?" He said, "I heard the sound of you in the garden, and I was afraid, because I was naked; and I hid myself." He said, "Who told you that you were naked? Have you eaten from the tree of which I commanded you not to eat?" The man said, "The woman whom you gave to be with me, she gave me fruit from the tree, and I ate." Then the LORD God said to the woman, "What is this that you have done?" The woman said, "The serpent tricked me, and I ate." The LORD God said to the serpent,

"Because you have done this,
    cursed are you among all animals
    and among all wild creatures;
upon your belly you shall go,
    and dust you shall eat
    all the days of your life.
I will put enmity between you and the woman,
    and between your offspring and hers;
he will strike your head,
    and you will strike his heel."

To the woman he said,

"I will greatly increase your pangs in childbearing;
    in pain you shall bring forth children,
yet your desire shall be for your husband,
    and he shall rule over you."

And to the man he said,

"Because you have listened to the voice of your wife,
    and have eaten of the tree
about which I commanded you,
    'You shall not eat of it,'
cursed is the ground because of you;
    in toil you shall eat of it all the days of your life;
thorns and thistles it shall bring forth for you;
    and you shall eat the plants of the field.
By the sweat of your face
    you shall eat bread
until you return to the ground,
    for out of it you were taken;
you are dust,
    and to dust you shall return."

The man named his wife Eve, because she was the mother of all living. And the Lord God made garments of skins for the man and for his wife, and clothed them.

Then the LORD God said, "See, the man has become like one of us, knowing good and evil; and now, he might reach out his hand and take also from the tree of life, and eat, and live forever"—therefore the LORD God sent him forth from the garden of Eden, to till the ground from which he was taken. He drove out the man; and at the east of the garden of Eden he placed the cherubim, and a sword flaming and turning to guard the way to the tree of life.

> **And, cowering in darkness and abject, he prayed mutely to his guardian angel to drive away with his sword the demon that was whispering to his brain.**
>
> —Stephen, struggling with sexual temptation, in James Joyce's *A Portrait of the Artist as a Young Man*

EAST OF EDEN

Relationships between brothers are always complicated. And it never helps when one seems to get all the breaks. It's been known to drive a young man to murder, especially when mom and dad are out of the picture, doing who knows what. The first family couldn't make it one generation without things going that far. And so we meet our first brooding, tormented hero and original outlaw, Cain.

Cain was the perfect biblical part for the popular icon of teen angst, James Dean, in *East of Eden.* But what makes that movie something more than a vehicle for this rising dark star is John Steinbeck's insightful use of the biblical story in the novel on which the movie was based. He saw Cain's story as a powerfully concentrated version of the universal human story: "Humans are caught—in their lives, in their thoughts, in their hungers and ambitions, in their avarice and cruelty, and in their kindness and generosity too—in a net of good and evil." We are never destined to evil or good; determinism and free will are both at work.

Do you agree? Is Cain free to act other than he does? With so few windows into the emotions and moral struggles of our main character, how can we know? Perhaps that is part of what draws us to him.

GENESIS 4:1-16

Now the man knew his wife Eve, and she conceived and bore Cain, saying, "I have produced a man with the help of the LORD." Next she bore his brother Abel. Now Abel was a keeper of sheep, and Cain a tiller of the ground. In the course of time Cain brought to the LORD an offering of the fruit of the ground, and Abel for his part brought of the firstlings of his flock, their fat portions. And the LORD had regard for Abel and his offering, but for Cain and his offering he had no regard. So Cain was very angry, and his countenance fell. The LORD said to Cain, "Why are you angry, and why has your countenance fallen? If you do well, will you not be accepted? And if you do not do well, sin is lurking at the door; its desire is for you, but you must master it."

> **[He] sluiced out his innocent soul through streams of blood:**
> **Which blood, like sacrificing Abel's, cries**
> **Even from the tongueless caverns of the earth**
> **To me for justice, and rough chastisement.**
> —William Shakespeare, *Richard II*

Cain said to his brother Abel, "Let us go out to the field." And when they were in the field, Cain rose up against his brother Abel, and killed him. Then the LORD said to Cain, "Where is your brother Abel?" He said, "I do not know; am I my brother's keeper?" And the LORD said, "What have you done? Listen; your brother's blood is crying out to me from the ground! And now you are cursed from the ground, which has opened its mouth to receive your brother's blood from your hand. When you

> **I am not my brother's keeper.**
> —James Dean, as Cal, moving in and out of the picture on a swing in Elia Kazan's *East of Eden*

till the ground, it will no longer yield to you its strength; you will be a fugitive and a wanderer on the earth." Cain said to the LORD, "My punishment is greater than I can bear! Today you have driven me away from the soil, and I shall be hidden from your face; I shall be a fugitive and a wanderer on the earth, and anyone who meets me may kill me." Then the LORD said to him, "Not so! Whoever kills Cain will suffer a sevenfold vengeance." And the LORD put a mark on Cain, so that no one who came upon him would kill him. Then Cain went away from the presence of the LORD, and settled in the land of Nod, east of Eden.

THE FLOOD

Whether making a soufflé, writing a research paper, or parenting, we've all felt at times like scrapping our work in progress and starting over. The biblical story of the flood is about the potential disaster of acting on that desire. It begins with disgust at the rottenness of things as they are, and it ends with regret for thinking it could ever be otherwise.

Yet the fantasy still holds water. Perhaps that's because so many of us identify with Noah and his tiny arkful of survivors rather than the drowning masses. Like Robert De Niro's character, Travis Bickle, in Martin Scorcese's 1976 film, *Taxi Driver,* we like to see ourselves as the lone righteous one, surrounded by a lot of fools and criminals, waiting for the apocalyptic flood waters to rise and wash the world clean again. As you read, ask whether the story encourages such fantasies.

GENESIS 6:11–22; 7:11–9:17

Now the earth was corrupt in God's sight, and the earth was filled with violence. And God saw that the earth was corrupt; for all flesh had corrupted its ways upon the earth. And God said to Noah, "I have determined to make an end of all flesh, for the earth is filled with violence because of them; now I am going to destroy them along with the earth. Make yourself an ark of cypress wood; make rooms in the ark, and cover it inside and out with pitch. This is how you are to make it: the length of the ark three hundred cubits, its width fifty cubits, and its height thirty cubits. Make a roof for the ark, and finish it to a cubit above; and put the door of the ark in its side; make it with lower, second, and third decks. For my part, I am going to bring a flood of waters on the earth, to destroy from under heaven all flesh in which is the breath of life; everything that is on the earth shall die. But I will establish my covenant with you; and you shall come into the ark, you, your sons, your wife, and your sons' wives with you. And of every living thing, of all flesh, you shall bring two of every kind into the ark, to keep them alive with you; they shall be male and female. Of the birds according to their kinds, and of the animals according to their kinds, of every creeping thing of the ground according to its kind, two of every kind shall come in to you, to keep them alive. Also take with you every kind of food that is eaten, and store it up; and it shall serve as food for you and for them." Noah did this; he did all that God commanded him.

. . . In the six hundredth year of Noah's life, in the second month, on the seventeenth day of the month, on that day all the fountains of the great deep burst forth, and the windows of the heavens were opened. The rain fell on the earth forty days and forty nights. On the very same day Noah with his sons, Shem and Ham and Japheth, and Noah's wife and the three wives of his sons entered the ark, they and every wild animal of every kind, and all domestic animals of every kind, and every creeping thing that creeps on the earth, and every bird of every kind—every bird, every winged creature. They went into the ark with Noah, two and two of all flesh in which there was the breath of life. And those that entered, male and female of all flesh, went in as God had commanded him; and the LORD shut him in.

The flood continued forty days on the earth; and the waters increased, and bore up the ark, and it rose high above the earth. The waters swelled and increased greatly on the earth; and the ark floated on the face of the waters. The waters swelled so mightily on the earth that all the high mountains under the whole heaven were covered; the waters swelled above the mountains, covering them fifteen cubits deep. And all flesh died that moved on the earth, birds, domestic animals, wild animals, all swarming creatures that swarm on the earth, and all human beings; everything on dry land in whose nostrils was the breath of life died. He blotted out every living thing that was on the face of the ground, human beings and animals and creeping things and birds of the air; they were blotted out from the earth. Only Noah was left, and those

---

All the animals come out at night—whores, skunk pussies, buggers, queens, fairies, dopers, junkies, sick, venal. Someday a real rain will come and wash all this scum off the streets.

> —Robert De Niro, as the loner vigilante Travis Bickle in *Taxi Driver*

---

that were with him in the ark. And the waters swelled on the earth for one hundred fifty days.

But God remembered Noah and all the wild animals and all the domestic animals that were with him in the ark. And God made a wind blow over the earth, and the waters subsided; the fountains of the deep and the windows of the heavens were closed, the rain from the heavens was restrained, and the waters gradually receded from the earth. At the end of one hundred fifty days the waters had abated; and in the seventh month, on the seventeenth day of the month, the ark came to rest on the mountains of Ararat. The waters continued to abate until the tenth month; in the tenth month, on the first day of the month, the tops of the mountains appeared.

At the end of forty days Noah opened the window of the ark that he had made and sent out the raven; and it went to and fro until the waters were dried up from the earth. Then he sent out the dove from him, to see if the waters had subsided from the face of the ground; but the dove found no place to set its foot, and it returned to him to the ark, for the waters were still on the face of the whole earth. So he put out his hand and took it and brought it into the ark with him. He waited another seven days, and again he sent out the dove from the ark; and the dove came back to him in the evening, and there in its beak was a freshly plucked olive leaf; so Noah knew that the waters had subsided from the earth. Then he waited another seven days, and sent out the dove; and it did not return to him any more.

In Kurt Vonnegut's novel *Galápagos,* a small boatful of humans survives worldwide sterilization on the Galápagos Islands. In the course of their evolution, natural selection eventually eliminates the human problem of the "oversized brain," and they come to resemble something closer to walking seals.

In the six hundred first year, in the first month, on the first day of the month, the waters were dried up from the earth; and Noah removed the covering of the ark, and looked, and saw that the face of the ground was drying. In the second month, on the twenty-seventh day of the month, the earth was dry. Then God said to Noah, "Go out of the ark, you and your wife, and your sons and your sons' wives with you. Bring out with you every living thing that is with you of all flesh—birds and animals and every creeping thing that creeps on the earth—so that they may abound on the earth, and be fruitful and multiply on the earth." So Noah went out with his sons and his wife and his sons' wives. And every animal, every creeping thing, and every bird, everything that moves on the earth, went out of the ark by families.

In the first creation story, God gives humans plants to eat. They don't start eating meat until after the flood.

Then Noah built an altar to the LORD, and took of every clean animal and of every clean bird, and offered burnt offerings on the altar. And when the LORD smelled the pleasing odor, the LORD said in his heart, "I will never again curse the ground because of humankind, for the inclination of the human heart is evil from youth; nor will I ever again destroy every living creature as I have done.

> As long as the earth endures,
>   seedtime and harvest, cold and heat,
> summer and winter, day and night,
>   shall not cease."

God blessed Noah and his sons, and said to them, "Be fruitful and multiply, and fill the earth. The fear and dread of you shall rest on every animal of the earth, and on every bird of the air, on everything that creeps on the ground, and on all the fish of the sea; into your hand they are delivered. Every moving thing that lives shall be food for you; and just as I gave you the green plants, I give you everything. Only, you shall not eat flesh with its life, that is, its blood. For your own lifeblood I will surely require a reckoning: from every animal I will require it and from human beings, each one for the blood of another, I will require a reckoning for human life.

The blood is the life!
—Bram Stoker, *Dracula*

> Whoever sheds the blood of a human,
>   by a human shall that person's blood be shed;

for in his own image
  God made humankind.

And you, be fruitful and multiply, abound on the earth and multiply in it."

Then God said to Noah and to his sons with him, "As for me, I am establishing my covenant with you and your descendants after you, and with every living creature that is with you, the birds, the domestic animals, and every animal of the earth with you, as many as came out of the ark. I establish my covenant with you, that never again shall all flesh be cut off by the waters of a flood, and never again shall there be a flood to destroy the earth." God said, "This is the sign of the covenant that I make between me and you and every living creature that is with you, for all future generations: I have set my bow in the clouds, and it shall be a sign of the covenant between me and the earth. When I bring clouds over the earth and the bow is seen in the clouds, I will remember my covenant that is between me and you and every living creature of all flesh; and the waters shall never again become a flood to destroy all flesh. When the bow is in the clouds, I will see it and remember the everlasting covenant between God and every living creature of all flesh that is on the earth." God said to Noah, "This is the sign of the covenant that I have established between me and all flesh that is on the earth."

THE TOWER OF BABEL

We all desire community, connection. And we dread isolation and alienation. The story of the Tower of Babel is more than an ancient story about why there are different languages in the world. It speaks to that desire for mutual understanding and our inability to achieve it.

Alejandro González Iñárritu's 2006 multilingual film, *Babel,* starring Brad Pitt and Cate Blanchett, alludes to the Bible story as a monument to broken communication. Everyone wants to be understood, but no one is listening. At the same time, and from a very different perspective, the story has inspired many meditations on the devastating effects of human pride and ambition. In this light, famously evoked by Brueghel's painting, Babel becomes a symbol of our arrogant reaching for the heavens, our aspiring to divinity. Chillingly, many saw the destruction of the twin towers of the World Trade Center as judgment on a new Tower of Babel.

As you read the story, ask how it opens itself to both interpretations. Where do you read desire? Fear? Hubris?

GENESIS 11:1–9

Now the whole earth had one language and the same words. And as they migrated from the east, they came upon a plain in the land of Shinar and settled there. And they said to one another, "Come, let us make bricks, and burn them thoroughly." And they had brick for stone, and bitumen for mortar. Then they said, "Come, let us build ourselves a city, and a tower with its top in the heavens, and let us make a name for ourselves; otherwise we shall be scattered abroad upon the face of the whole earth." The LORD came down to see the city and the tower, which mortals had built. And the LORD said, "Look, they are one people, and they have all one language; and this is only the beginning of what they will do; nothing that they propose to do will now be impossible for them. Come, let us go down, and confuse their language there, so that they will not understand one another's speech."

> Babel: everyone developing
> A language of his own to
>   write his book in,
> And one to cap the climax by
>   combining
> All language in a one-man
>   tongue-confusion.
>   —Robert Frost, describing
>   New York City, in *A Masque
>   of Mercy*

So the LORD scattered them abroad from there over the face of all the earth, and they left off building the city. Therefore it was called Babel, because there the LORD confused the language of all the earth; and from there the LORD scattered them abroad over the face of all the earth.

HAGAR AND ISHMAEL

"Call me Ishmael." So famously begins *Moby Dick*. Ishmael, Abraham's first son by the servant girl Hagar, has come to stand in Western culture for the orphan and the outcast, always at odds with society. Melville's Ishmael is a good example: a resident alien of civil society, avoiding his penchant for conflict by taking to the wilderness of the sea.

The story of Hagar and Ishmael is in the second main part of Genesis, the so-called ancestral history, which focuses on the promise to make a great nation of Abram (soon to be renamed Abraham, "father of many"). But here the Bible turns to those on the margins of that grand narrative, a slave girl, persecuted by her mistress, and her helpless baby.

In both biblical and Islamic tradition, Ishmael is the ancestor of the Arab people (thus references to Judaism, Christianity, and Islam as the three "Abrahamic religions"). In Islamic tradition, moreover, it was Ishmael, not Isaac, who was nearly sacrificed by Abraham (see "The Binding of Isaac," below). He is believed to have settled in Mecca, where he and Abraham built the foundation of the Kaaba, the focal point of the world's largest annual pilgrimage.

GENESIS 16:1-16

Now Sarai, Abram's wife, bore him no children. She had an Egyptian slave-girl whose name was Hagar, and Sarai said to Abram, "You see that the LORD has prevented me from bearing children; go in to my slave-girl; it may be that I shall obtain children by her." And Abram listened to the voice of Sarai. So, after Abram had lived ten years in the land of Canaan, Sarai, Abram's wife, took Hagar the Egyptian, her slave-girl, and gave her to her husband Abram as a wife. He went in to Hagar, and she conceived; and when she saw that she had conceived, she looked with contempt on her mistress. Then Sarai said to Abram, "May the wrong done to me be on you! I gave my slave-girl to your embrace, and when she saw that she had conceived, she looked on me with

> Call me Ishmael. Some years ago—never mind how long precisely—having little or no money in my purse, and nothing particular to interest me on shore, I thought I would sail about a little and see the watery part of the world.
>
> —Opening lines of Herman Melville's *Moby Dick*

contempt. May the LORD judge between you and me!" But Abram said to Sarai, "Your slave-girl is in your power; do to her as you please." Then Sarai dealt harshly with her, and she ran away from her.

The angel of the LORD found her by a spring of water in the wilderness, the spring on the way to Shur. And he said, "Hagar, slave-girl of Sarai, where have you come from and where are you going?" She said, "I am running away from my mistress Sarai." The angel of the LORD said to her, "Return to your mistress, and submit to her." The angel of the LORD also said to her, "I will so greatly multiply your offspring that they cannot be counted for multitude." And the angel of the LORD said to her,

> "Now you have conceived and shall bear a son;
>   you shall call him Ishmael,
>   for the LORD has given heed to your affliction.
> He shall be a wild ass of a man,
> with his hand against everyone,
>   and everyone's hand against him;
> and he shall live at odds with all his kin."

So she named the LORD who spoke to her, "You are El-roi"; for she said, "Have I really seen God and remained alive after seeing him?" Therefore the well was called Beer-lahai-roi; it lies between Kadesh and Bered.

Hagar bore Abram a son; and Abram named his son, whom Hagar bore, Ishmael. Abram was eighty-six years old when Hagar bore him Ishmael.

SARAH LAUGHED

Hospitality changes everything. Opening your home and your life to strangers means opening yourself to the unexpected— perhaps even the impossible. So it goes in this story, the annunciation of Sarah's son, Isaac.

How do you imagine the scene? Did Abraham see God *and* the three men? Or did he see God in the form of three men? Notice how he talks to them as if they are one person ("My lord, . . ."), to which "they" respond as a collective. Later, however, it is God, not "they," who speak. And where do you imagine Sarah? What does she see and hear? She becomes the subject of this strange visit before she ever speaks or acts for herself. And when she does respond, it is with a skeptical chuckle to herself.

The story ends abruptly, with Sarah fearing that her laughter has offended. But it appears God had a sense of humor about it: her son is to be named Isaac, "laughter."

GENESIS 18:1–15

The Lord appeared to Abraham by the oaks of Mamre, as he sat at the entrance of his tent in the heat of the day. He looked up and saw three men standing near him. When he saw them, he ran from the tent entrance to meet them, and bowed down to the ground. He said, "My lord, if I find favor with you, do not pass by your servant. Let a little water be brought, and wash your feet, and rest yourselves under the tree. Let me bring a little bread, that you may refresh yourselves, and after that you may pass on—since you have come to your servant." So they said, "Do as you have said." And Abraham hastened into the tent to Sarah, and said, "Make ready quickly three measures of choice flour, knead it, and make cakes." Abraham ran to the herd, and took a calf, tender and good, and gave it to the servant, who hastened to prepare it. Then he took curds and milk and the calf that he had prepared, and set it before them; and he stood by them under the tree while they ate.

They said to him, "Where is your wife Sarah?" And he said, "There, in the tent." Then one said, "I will surely return to you in due season, and your wife Sarah shall have a son." And Sarah was listening at the tent entrance behind him. Now Abraham and Sarah were old, advanced in age; it had ceased to be with Sarah after the manner of women. So Sarah laughed to herself, saying, "After I have grown old, and my husband is old, shall I have pleasure?" The Lord said to Abraham, "Why did Sarah laugh, and say, 'Shall I indeed bear a child, now that I am old?' Is anything too wonderful for the Lord? At the set time I will return to you, in due season, and Sarah shall have a son." But Sarah denied, saying, "I did not laugh"; for she was afraid. He said, "Oh yes, you did laugh."

SODOM AND GOMORRAH

Biblical names often take on lives of their own quite apart from the stories in which they first appear. So it is with the infamous cities of Sodom and Gomorrah. Ask most people today why they were destroyed and they'll say something about homosexuality. Indeed, a "sodomy law" is a law that prohibits homosexuality. And the slang word "sod," as in "you old sod," is short for "sodomite," a derogatory term for a homosexual.

But what draws judgment on Sodom and Gomorrah? The "outcry" of people therein—a word used elsewhere, as in the Exodus story, for the cry of the oppressed. Although the attempted rape of Lot's male guests is an indication of how bad some of its men are, the "sin of Sodom" is never identified as homosexuality.

And what of those in the city who cried out about its wickedness? Perhaps they are the ones Lot's wife was thinking about when she looked back. No wonder so many cultural retellings of this story in movies and books focus on her, the one who disobeyed and looked back. On the other hand, as comedians Andy Samberg and Will Ferrell aptly observe, in action movies, "cool guys don't look at explosions. The flames are hot but their heart is chill." They just keep walking away. Is Lot their biblical predecessor?

GENESIS 18:16-19:29

Then the men set out from there, and they looked toward Sodom; and Abraham went with them to set them on their way. The LORD said, "Shall I hide from Abraham what I am about to do, seeing that Abraham shall become a great and mighty nation, and all the nations of the earth shall be blessed in him? No, for I have chosen him, that he may charge his children and his household after him to keep the way of the LORD by doing righteousness and justice; so that the LORD may bring about for Abraham what he has promised him." Then the LORD said, "How great is the outcry against Sodom and Gomorrah and how very grave their sin! I must go down and see whether they have done altogether according to the outcry that has come to me; and if not, I will know."

So the men turned from there, and went toward Sodom, while Abraham remained standing before the LORD. Then Abraham came near and said, "Will you indeed sweep away the righteous with the wicked? Suppose there are fifty righteous within the city; will you then sweep away the place and not forgive it for the fifty righteous who are in it? Far be it from you to do such a thing, to slay the righteous with the wicked, so that the righteous fare as the wicked! Far be that from you! Shall not the Judge of all the earth do what is just?" And the LORD said, "If I find at Sodom fifty righteous in the city, I will forgive the whole place for their sake." Abraham answered, "Let me take it upon myself to speak to the LORD, I who am but dust and ashes. Suppose five of the fifty righteous are lacking? Will you destroy the whole city for lack of five?" And he said, "I will not destroy it if I find forty-five there." Again he spoke to him, "Suppose forty are found there." He answered, "For the sake of forty I will not do it." Then he said, "Oh do not let the LORD be angry if I speak. Suppose thirty are found there." He answered, "I will not do it, if I find thirty there." He said, "Let me take it upon myself to speak to the LORD. Suppose twenty are found there." He answered, "For the sake of twenty I will not destroy it." Then he said, "Oh do not let the LORD be angry if I speak just once more. Suppose ten are found there." He answered, "For the sake of ten I will not destroy it." And the LORD went his way, when he had finished speaking to Abraham; and Abraham returned to his place.

The two angels came to Sodom in the evening, and Lot was sitting in the gateway of Sodom. When Lot saw them, he rose to meet them, and bowed down with his face to the ground. He said, "Please, my lords, turn aside to your servant's house and spend the night, and wash your feet; then you can rise early and go on your way." They said, "No; we will spend the night in the square." But he urged them strongly; so they turned aside to him and entered his house; and he made them a feast, and baked unleavened bread, and they ate. But before they lay down, the men of the city, the men of Sodom, both young and old, all the people to the last man, surrounded the house; and they called to Lot, "Where are the men who came to you tonight? Bring them out to us, so that we may know them." Lot went out of the door to the men, shut the door after him, and said, "I beg you, my brothers, do not act so wickedly. Look, I have two daughters who have not known a man; let me bring them out to you, and do to them as you please; only do nothing to these men, for they have come under the shelter of my roof." But they replied, "Stand back!" And they said, "This fellow came here as an alien, and he would play the judge! Now we will deal worse with you than with them." Then they pressed hard against the man Lot, and came near the door to break it down. But the men inside reached out their hands and brought Lot into the house with them, and shut the door. And they struck with blindness the men who were at the door of the house, both small and great, so that they were unable to find the door.

> Still, the kiss was a touch of bitterness in my mouth
> Like salt, burning in.
> And my hand withered in
>   your hand.
> For you were straining with
>   a wild heart, back, back
>   again.
> Back to those children you
>   had left behind, to all the
>   aeons of the past.
> —D. H. Lawrence,
>   "She Looks Back"

Then the men said to Lot, "Have you anyone else here? Sons-in-law, sons, daughters, or anyone you have in the city—bring them out of the place. For we are about to destroy this place, because the outcry against its people has become great before the LORD, and the LORD has sent us to destroy it." So Lot went out and said to his sons-in-law, who were to marry his daughters, "Up, get out of this place; for the LORD is about to destroy the city." But he seemed to his sons-in-law to be jesting.

When morning dawned, the angels urged Lot, saying, "Get up, take your wife and your two daughters who are here, or else you will be consumed in the punishment of the city." But he lingered; so the men seized him and his wife and his two daughters by the hand, the LORD being merciful to him, and they brought him out and left him outside the city. When they had brought them outside, they said, "Flee for your life; do not look back or stop anywhere in the Plain; flee to the hills, or else you will be consumed." And Lot said to them, "Oh, no, my lords; your servant has found favor with you, and you have shown me great kindness in saving my life; but I cannot flee to the hills, for fear the disaster will overtake me and I die. Look, that city is near enough to flee to, and it is a little one. Let me escape there—is it not a little one?—and my life will be saved!" He said to him, "Very well, I grant you this favor too, and will not overthrow the city of which you have spoken. Hurry, escape there, for I can do nothing until you arrive there." Therefore the city was called Zoar. The sun had risen on the earth when Lot came to Zoar.

Then the LORD rained on Sodom and Gomorrah sulfur and fire from the LORD out of heaven; and he overthrew those cities, and all the Plain, and all the inhabitants of the cities, and what grew on the ground. But Lot's wife, behind him, looked back, and she became a pillar of salt.

Abraham went early in the morning to the place where he had stood before the LORD; and he looked down toward Sodom and Gomorrah and toward all the land of the Plain and saw the smoke of the land going up like the smoke of a furnace.

So it was that, when God destroyed the cities of the Plain, God remembered Abraham, and sent Lot out of the midst of the overthrow, when he overthrew the cities in which Lot had settled.

THE BINDING OF ISAAC

"Abe says, 'Man you must be puttin' me on.'" If only Abraham had protested even as much as Bob Dylan imagines. Why doesn't he? What was he thinking? What, for that matter, was Isaac thinking? And what about his mother, Sarah?

The story of the binding of Isaac, known in Jewish tradition as the Akeda ("binding"), leaves more unsaid than it says. It is, as critic Erich Auerbach famously put it, "fraught with background," inviting readers to fill in the gaps by their own imaginations. In *Fear and Trembling,* Søren Kierkegaard retells the story four different ways, each time re-imagining it from another perspective. In one, he imagines that Abraham decided to hide the fact that God had commanded the sacrifice, so that Isaac would think that he, rather than God, was the monster. Others, like Bob Dylan and Leonard Cohen, have made the story a contemporary parable of child sacrifice.

What gaps do you find in the story? What is left unsaid? Some have even wondered whether Abraham actually failed the test—that God had hoped that he would protest, even refuse. What do you think? Did he pass or fail?

GENESIS 22:1–19

After these things God tested Abraham. He said to him, "Abraham!" And he said, "Here I am." He said, "Take your son, your only son Isaac, whom you love, and go to the land of Moriah, and offer him there as a burnt offering on one of the mountains that I shall show you." So Abraham rose early in the morning, saddled his donkey, and took two of his young men with him, and his son Isaac; he cut the wood for the burnt offering, and set out and went to the place in the distance that God had shown him. On the third day Abraham looked up and saw the place far away. Then Abraham said to his young men, "Stay here with the donkey; the boy and I will go over there; we will worship, and then we will come back to you." Abraham took the wood of the burnt offering and laid it on his son Isaac, and he himself carried the fire and the knife. So the two of them walked on together. Isaac said to his father Abraham, "Father!" And he said, "Here I am, my son." He said, "The fire and the wood are here, but where is the lamb for a burnt offering?" Abraham said, "God himself will provide the lamb for a burnt offering, my son." So the two of them walked on together.

In his 1969 antiwar song, "Story of Isaac," Jewish poet and recording artist Leonard Cohen retells this tale from the son's point of view. After recollecting that chilling moment with his father on the mountain, Isaac turns suddenly to confront those "who build the altars now," willing to sacrifice a new generation of children as though by divine command. "A scheme is not a vision," Isaac warns, prophetically, "and you have not been tempted by a demon or a god."

When they came to the place that God had shown him, Abraham built an altar there and laid the wood in order. He bound his son Isaac, and laid him on the altar, on top of the wood. Then Abraham reached out his hand and took the knife to kill his son. But the angel of the LORD called to him from heaven, and said, "Abraham, Abraham!" And he said, "Here I am." He said, "Do not lay your hand on the boy or do anything to him; for now I know that you fear God, since you have not withheld your son, your only son, from me." And Abraham looked up and saw a ram, caught in a thicket by its horns. Abraham went and took the ram and offered it up as a burnt offering instead of his son. So Abraham called that place "The LORD will provide"; as it is said to this day, "On the mount of the LORD it shall be provided."

The angel of the LORD called to Abraham a second time from heaven, and said, "By myself I have sworn, says the LORD: Because you have done this, and have not withheld your son, your only son, I will indeed bless you, and I will make your offspring as numerous as the stars of heaven and as the sand that is on the seashore. And your offspring shall possess the gate of their enemies, and by your offspring shall all the nations of the earth gain blessing for themselves, because you have obeyed my voice." So Abraham returned to his young men, and they arose and went together to Beer-sheba; and Abraham lived at Beer-sheba.

JACOB'S LADDER

There's competition enough between twins when parents stay out of it. There's even more when mom takes sides. So it is with Isaac and Rebekah's twin sons, Jacob and Esau. Jacob is mama's boy. Esau was born first, and so was the elder. But Jacob and Rebekah conspire to trick Esau out of his birthright and blessing.

Fleeing for his life from Esau, Jacob finds himself sleeping under the stars with nothing but a rock for a pillow. There he dreams of what has come to be known as "Jacob's Ladder." Described only very briefly, almost in passing, in the biblical story itself, this vision has captured the imaginations of many since, often representing the hope for release from the present world of suffering. As in the black spiritual "We Are Climbing Jacob's Ladder" and in the final scene of a Vietnam soldier's death in the 1990 thriller *Jacob's Ladder,* we tend to identify with those ascending the ladder into the heavens rather than with Jacob himself, who stands and watches.

GENESIS 28:10-22

Jacob left Beer-sheba and went toward Haran. He came to a certain place and stayed there for the night, because the sun had set. Taking one of the stones of the place, he put it under his head and lay down in that place. And he dreamed that there was a ladder set up on the earth, the top of it reaching to heaven; and the angels of God were ascending and descending on it. And the LORD stood beside him and said, "I am the LORD, the God of Abraham your father and the God of Isaac; the land on which you lie I will give to you and to your offspring; and your offspring shall be like the dust of the earth, and you shall spread abroad to the west and to the east and to the north and to the south; and all the families of the earth shall be blessed in you and in your offspring. Know that I am with you and will keep you wherever you go, and will bring you back to this land; for I will not leave you until I have done what I have promised you." Then Jacob woke from his sleep and said, "Surely the LORD is in this place—and I did not know it!" And he was afraid, and said, "How awesome is this place! This is none other than the house of God, and this is the gate of heaven."

So Jacob rose early in the morning, and he took the stone that he had put under his head and set it up for a pillar and poured oil on the top of it. He called that place Bethel; but the name of the city was Luz at the first. Then Jacob made a vow, saying, "If God will be with me, and will keep me in this way that I go, and will give me bread to eat and clothing to wear, so that I come again to my father's house in peace, then the LORD shall be my God, and this stone, which I have set up for a pillar, shall be God's house; and of all that you give me I will surely give one-tenth to you."

WRESTLING JACOB

Sooner or later, we all find ourselves alone, out of tricks and charms, lying in the uncomfortable bed we have made for ourselves.

In this story, Jacob is older and in many ways more secure. After years of working for his uncle Laban, he has become wealthy. He has married, twice, and has many children. Now he is on his way back home, hoping to reconcile with the brother he badly wronged. It is during his anxious journey that we find the famous story of his all-night wrestling match with a stranger who ultimately wounds him, blesses him, and renames him Israel.

Who is this opponent? Is it a man, as the story says? An angel, as so many paintings and sculptures have depicted? God? Jacob himself? Some sleepless nights, it's hard to know exactly who or what we're really wrestling.

GENESIS 32:22-32

The same night he got up and took his two wives, his two maids, and his eleven children, and crossed the ford of the Jabbok. He took them and sent them across the stream, and likewise everything that he had. Jacob was left alone; and a man wrestled with him until daybreak. When the man saw that he did not prevail against Jacob, he struck him on the hip socket; and Jacob's hip was put out of joint as he wrestled with him. Then he said, "Let me go, for the day is breaking." But Jacob said, "I will not let you go, unless you bless me." So he said to him, "What is your name?" And he said, "Jacob." Then the man said, "You shall no longer be called Jacob, but Israel, for you have striven with God and with humans, and have prevailed." Then Jacob asked him, "Please tell me your name." But he said, "Why is it that you ask my name?" And there he blessed him. So Jacob called the place Peniel, saying, "For I have seen God face to face, and yet my life is preserved." The sun rose upon him as he passed Penuel, limping because of his hip. Therefore to this day the Israelites do not eat the thigh muscle that is on the hip socket, because he struck Jacob on the hip socket at the thigh muscle.

> In the locust wind
> comes a rattle and hum
> Jacob wrestled the angel
> and the angel was overcome
> —U2, "Bullet the Blue Sky"

DINAH

Dinah's name means "judgment" or "vindication." Is that what she finds? Or is her name an ironic title for her story, a subtle commentary on the lack of justice for women in a patriarchal world?

The story of Dinah is brief, offering few windows into the thoughts and intentions of its characters. Indeed, the main characters are the men around Dinah; she never speaks for herself.

Anita Diamant's bestselling novel *The Red Tent* offers a retelling from Dinah's perspective, suggesting several questions we might bring back to the biblical account. For example, what would Dinah have wanted? What, indeed, were her options? And what were the true motives of her brothers? Did they have Dinah's best interests at heart, or were they using her to their advantage?

GENESIS 34:1–31

Now Dinah the daughter of Leah, whom she had borne to Jacob, went out to visit the women of the region. When Shechem son of Hamor the Hivite, prince of the region, saw her, he seized her and lay with her by force. And his soul was drawn to Dinah daughter of Jacob; he loved the girl, and spoke tenderly to her. So Shechem spoke to his father Hamor, saying, "Get me this girl to be my wife."

Now Jacob heard that Shechem had defiled his daughter Dinah; but his sons were with his cattle in the field, so Jacob held his peace until they came. And Hamor the father of Shechem went out to Jacob to speak with him, just as the sons of Jacob came in from the field. When they heard of it, the men were indignant and very angry, because he had committed an outrage in Israel by lying with Jacob's daughter, for such a thing ought not to be done.

But Hamor spoke with them, saying, "The heart of my son Shechem longs for your daughter; please give her to him in marriage. Make marriages with us; give your daughters to us, and take our daughters for yourselves. You shall live with us; and the land shall be open to you; live and trade in it, and get property in it." Shechem also said to her father and to her brothers, "Let me find favor with you, and whatever you say to me I will give. Put the marriage present and gift as high as you like, and I will give whatever you ask me; only give me the girl to be my wife."

The sons of Jacob answered Shechem and his father Hamor deceitfully, because he had defiled their sister Dinah. They said to them, "We cannot do this thing, to give our sister to one who is uncircumcised, for that would be a disgrace to us. Only on this condition will we consent to you: that you will become as we are and every male among you be circumcised. Then we will give our daughters to you, and we will take your daughters for ourselves, and we will live among you and become one

"OLD TESTAMENT" OR "HEBREW BIBLE"?

In biblical stories, naming is often an act of power. Abram is renamed Abraham at the very moment God promises that his descendants will become a great nation, and Sarai is renamed Sarah when she is told that she will, in her old age, bear the child that will continue that promise. Jacob is renamed Israel when he receives the same promise. And so on.

So too when it comes to the naming of this literature itself. Christians have traditionally called it the "Old Testament," because it is read in light of and with an eye toward the "New Testament" that follows. It's a Christian name and implies a Christian way of reading it. It isn't inclusive of all readers, especially Jews, who read it without reference to the New Testament. It has become common, therefore, to use the more generic name "Hebrew Bible," which neither excludes nor privileges particular religious or nonreligious perspectives and interests.

people. But if you will not listen to us and be circumcised, then we will take our daughter and be gone."

Their words pleased Hamor and Hamor's son Shechem. And the young man did not delay to do the thing, because he was delighted with Jacob's daughter. Now he was the most honored of all his family. So Hamor and his son Shechem came to the gate of their city and spoke to the men of their city, saying, "These people are friendly with us; let them live in the land and trade in it, for the land is large enough for them; let us take their daughters in marriage, and let us give them our daughters. Only on this condition will they agree to live among us, to become one people: that every male among us be circumcised as they are circumcised. Will not their livestock, their property, and all their animals be ours? Only let us agree with them, and they will live among us." And all who went out of the city gate heeded Hamor and his son Shechem; and every male was circumcised, all who went out of the gate of his city.

On the third day, when they were still in pain, two of the sons of Jacob, Simeon and Levi, Dinah's brothers, took their swords and came against the city unawares, and killed all the males. They killed Hamor and his son Shechem with the sword, and took Dinah out of Shechem's house, and went away. And the other sons of Jacob came upon the slain, and plundered the city, because their sister had been defiled. They took their flocks and their herds, their donkeys, and whatever was in the city and in the field. All their wealth, all their little ones and their wives, all that was in the houses, they captured and made their prey. Then Jacob said to Simeon and Levi, "You have brought trouble on me by making me odious to the inhabitants of the land, the Canaanites and the Perizzites; my numbers are few, and if they gather themselves against me and attack me, I shall be destroyed, both I and my household." But they said, "Should our sister be treated like a whore?"

JOSEPH: THE FAVORED ONE

Joseph's is a rags-to-riches immigrant story, which is at least partly why it resonates in pop culture, from Tim Rice and Andrew Lloyd Webber's musical *Joseph and the Amazing Technicolor Dreamcoat* (1968) to the DreamWorks animated film *Joseph: King of Dreams* (2000). But the story's hero is no Cinderella. Favored by his father, he has great expectations for himself from the start. Nor is he reluctant to share his self-aggrandizing dreams with his resentful brothers. Which is how he goes from fancy clothes to rags in the first place.

The best-known thing about Joseph is his "coat of many colors," as the King James Version puts it. Unfortunately, that's a mistranslation. It was not multicolored, but long-sleeved. Perhaps it's just as well that Webber and Rice didn't take that fact into account, as it would be difficult to come up with an exaggeratedly mod version of long sleeves.

Joseph's story takes up nearly one-third of the book of Genesis. As you read about him in different contexts at different points in his life, do you see him change and develop as a character?

Selling Little Brother

GENESIS 37:3-36

Now Israel [Jacob] loved Joseph more than any other of his children, because he was the son of his old age; and he had made him a long robe with sleeves. But when his brothers saw that their father loved him more than all his brothers, they hated him, and could not speak peaceably to him.

Once Joseph had a dream, and when he told it to his brothers, they hated him even more. He said to them, "Listen to this dream that I dreamed. There we were, binding sheaves in the field. Suddenly my sheaf rose and stood upright; then your sheaves gathered around it, and bowed down to my sheaf." His brothers said to him, "Are you indeed to reign over us? Are you indeed to have dominion over us?" So they hated him even more because of his dreams and his words.

He had another dream, and told it to his brothers, saying, "Look, I have had another dream: the sun, the moon, and eleven stars were bowing down to me." But when he told it to his father and to his brothers, his father rebuked him, and said to him, "What kind of dream is this that you have had? Shall we indeed come, I and your mother and your brothers, and bow to the ground before you?" So his brothers were jealous of him, but his father kept the matter in mind.

Now his brothers went to pasture their father's flock near Shechem. And Israel said to Joseph, "Are not your brothers pasturing the flock at Shechem? Come, I will send you to them." He answered, "Here I am." So he said to him, "Go now, see if it is well with your brothers and with the flock; and bring word back to me." So he sent him from the valley of Hebron. He came to Shechem, and a man found him wandering in the fields; the man asked him, "What are you seeking?" "I am seeking my brothers," he said; "tell me, please, where they are pasturing the flock." The man said, "They have gone away, for I heard them say, 'Let us go to Dothan.'" So Joseph went after his brothers, and found them at Dothan. They saw him from a distance, and before he came near to them, they conspired to kill him. They said to one another, "Here comes this dreamer. Come now, let us kill him and throw him into one of the pits; then we shall say that a wild animal has devoured him, and we shall see what will become of his dreams." But when Reuben heard it, he delivered him out of their hands, saying, "Let us not take his life." Reuben said to them, "Shed no blood; throw him into this pit here in the wilderness, but lay no hand on him"—that he might rescue him out of their hand and restore him to his father. So when Joseph came to his brothers, they stripped him of his robe, the long robe with sleeves that he wore; and they took him and threw him into a pit. The pit was empty; there was no water in it.

Then they sat down to eat; and looking up they saw a caravan of Ishmaelites coming from Gilead, with their camels carrying gum, balm, and resin, on their way to carry it down to Egypt. Then Judah said to his brothers, "What profit is it if we kill our brother and conceal his blood? Come, let us sell him to the Ishmaelites, and not lay our hands on him, for he is our brother, our own flesh." And his brothers agreed. When some Midianite traders passed by, they drew Joseph up, lifting him out of the pit, and sold him to the Ishmaelites for twenty pieces of silver. And they took Joseph to Egypt.

When Reuben returned to the pit and saw that Joseph was not in the pit, he tore his clothes. He returned to his brothers, and said, "The boy is gone; and I, where can I turn?" Then they took Joseph's robe, slaughtered a goat, and dipped the robe in the blood. They had the long robe with sleeves taken to their father, and they said, "This we have found; see now whether it is your son's robe or not." He recognized it, and said, "It is my son's robe! A wild animal has devoured him; Joseph is without doubt torn to pieces." Then Jacob tore his garments, and put sackcloth on his loins, and mourned for his son many days. All his sons and all his daughters sought to comfort him; but he refused to be comforted, and said, "No, I shall go down to Sheol to my son, mourning." Thus his father bewailed him. Meanwhile the Midianites had sold him in Egypt to Potiphar, one of Pharaoh's officials, the captain of the guard.

In Potiphar's House

GENESIS 39:1-23

Now Joseph was taken down to Egypt, and Potiphar, an officer of Pharaoh, the captain of the guard, an Egyptian, bought him from the Ishmaelites who had brought him down there. The LORD was with Joseph, and he became a successful man; he was in the house of his Egyptian master. His master saw that the LORD was with him, and that the LORD caused all that he did to prosper in his hands. So Joseph found favor in his sight and attended him; he made him overseer of his house and put him in charge of all that he had. From the time that he made him overseer in his house and over all that he had, the LORD blessed the Egyptian's house for Joseph's sake; the blessing of the LORD was on all that he had, in house and field. So he left all that he had in Joseph's charge; and, with him there, he had no concern for anything but the food that he ate.

> And then his only garment
>   quite gave way;
> He fled, like Joseph, leaving
>   it; but there,
> I doubt, all likeness ends
>   between the pair.
> —Lord Byron, *Don Juan*

Now Joseph was handsome and good-looking. And after a time his master's wife cast her eyes on Joseph and said, "Lie with me." But he refused and said to his master's wife, "Look, with me here, my master has no concern about anything in the house, and he has put everything that he has in my hand. He is not greater in this house than I am, nor has he kept back anything from me except yourself, because you are his wife. How then could I do this great wickedness, and sin against God?" And although she spoke to Joseph day after day, he would not consent to lie beside her or to be with her. One day, however, when he went into the house to do his work, and while no one else was in the house, she caught hold of his garment, saying, "Lie with me!" But he left his garment in her hand, and fled and ran outside. When she saw that he had left his garment in her hand and had fled outside, she called out to the members of her household and said to them, "See, my husband has brought among us a Hebrew to insult us! He came in to me to lie with me, and I cried out with a loud voice; and when he heard me raise my voice and cry out, he left his garment beside me, and fled outside." Then she kept his garment by her until his master came home, and she told him the same story, saying, "The Hebrew servant, whom you have brought among us, came in to me to insult me; but as soon as I raised my voice and cried out, he left his garment beside me, and fled outside."

When his master heard the words that his wife spoke to him, saying, "This is the way your servant treated me," he became enraged. And Joseph's master took him and put him into the prison, the place where the king's prisoners were confined; he remained there in prison. But the LORD was with Joseph and showed him steadfast love; he gave him favor in the sight of the chief jailer. The chief jailer committed to Joseph's care all the prisoners who were in the prison, and whatever was done there, he was the one who did it. The chief jailer paid no heed to anything that was in Joseph's care, because the LORD was with him; and whatever he did, the LORD made it prosper.

Joseph Unveiled

GENESIS 45:1-28

Then Joseph could no longer control himself before all those who stood by him, and he cried out, "Send everyone away from me." So no one stayed with him when Joseph made himself known to his brothers. And he wept so loudly that the Egyptians heard it, and the household of Pharaoh heard it. Joseph said to his brothers, "I am Joseph. Is my father still alive?" But his brothers could not answer him, so dismayed were they at his presence.

Then Joseph said to his brothers, "Come closer to me." And they came closer. He said, "I am your brother, Joseph, whom you sold into Egypt. And now do not be

Even while in prison, Joseph thrives. When Pharaoh has two dreams that his sages are unable to interpret, a baker who had been in jail with Joseph suggests that he be allowed to try. Joseph succeeds, realizing that they are divine portents of a coming famine and encouraging Pharaoh to prepare for it. Pleased, Pharaoh promotes him to second-in-command. When the famine comes, Joseph's brothers visit from Canaan to buy food. Joseph recognizes them, but they don't recognize him. After toying with them during two separate visits, he finally reveals his true identity. Soon his brothers and his father, Jacob (Israel), have all moved to Egypt, which is where we find their descendants, many generations later, at the beginning of the book of Exodus.

distressed, or angry with yourselves, because you sold me here; for God sent me before you to preserve life. For the famine has been in the land these two years; and there are five more years in which there will be neither plowing nor harvest. God sent me before you to preserve for you a remnant on earth, and to keep alive for you many survivors. So it was not you who sent me here, but God; he has made me a father to Pharaoh, and lord of all his house and ruler over all the land of Egypt. Hurry and go up to my father and say to him, 'Thus says your son Joseph, God has made me lord of all Egypt; come down to me, do not delay. You shall settle in the land of Goshen, and you shall be near me, you and your children and your children's children, as well as your flocks, your herds, and all that you have. I will provide for you there—since there are five more years of famine to come—so that you and your household, and all that you have, will not come to poverty.' And now your eyes and the eyes of my brother Benjamin see that it is my own mouth that speaks to you. You must tell my father how greatly I am honored in Egypt, and all that you have seen. Hurry and bring my father down here." Then he fell upon his brother Benjamin's neck and wept, while Benjamin wept upon his neck. And he kissed all his brothers and wept upon them; and after that his brothers talked with him.

When the report was heard in Pharaoh's house, "Joseph's brothers have come," Pharaoh and his servants were pleased. Pharaoh said to Joseph, "Say to your brothers, 'Do this: load your animals and go back to the land of Canaan. Take your father and your households and come to me, so that I may give you the best of the land of Egypt, and you may enjoy the fat of the land.' You are further charged to say, 'Do this: take wagons from the land of Egypt for your little ones and for your wives, and bring your father, and come. Give no thought to your possessions, for the best of all the land of Egypt is yours.'"

The sons of Israel did so. Joseph gave them wagons according to the instruction of Pharaoh, and he gave them provisions for the journey. To each one of them he gave a set of garments; but to Benjamin he gave three hundred pieces of silver and five sets of garments. To his father he sent the following: ten donkeys loaded with the good things of Egypt, and ten female donkeys loaded with grain, bread, and provision for his father on the journey. Then he sent his brothers on their way, and as they were leaving he said to them, "Do not quarrel along the way."

So they went up out of Egypt and came to their father Jacob in the land of Canaan. And they told him, "Joseph is still alive! He is even ruler over all the land of Egypt." He was stunned; he could not believe them. But when they told him all the words of Joseph that he had said to them, and when he saw the wagons that Joseph had sent to carry him, the spirit of their father Jacob revived. Israel said, "Enough! My son Joseph is still alive. I must go and see him before I die."

Israel Moves to Egypt

GENESIS 47:1-6, 27-31; 50:15-21

So Joseph went and told Pharaoh, "My father and my brothers, with their flocks and herds and all that they possess, have come from the land of Canaan; they are now in the land of Goshen." From among his brothers he took five men and presented them to Pharaoh. Pharaoh said to his brothers, "What is your occupation?" And they said to Pharaoh, "Your servants are shepherds, as our ancestors were." They said to Pharaoh, "We have come to reside as aliens in the land; for there is no pasture for your servants' flocks because the famine is severe in the land of Canaan. Now, we ask you, let your servants settle in the land of Goshen." Then Pharaoh said to Joseph, "Your father and your brothers have come to you. The land of Egypt is before you; settle your father and your brothers in the best part of the land; let them live in the land of Goshen; and if you know that there are capable men among them, put them in charge of my livestock."

. . . Thus Israel settled in the land of Egypt, in the region of Goshen; and they gained possessions in it, and were fruitful and multiplied exceedingly. Jacob lived in the land of Egypt seventeen years; so the days of Jacob, the years of his life, were one hundred forty-seven years.

When the time of Israel's death drew near, he called his son Joseph and said to him, "If I have found favor with you, put your hand under my thigh and promise to deal loyally and truly with me. Do not bury me in Egypt. When I lie down with my ancestors, carry me out of Egypt and bury me in their burial place." He answered, "I will do as you have said." And he said, "Swear to me"; and he swore to him. Then Israel bowed himself on the head of his bed.

. . . Realizing that their father was dead, Joseph's brothers said, "What if Joseph still bears a grudge against us and pays us back in full for all the wrong that we did to him?" So they approached Joseph, saying, "Your father gave this instruction before he died, 'Say to Joseph: I beg you, forgive the crime of your brothers and the wrong they did in harming you.' Now therefore please forgive the crime of the servants of the God of your father." Joseph wept when they spoke to him. Then his brothers also wept, fell down before him, and said, "We are here as your slaves." But Joseph said to them, "Do not be afraid! Am I in the place of God? Even though you intended to do harm to me, God intended it for good, in order to preserve a numerous people, as he is doing today. So have no fear; I myself will provide for you and your little ones." In this way he reassured them, speaking kindly to them.

EXODUS: "LET MY PEOPLE GO"

From Cecil B. DeMille's morality film *The Ten Commandments* (1923) to DreamWorks' animated coming-of-age story *The Prince of Egypt* (1998), popular culture has been fascinated by Moses, the unlikely leader of Israel's liberation from bondage in Egypt as told in the book of Exodus.

What makes him such a successful revolutionary leader? The opening scenes of the story are suggestive. Moses, the soon-to-be head of this band of former slaves, is an in-between person, a hybrid of two incompatible identities. Born to one of Pharaoh's slaves, he is adopted by Pharaoh's daughter, then nursed by his Hebrew mother, then taken into the home of Pharaoh as a member of the family. It seems his in-betweenness puts him in a unique position to lead one side out of bondage under the other. Yet his process of coming into his own will be painful and conflicted.

While reading, try mapping Moses's back-and-forth movement between the Israelites and the Egyptians. Where does that leave him by the time of his calling? How does his position inform his response to that call?

Moses's Early Years

EXODUS 1:8-2:22

Now a new king arose over Egypt, who did not know Joseph. He said to his people, "Look, the Israelite people are more numerous and more powerful than we. Come, let us deal shrewdly with them, or they will increase and, in the event of war, join our enemies and fight against us and escape from the land." Therefore they set taskmasters over them to oppress them with forced labor. They built supply cities, Pithom and Rameses, for Pharaoh. But the more they were oppressed, the more they multiplied and spread, so that the Egyptians came to dread the Israelites. The Egyptians became ruthless in imposing tasks on the Israelites, and made their lives bitter with hard service in mortar and brick and in every kind of field labor. They were ruthless in all the tasks that they imposed on them.

The king of Egypt said to the Hebrew midwives, one of whom was named Shiphrah and the other Puah, "When you act as midwives to the Hebrew women, and see them on the birthstool, if it is a boy, kill him; but if it is a girl, she shall live." But the midwives feared God; they did not do as the king of Egypt commanded them, but they let the boys live. So the king of Egypt summoned the midwives and said to them, "Why have you done this, and allowed the boys to live?" The midwives said to Pharaoh, "Because the Hebrew women are not like the Egyptian women; for they are vigorous and give birth before the midwife comes to them." So God dealt well with the midwives; and the people multiplied and became very strong. And because the midwives feared God, he gave them families. Then Pharaoh commanded all his people, "Every boy that is born to the Hebrews you shall throw into the Nile, but you shall let every girl live."

Now a man from the house of Levi went and married a Levite woman. The woman conceived and bore a son; and when she saw that he was a fine baby, she hid him three months. When she could hide him no longer she got a papyrus basket for him, and plastered it with bitumen and pitch; she put the child in it and placed it among the reeds on the bank of the river. His sister stood at a distance, to see what would happen to him.

The daughter of Pharaoh came down to bathe at the river, while her attendants walked beside the river. She saw the basket among the reeds and sent her maid to bring it. When she opened it, she saw the child. He was crying, and she took pity on him. "This must be one of the Hebrews' children," she said. Then his sister said to Pharaoh's daughter, "Shall I go and get you a nurse from the Hebrew women to nurse the child for you?" Pharaoh's daughter said to her, "Yes." So the girl went and called the child's mother. Pharaoh's daughter said to her, "Take this child and nurse it for me, and I will give you your wages." So the woman took the child and nursed it. When the child grew up, she brought him to Pharaoh's daughter, and she took him as her son. She named him Moses, "because," she said, "I drew him out of the water."

One day, after Moses had grown up, he went out to his people and saw their forced labor. He saw an Egyptian beating a Hebrew, one of his kinsfolk. He looked this way and that, and seeing no one he killed the Egyptian and hid him in the sand. When he went out the next day, he saw two Hebrews fighting; and he said to the one who was in the wrong, "Why do you strike your fellow Hebrew?" He answered, "Who made you a ruler and judge over us? Do you mean to kill me as you killed the Egyptian?" Then Moses was afraid and thought, "Surely the thing is known." When Pharaoh heard of it, he sought to kill Moses.

But Moses fled from Pharaoh. He settled in the land of Midian, and sat down by a well. The priest of Midian had seven daughters. They came to draw water, and filled the troughs to water their father's flock. But some shepherds came and drove them away. Moses got up and came to their defense and watered their flock. When they returned to their father Reuel, he said, "How is it that you have come back so soon today?" They said, "An Egyptian helped us against the shepherds; he even drew water for us and watered the flock." He said to his daughters, "Where is he? Why did you leave the man? Invite him to break bread." Moses agreed to

> Pharaoh's daughter here parallels God in the next story. Just as she hears baby Moses crying, recognizes him as one of the Hebrew children (condemned to death), and determines to deliver him, so God hears the cries of the oppressed Hebrew people, remembers the covenant with their ancestors, and determines to deliver them.

stay with the man, and he gave Moses his daughter Zipporah in marriage. She bore a son, and he named him Gershom; for he said, "I have been an alien residing in a foreign land."

The Burning Bush

EXODUS 2:23-3:15

After a long time the king of Egypt died. The Israelites groaned under their slavery, and cried out. Out of the slavery their cry for help rose up to God. God heard their groaning, and God remembered his covenant with Abraham, Isaac, and Jacob. God looked upon the Israelites, and God took notice of them.

Moses was keeping the flock of his father-in-law Jethro, the priest of Midian; he led his flock beyond the wilderness, and came to Horeb, the mountain of God. There the angel of the LORD appeared to him in a flame of fire out of a bush; he looked, and the bush was blazing, yet it was not consumed. Then Moses said, "I must turn aside and look at this great sight, and see why the bush is not burned up." When the LORD saw that he had turned aside to see, God called to him out of the bush, "Moses, Moses!" And he said, "Here I am." Then he said, "Come no closer! Remove the sandals from your feet, for the place on which you are standing is holy ground." He said further, "I am the God of your father, the God of Abraham, the God of Isaac, and the God of Jacob." And Moses hid his face, for he was afraid to look at God.

Then the LORD said, "I have observed the misery of my people who are in Egypt; I have heard their cry on account of their taskmasters. Indeed, I know their sufferings, and I have come down to deliver them from the Egyptians, and to bring them up out of that land to a good and broad land, a land flowing with milk and honey, to the country of the Canaanites, the Hittites, the Amorites, the Perizzites, the Hivites, and the Jebusites. The cry of the Israelites has now come to me; I have also seen how the Egyptians oppress them. So come, I will send you to Pharaoh to bring my people, the Israelites, out of Egypt." But Moses said to God, "Who am I that I should go to Pharaoh, and bring the Israelites out of Egypt?" He said, "I will be with you; and this shall be the sign for you that it is I who sent you: when you have brought the people out of Egypt, you shall worship God on this mountain."

But Moses said to God, "If I come to the Israelites and say to them, 'The God of your ancestors has sent me to you,' and they ask me, 'What is his name?' what shall I say to them?" God said to Moses, "I Am Who I Am." He said further, "Thus you shall say to the Israelites, 'I Am has sent me to you.'" God also said to Moses, "Thus you shall say to the Israelites, 'The Lord, the God of your ancestors, the God of Abraham, the God of Isaac, and the God of Jacob, has sent me to you':

This is my name forever,
and this my title for all generations.

"Why Me?"

EXODUS 4:1-17

Then Moses answered, "But suppose they do not believe me or listen to me, but say, 'The Lord did not appear to you.'" The Lord said to him, "What is that in your hand?" He said, "A staff." And he said, "Throw it on the ground." So he threw the staff on the ground, and it became a snake; and Moses drew back from it. Then the Lord said to Moses, "Reach out your hand, and seize it by the tail"—so he reached out his hand and grasped it, and it became a staff in his hand—"so that they may believe that the Lord, the God of their ancestors, the God of Abraham, the God of Isaac, and the God of Jacob, has appeared to you."

Again, the Lord said to him, "Put your hand inside your cloak." He put his hand into his cloak; and when he took it out, his hand was leprous, as white as snow. Then God said, "Put your hand back into your cloak"—so he put his hand back into his cloak, and when he took it out, it was restored like the rest of his body—"If they will not believe you or heed the first sign, they may believe the second sign. If they will not believe even these two signs or heed you, you shall take some water from the Nile and pour it on the dry ground; and the water that you shall take from the Nile will become blood on the dry ground."

But Moses said to the Lord, "O my Lord, I have never been eloquent, neither in the past nor even now that you have spoken to your servant; but I am slow of speech and slow of tongue." Then the LORD said to him, "Who gives speech to mortals? Who makes them mute or deaf, seeing or blind? Is it not I, the LORD? Now go, and I will be with your mouth and teach you what you are to speak." But he said, "O my Lord, please send someone else." Then the anger of the LORD was kindled against Moses and he said, "What of your brother Aaron the Levite? I know that he can speak fluently; even now he is coming out to meet you, and when he sees you his heart will be glad. You shall speak to him and put the words in his mouth; and I will be with your mouth and with his mouth, and will teach you what you shall do. He indeed shall speak for you to the people; he shall serve as a mouth for you, and you shall serve as God for him. Take in your hand this staff, with which you shall perform the signs."

EXODUS AND REVOLUTION

The dramatic story of the Exodus, the liberation of the Israelites from slavery in Egypt, is the core story of Judaism, remembered every year during Passover. At the same time, it has inspired many other liberation movements in other cultural and religious contexts, from the Puritan revolution of the seventeenth century, to the liberation theology movement in Central America, to the Rastafarian movement in Jamaica. In the last, Bob Marley helped reimagine the Exodus as a spiritual as well as political emancipation. "Emancipate yourselves from mental slavery," declares this modern-day Moses in his Rastafarian manifesto, "Redemption Song."

On the other hand, the Exodus story has also inspired what political philosopher Michael Walzer calls a "messianic" politics of liberation, which leads some radical groups to see themselves as waging a revolutionary holy war of good against evil, thereby justifying any means necessary to triumph.

As you read, pay attention to the repetition of phrases and images. How do they lead to the story's dramatic climax? At the same time, don't shy away from the tough questions. One repeated image is that of God hardening Pharaoh's heart so that he won't let the people go. Is it necessary, let alone right, to harden Pharaoh's heart to the point that it cost the lives of all the firstborn in Egypt?

The Plagues

EXODUS 7:1–24

The LORD said to Moses, "See, I have made you like God to Pharaoh, and your brother Aaron shall be your prophet. You shall speak all that I command you, and your brother Aaron shall tell Pharaoh to let the Israelites go out of his land. But I will harden Pharaoh's heart, and I will multiply my signs and wonders in the land of Egypt. When Pharaoh does not listen to you, I will lay my hand upon Egypt and bring my people the Israelites, company by company, out of the land of Egypt by great acts of judgment. The Egyptians shall know that I am the LORD, when I stretch out my hand against Egypt and bring the Israelites out from among them." Moses and Aaron did so; they did just as the LORD commanded them. Moses was eighty years old and Aaron eighty-three when they spoke to Pharaoh.

The LORD said to Moses and Aaron, "When Pharaoh says to you, 'Perform a wonder,' then you shall say to Aaron, 'Take your staff and throw it down before Pharaoh, and it will become a snake.'" So Moses and Aaron went to Pharaoh and did as the LORD had commanded; Aaron threw down his staff before Pharaoh and his officials, and it became a snake. Then Pharaoh summoned the wise men and the sorcerers; and they also, the magicians of Egypt, did the same by their secret arts. Each one threw down his staff, and they became snakes; but Aaron's staff swallowed up theirs. Still Pharaoh's heart was hardened, and he would not listen to them, as the LORD had said.

> In business (this all-devouring word, business) the one sole object is, by any means, pecuniary gain. The magician's serpent in the fable ate up all the other serpents; and money-making is our magician's serpent, remaining sole master of the field.
>
> —Walt Whitman, *Democratic Vistas*

Then the LORD said to Moses, "Pharaoh's heart is hardened; he refuses to let the people go. Go to Pharaoh in the morning, as he is going out to the water; stand by at the river bank to meet him, and take in your hand the staff that was turned into a snake. Say to him, 'The LORD, the God of the Hebrews, sent me to you to say, "Let my people go, so that they may worship me in the wilderness." But until now you have not listened. Thus says the LORD, "By this you shall know that I am the LORD." See, with the staff that is in my hand I will strike the water that is in the Nile, and it shall be turned to blood. The fish in the river shall die, the river itself shall stink, and the Egyptians shall be unable to drink water from the Nile.'" The LORD said to Moses, "Say to Aaron, 'Take your staff and stretch out your hand over the waters of Egypt—over its rivers, its canals, and its ponds, and all its pools of water—so that they may become blood; and there shall be blood throughout the whole land of Egypt, even in vessels of wood and in vessels of stone.'"

The Ten Plagues

1. Water turned to blood
2. Frogs
3. Gnats
4. Flies
5. Death of livestock from disease
6. Boils on people and animals
7. Thunder and hail
8. Locusts
9. Darkness that can be felt
10. Death of all Egyptian firstborn, including animals

Moses and Aaron did just as the LORD commanded. In the sight of Pharaoh and of his officials he lifted up the staff and struck the water in the river, and all the water in the river was turned into blood, and the fish in the river died. The river stank so that the Egyptians could not drink its water, and there was blood throughout the whole land of Egypt. But the magicians of Egypt did the same by their secret arts; so Pharaoh's heart remained hardened, and he would not listen to them, as the LORD had said. Pharaoh turned and went into his house, and he did not take even this to heart. And all the Egyptians had to dig along the Nile for water to drink, for they could not drink the water of the river.

Passover and the Tenth Plague

EXODUS 11:1-12:42

The LORD said to Moses, "I will bring one more plague upon Pharaoh and upon Egypt; afterwards he will let you go from here; indeed, when he lets you go, he will drive you away. Tell the people that every man is to ask his neighbor and every woman is to ask her neighbor for objects of silver and gold." The LORD gave the people favor in the sight of the Egyptians. Moreover, Moses himself was a man of great importance in the land of Egypt, in the sight of Pharaoh's officials and in the sight of the people.

Moses said, "Thus says the LORD: About midnight I will go out through Egypt. Every firstborn in the land of Egypt shall die, from the firstborn of Pharaoh who sits on his throne to the firstborn of the female slave who is behind the handmill, and all the firstborn of the livestock. Then there will be a loud cry throughout the whole land of Egypt, such as has never been or will ever be again. But not a dog shall growl at any of the Israelites—not at people, not at animals—so that you may know that the LORD makes a distinction between Egypt and Israel. Then all these officials of yours shall come down to me, and bow low to me, saying, 'Leave us, you and all the people who follow you.' After that I will leave." And in hot anger he left Pharaoh.

The LORD said to Moses, "Pharaoh will not listen to you, in order that my wonders may be multiplied in the land of Egypt." Moses and Aaron performed all these wonders before Pharaoh; but the LORD hardened Pharaoh's heart, and he did not let the people of Israel go out of his land.

The LORD said to Moses and Aaron in the land of Egypt: This month shall mark for you the beginning of months; it shall be the first month of the year for you. Tell the whole congregation of Israel that on the tenth of this month they are to take a lamb for each family, a lamb for each household. If a household is too small for a whole lamb, it shall join its closest neighbor in obtaining one; the lamb shall be divided in proportion to the number of people who eat of it. Your lamb shall be without blemish, a year-old male; you may take it from the sheep or from the goats. You shall keep it until the fourteenth day of this month; then the whole assembled congregation of Israel shall slaughter it at twilight. They shall take some of the blood and put it on the two doorposts and the lintel of the houses in which they eat it. They shall eat the lamb that same night; they shall eat it roasted over the fire with unleavened bread and bitter herbs. Do not eat any of it raw or boiled in water, but roasted over the fire, with its head, legs, and inner organs. You shall let none of it remain until the morning; anything that remains until the morning you shall burn. This is how you shall eat it: your loins girded, your sandals on your feet, and your staff in your hand; and you shall eat it hurriedly. It is the passover of the LORD. For I will pass through the land of Egypt that night, and I will strike down every firstborn in the land of Egypt, both human beings and animals; on all the gods of Egypt I will execute judgments: I am the LORD. The blood shall be a sign for you on the houses where you live: when I see the blood, I will pass over you, and no plague shall destroy you when I strike the land of Egypt.

This day shall be a day of remembrance for you. You shall celebrate it as a festival to the LORD; throughout your generations you shall observe it as a perpetual ordinance. Seven days you shall eat unleavened bread; on the first day you shall remove leaven from your houses, for whoever eats leavened bread from the first day until the seventh day shall be cut off from Israel. On the first day you shall hold a solemn assembly, and on the seventh day a solemn assembly; no work shall be done on those days; only what everyone must eat, that alone may be prepared by you. You shall observe the festival of unleavened bread, for on this very day I brought your companies out of the land of Egypt: you shall observe this day throughout your generations as a perpetual ordinance. In the first month, from the evening of the fourteenth day until the evening of the twenty-first day, you shall eat unleavened bread. For seven days no leaven shall be found in your houses; for whoever eats what is leavened shall be cut off from the congregation of Israel, whether an alien or a native of the land. You shall eat nothing leavened; in all your settlements you shall eat unleavened bread.

Then Moses called all the elders of Israel and said to them, "Go, select lambs for your families, and slaughter the passover lamb. Take a bunch of hyssop, dip it in the blood that is in the basin, and touch the lintel and the two doorposts with the blood in the basin. None of you shall go outside the door of your house until morning. For the LORD will pass through to strike down the Egyptians; when he sees the blood on the lintel and on the two doorposts, the LORD will pass over that door and will not allow the destroyer to enter your houses to strike you down. You shall observe this rite as a perpetual ordinance for you and your children. When you come to the land that the LORD will give you, as he has promised, you shall keep this observance. And when your children ask you, 'What do you mean by this observance?' you shall say, 'It is the passover sacrifice to the LORD, for he passed over the houses of the Israelites in Egypt, when he struck down the Egyptians but spared our houses.'" And the people bowed down and worshiped.

The Israelites went and did just as the LORD had commanded Moses and Aaron.

At midnight the LORD struck down all the firstborn in the land of Egypt, from the firstborn of Pharaoh who sat on his throne to the firstborn of the prisoner who was in the dungeon, and all the firstborn

> My hopes were all dead— struck with a subtle doom, such as, in one night, fell on all the first-born in the land of Egypt. I looked on my cherished wishes, yesterday so blooming and glowing; they lay stark, chill, livid corpses that could never revive.
>
> —Charlotte Brontë, *Jane Eyre*

of the livestock. Pharaoh arose in the night, he and all his officials and all the Egyptians; and there was a loud cry in Egypt, for there was not a house without someone dead. Then he summoned Moses and Aaron in the night, and said, "Rise up, go away from my people, both you and the Israelites! Go, worship the LORD, as you said. Take your flocks and your herds, as you said, and be gone. And bring a blessing on me too!"

The Egyptians urged the people to hasten their departure from the land, for they said, "We shall all be dead." So the people took their dough before it was leavened, with their kneading bowls wrapped up in their cloaks on their shoulders. The Israelites had done as Moses told them; they had asked the Egyptians for jewelry of silver and gold, and for clothing, and the LORD had given the people favor in the sight of the Egyptians, so that they let them have what they asked. And so they plundered the Egyptians.

The Israelites journeyed from Rameses to Succoth, about six hundred thousand men on foot, besides children. A mixed crowd also went up with them, and livestock in great numbers, both flocks and herds. They baked unleavened cakes of the dough that they had brought out of Egypt; it was not leavened, because they were driven out of Egypt and could not wait, nor had they prepared any provisions for themselves.

The time that the Israelites had lived in Egypt was four hundred thirty years. At the end of four hundred thirty years, on that very day, all the companies of the LORD went out from the land of Egypt. That was for the LORD a night of vigil, to bring them out of the land of Egypt. That same night is a vigil to be kept for the LORD by all the Israelites throughout their generations.

Parting the Waters

EXODUS 14:1-31; 15:20-21

Then the LORD said to Moses: Tell the Israelites to turn back and camp in front of Pi-hahiroth, between Migdol and the sea, in front of Baal-zephon; you shall camp opposite it, by the sea. Pharaoh will say of the Israelites, "They are wandering aimlessly in the land; the wilderness has closed in on them." I will harden Pharaoh's heart, and he will pursue them, so that I will gain glory for myself over Pharaoh and all his army; and the Egyptians shall know that I am the LORD. And they did so.

When the king of Egypt was told that the people had fled, the minds of Pharaoh and his officials were changed toward the people, and they said, "What have we done, letting Israel leave our service?" So he had his chariot made ready, and took his army with him; he took six hundred picked chariots and all the other chariots of Egypt with officers over all of them. The LORD hardened the heart of Pharaoh king of Egypt and he pursued the Israelites, who were going out boldly. The Egyptians pursued them, all Pharaoh's horses and chariots, his chariot drivers and his army; they overtook them camped by the sea, by Pi-hahiroth, in front of Baal-zephon.

As Pharaoh drew near, the Israelites looked back, and there were the Egyptians advancing on them. In great fear the Israelites cried out to the LORD. They said to Moses, "Was it because there were no graves in Egypt that you have taken us away to die in the wilderness? What have you done to us, bringing us out of Egypt? Is this not the very thing we told you in Egypt, 'Let us alone and let us serve the Egyptians'? For it would have been better for us to serve the Egyptians than to die in the wilderness." But Moses said to the people, "Do not be afraid, stand firm, and see the deliverance that the LORD will accomplish for you today; for the Egyptians whom you see today you shall never see again. The LORD will fight for you, and you have only to keep still."

Then the LORD said to Moses, "Why do you cry out to me? Tell the Israelites to go forward. But you lift up your staff, and stretch out your hand over the sea and divide it, that the Israelites may go into the sea on dry ground. Then I will harden the hearts of the Egyptians so that they will go in after them; and so I will gain glory for myself over Pharaoh and all his army, his chariots, and his chariot drivers. And the Egyptians shall know that I am the LORD, when I have gained glory for myself over Pharaoh, his chariots, and his chariot drivers."

The angel of God who was going before the Israelite army moved and went behind them; and the pillar of cloud moved from in front of them and took its place behind them. It came between the army of Egypt and the army of Israel. And so the cloud was there with the darkness, and it lit up the night; one did not come near the other all night.

With its huge budget, its cast of thousands, and its use of early Technicolor, Cecil B. DeMille's first version of *The Ten Commandments* (1923) was heralded as a cinematic spectacle to top all spectacles. The celebrated scene of the parting of the sea was done by filming the melting of gelatin that was formed to look like a divided sea and then running the film backwards.

Then Moses stretched out his hand over the sea. The LORD drove the sea back by a strong east wind all night, and turned the sea into dry land; and the waters were divided. The Israelites went into the sea on dry ground, the waters forming a wall for them on their right and on their left. The Egyptians pursued, and went into the sea after them, all of Pharaoh's horses, chariots, and chariot drivers. At the morning watch the LORD in the pillar of fire and cloud looked down upon the Egyptian army, and threw the Egyptian army into panic. He clogged their chariot wheels so that they turned with difficulty. The Egyptians said, "Let us flee from the Israelites, for the LORD is fighting for them against Egypt."

Then the LORD said to Moses, "Stretch out your hand over the sea, so that the water may come back upon the Egyptians, upon their chariots and chariot drivers." So Moses stretched out his hand over the sea, and at dawn the sea returned to its normal depth. As the Egyptians fled before it, the LORD tossed the Egyptians into the sea. The waters returned and covered the chariots and the chariot drivers, the entire army of Pharaoh that had followed them into the sea; not one of them remained. But the Israelites walked on dry ground through the sea, the waters forming a wall for them on their right and on their left.

Miriam's brief song is probably one of the oldest poems in the Hebrew Bible. It is likely that women were the original poets of ancient Israel, and that their songs, like this one, served ritual functions within the community—celebrating victory and deliverance, lamenting death and loss, for example.

Thus the LORD saved Israel that day from the Egyptians; and Israel saw the Egyptians dead on the seashore. Israel saw the great work that the LORD did against the Egyptians. So the people feared the LORD and believed in the LORD and in his servant Moses.

. . . Then the prophet Miriam, Aaron's sister, took a tambourine in her hand; and all the women went out after her with tambourines and with dancing. And Miriam sang to them:

"Sing to the LORD, for he has triumphed gloriously;
horse and rider he has thrown into the sea."

MANNA FROM HEAVEN

Manna **is the Hebrew equivalent of "whatchamacallit." It literally means "What is it?" Thanks to this story, however,** *manna* **has become another name for divine sustenance, which not only satisfies hunger, but tastes downright heavenly. Interestingly, the story itself says little about the flavor, just that it tasted like sweetened wafers and provided the wilderness wanderers with their daily nutritional needs.**

A central theme here is dependence and trust. There's no returning to the fleshpots of Egypt. The Promised Land is a long way away. Provision is given day to day, but the people cannot create long-term security for themselves. Insecurity is the way of the wilderness.

EXODUS 16:1–35

The whole congregation of the Israelites set out from Elim; and Israel came to the wilderness of Sin, which is between Elim and Sinai, on the fifteenth day of the second month after they had departed from the land of Egypt. The whole congregation of the Israelites complained against Moses and Aaron in the wilderness. The Israelites said to them, "If only we had died by the hand of the Lord in the land of Egypt, when we sat by the fleshpots and ate our fill of bread; for you have brought us out into this wilderness to kill this whole assembly with hunger."

Then the Lord said to Moses, "I am going to rain bread from heaven for you, and each day the people shall go out and gather enough for that day. In that way I will test them, whether they will follow my instruction or not. On the sixth day, when they prepare what they bring in, it will be twice as much as they gather on other days." So Moses and Aaron said to all the Israelites, "In the evening you shall know that it was the Lord who brought you out of the land of Egypt, and in the morning you shall see the glory of the Lord, because he has heard your complaining against the Lord. For what are we, that you complain against us?" And Moses said, "When the Lord gives you meat to eat in the evening and your fill of bread in the morning, because the Lord has heard the complaining that you utter against him—what are we? Your complaining is not against us but against the Lord."

Then Moses said to Aaron, "Say to the whole congregation of the Israelites, 'Draw near to the Lord, for he has heard your complaining.'" And as Aaron spoke to the whole congregation of the Israelites, they looked toward the wilderness, and the glory of the Lord appeared in the cloud. The Lord spoke to Moses and said, "I have heard the complaining of the Israelites; say to them, 'At twilight you shall eat meat, and in the morning you shall have your fill of bread; then you shall know that I am the Lord your God.'"

In the evening quails came up and covered the camp; and in the morning there was a layer of dew around the camp. When the layer of dew lifted, there on the surface of the wilderness was a fine flaky substance, as fine as frost on the ground. When the Israelites saw it, they said to one another, "What is it?" For they did not know what it was. Moses said to them, "It is the bread that the LORD has given you to eat. This is what the LORD has commanded: 'Gather as much of it as each of you needs, an omer to a person according to the number of persons, all providing for those in their own tents.'" The Israelites did so, some gathering more, some less. But when they measured it with an omer, those who gathered much had nothing over, and those who gathered little had no shortage; they gathered as much as each of them needed. And Moses said to them, "Let no one leave any of it over until morning." But they did not listen to Moses; some left part of it until morning, and it bred worms

---

The extra manna provided on the sixth day makes possible the very first Sabbath for the newly liberated Israelites.

---

and became foul. And Moses was angry with them. Morning by morning they gathered it, as much as each needed; but when the sun grew hot, it melted.

On the sixth day they gathered twice as much food, two omers apiece. When all the leaders of the congregation came and told Moses, he said to them, "This is what the LORD has commanded: 'Tomorrow is a day of solemn rest, a holy sabbath to the LORD; bake what you want to bake and boil what you want to boil, and all that is left over put aside to be kept until morning.'" So they put it aside until morning, as Moses commanded them; and it did not become foul, and there were no worms in it. Moses said, "Eat it today, for today is a sabbath to the LORD; today you will not find it in the field. Six days you shall gather it; but on the seventh day, which is a sabbath, there will be none."

On the seventh day some of the people went out to gather, and they found none. The LORD said to Moses, "How long will you refuse to keep my commandments and instructions? See! The LORD has given you the sabbath, therefore on the sixth day he gives you food for two days; each of you stay where you are; do not leave your place on the seventh day." So the people rested on the seventh day.

The house of Israel called it manna; it was like coriander seed, white, and the taste of it was like wafers made with honey. Moses said, "This is what the LORD has commanded: 'Let an omer of it be kept throughout your generations, in order that they may see the food with which I fed you in the wilderness, when I brought you out of the land of Egypt.'" And Moses said to Aaron, "Take a jar, and put an omer of manna in it, and place it before the LORD, to be kept throughout your generations." As the LORD commanded Moses, so Aaron placed it before the covenant, for safekeeping. The Israelites ate manna forty years, until they came to a habitable land; they ate manna, until they came to the border of the land of Canaan.

THE TEN COMMANDMENTS

The two tablets of the Ten Commandments have become a cultural icon for the conservative Christian ideal of a God-fearing, morally upright nation. Indeed, the image of them is often more culturally significant than the words themselves. The politicians and activists who promote them, even erecting monuments of them in courthouses and schools, are not always able to recite all ten.

The Ten Commandments don't speak for themselves. Over the centuries, they've been interpreted in different ways. The third, prohibiting taking "the LORD's name in vain," as the King James Version put it, has come to refer to any sort of swearing or profanity. The fifth, "Honor your father and mother," is often directed to children these days, but it referred originally to the need for able adults to take care of their elderly parents, who were especially vulnerable. And many "keep the Sabbath" on Sunday rather than the actual biblical Sabbath, which is the seventh day of the week, Saturday.

How practical are these commandments as a foundation for society? What would a society based on them look like? Which ones are specifically religious, and which are more generally moral? Also, who is the implied subject of these laws? To whom are they addressed? Do they all speak to everyone, including women, children, and servants?

EXODUS 19:1–20:21

On the third new moon after the Israelites had gone out of the land of Egypt, on that very day, they came into the wilderness of Sinai. They had journeyed from Rephidim, entered the wilderness of Sinai, and camped in the wilderness; Israel camped there in front of the mountain. Then Moses went up to God; the LORD called to him from the mountain, saying, "Thus you shall say to the house of Jacob, and tell the Israelites: You have seen what I did to the Egyptians, and how I bore you on eagles' wings and brought you to myself. Now therefore, if you obey my voice and keep my covenant, you shall be my treasured possession out of all the peoples. Indeed, the whole earth is mine, but you shall be for me a priestly kingdom and a holy nation. These are the words that you shall speak to the Israelites."

So Moses came, summoned the elders of the people, and set before them all these words that the LORD had commanded him. The people all answered as one: "Everything that the LORD has spoken we will do." Moses reported the words of the people to the LORD. Then the LORD said to Moses, "I am going to come to you in a dense cloud, in order that the people may hear when I speak with you and so trust you ever after."

When Moses had told the words of the people to the LORD, the LORD said to Moses: "Go to the people and consecrate them today and tomorrow. Have them wash their clothes and prepare for the third day, because on the third day the LORD will come down upon Mount Sinai in the sight of all the people. You shall set limits for the people all around, saying, 'Be careful not to go up the mountain or to touch the edge of it. Any who touch the mountain shall be put to death. No hand shall touch them, but they shall be stoned or shot with arrows; whether animal or human being, they shall not live.' When the trumpet sounds a long blast, they may go up on the mountain." So Moses went down from the mountain to the people. He consecrated the people, and they washed their clothes. And he said to the people, "Prepare for the third day; do not go near a woman."

On the morning of the third day there was thunder and lightning, as well as a thick cloud on the mountain, and a blast of a trumpet so loud that all the people who were in the camp trembled. Moses brought the people out of the camp to meet God. They took their stand at the foot of the mountain. Now Mount Sinai was wrapped in smoke, because the

LORD had descended upon it in fire; the smoke went up like the smoke of a kiln, while the whole mountain shook violently. As the blast of the trumpet grew louder and louder, Moses would speak and God would answer him in thunder. When the LORD descended upon Mount Sinai, to the top of the mountain, the LORD summoned Moses to the top of the mountain, and Moses went up. Then the LORD said to Moses, "Go down and warn the people not to break through to the LORD to look; otherwise many of them will perish. Even the priests who approach the LORD must consecrate themselves or the LORD will break out against them." Moses said to the LORD, "The people are not permitted to come up to Mount Sinai; for you yourself warned us, saying, 'Set limits around the mountain and keep it holy.'" The LORD said to him, "Go down, and come up bringing Aaron with you; but do not let either the priests or the people break through to come up to the LORD; otherwise he will break out against them." So Moses went down to the people and told them.

Then God spoke all these words: I am the LORD your God, who brought you out of the land of Egypt, out of the house of slavery; you shall have no other gods before me.

You shall not make for yourself an idol, whether in the form of anything that is in heaven above, or that is on the earth beneath, or that is in the water under the earth. You shall not bow down to them or worship them; for I the LORD your God am a jealous God, punishing children for the iniquity of parents, to the third and the fourth generation of those who reject me, but showing steadfast love to the thousandth generation of those who love me and keep my commandments.

You shall not make wrongful use of the name of the LORD your God, for the LORD will not acquit anyone who misuses his name.

Remember the sabbath day, and keep it holy. Six days you shall labor and do all your work. But the seventh day is a sabbath to the LORD your God; you shall not do any work—you, your son or your daughter, your male or female slave, your livestock, or the alien resident in your towns. For in six days the LORD made heaven and earth, the sea, and all that is in them, but rested the seventh day; therefore the LORD blessed the sabbath day and consecrated it.

Honor your father and your mother, so that your days may be long in the land that the LORD your God is giving you.

You shall not murder.

You shall not commit adultery.

You shall not steal.

You shall not bear false witness against your neighbor.

You shall not covet your neighbor's house; you shall not covet your neighbor's wife, or male or female slave, or ox, or donkey, or anything that belongs to your neighbor.

When all the people witnessed the thunder and lightning, the sound of the trumpet, and the mountain smoking, they were afraid and trembled and stood at a distance, and said to Moses, "You speak to us, and we will listen; but do not let God speak to us, or we will die." Moses said to the people, "Do not be afraid; for God has come only to test you and to put the fear of him upon you so that you do not sin." Then the people stood at a distance, while Moses drew near to the thick darkness where God was.

The Ten Commandments

1. Do not have other gods.
2. Do not make idols.
3. Do not wrongfully use the LORD's name.
4. Honor the Sabbath.
5. Honor your father and mother.
6. Do not murder.
7. Do not commit adultery.
8. Do not steal.
9. Do not bear false witness.
10. Do not covet.

THE GOLDEN CALF

The story of the golden calf speaks to human insecurity and the desire for real presence. In our consumer culture, that insecurity and that desire are often manifest in materialism. The fact that Aaron's idol is made from gold suggests a connection.

Notice how the story moves back and forth between two scenes: up on the mountain, where God is talking with Moses, and down below, where the Israelites are anxiously awaiting Moses's return. Moses is the mediator between the two spaces and the two parties. Indeed, he argues with each on behalf of the other. How does this story develop his character in relation to each?

EXODUS 32:1-35; 34:1-9

When the people saw that Moses delayed to come down from the mountain, the people gathered around Aaron, and said to him, "Come, make gods for us, who shall go before us; as for this Moses, the man who brought us up out of the land of Egypt, we do not know what has become of him." Aaron said to them, "Take off the gold rings that are on the ears of your wives, your sons, and your daughters, and bring them to me." So all the people took off the gold rings from their ears, and brought them to Aaron. He took the gold from them, formed it in a mold, and cast an image of a calf; and they said, "These are your gods, O Israel, who brought you up out of the land of Egypt!" When Aaron saw this, he built an altar before it; and Aaron made proclamation and said, "Tomorrow shall be a festival to the Lord." They rose early the next day, and offered burnt offerings and brought sacrifices of well-being; and the people sat down to eat and drink, and rose up to revel.

The Lord said to Moses, "Go down at once! Your people, whom you brought up out of the land of Egypt, have acted perversely; they have been quick to turn aside from the way that I commanded them; they have cast for themselves an image of a calf, and have worshiped it and sacrificed to it, and said, 'These are your gods, O Israel, who brought you up out of the land of Egypt!'" The Lord said to Moses, "I have seen this people, how stiff-necked they are. Now let me alone, so that my wrath may burn hot against them and I may consume them; and of you I will make a great nation."

> This story literally says that God "repented of the evil [or bad] that he planned to bring on his people." Moses convinces God to repent of destructive intentions. Stories like this are why Moses is remembered as an extraordinary model of faith.

But Moses implored the Lord his God, and said, "O Lord, why does your wrath burn hot against your people, whom you brought out of the land of Egypt with great power and with a mighty hand? Why should the Egyptians say, 'It was with evil intent that he brought them out to kill them in the mountains, and to consume them from the face of the earth'? Turn from your fierce wrath; change your mind and do not bring disaster on your people. Remember Abraham, Isaac, and Israel, your servants, how you swore to them by your own self, saying to them, 'I will multiply your descendants like the stars of heaven, and all this land that I have promised I will give to your descendants, and they shall inherit it forever.'" And the LORD changed his mind about the disaster that he planned to bring on his people.

Then Moses turned and went down from the mountain, carrying the two tablets of the covenant in his hands, tablets that were written on both sides, written on the front and on the back. The tablets were the work of God, and the writing was the writing of God, engraved upon the tablets. When Joshua heard the noise of the people as they shouted, he said to Moses, "There is a noise of war in the camp." But he said,

> "It is not the sound made by victors,
> or the sound made by losers;
> it is the sound of revelers that I hear."

As soon as he came near the camp and saw the calf and the dancing, Moses' anger burned hot, and he threw the tablets from his hands and broke them at the foot of the mountain. He took the calf that they had made, burned it with fire, ground it to powder, scattered it on the water, and made the Israelites drink it.

Moses said to Aaron, "What did this people do to you that you have brought so great a sin upon them?" And Aaron said, "Do not let the anger of my lord burn hot; you know the people, that they are bent on evil. They said to me, 'Make us gods, who shall go before us; as for this Moses, the man who brought us up out of the land of Egypt, we do not know what has become of him.' So I said to them, 'Whoever has gold, take it off'; so they gave it to me, and I threw it into the fire, and out came this calf!"

When Moses saw that the people were running wild (for Aaron had let them run wild, to the derision of their enemies), then Moses stood in the gate of the camp, and said, "Who is on the LORD's side? Come to me!" And all the sons of Levi gathered around him. He said to them, "Thus says the LORD, the God of Israel, 'Put your sword on your side, each of you! Go back and forth from gate to gate throughout the camp, and each of you kill your brother, your friend, and your neighbor.'" The sons of

Levi did as Moses commanded, and about three thousand of the people fell on that day. Moses said, "Today you have ordained yourselves for the service of the LORD, each one at the cost of a son or a brother, and so have brought a blessing on yourselves this day."

On the next day Moses said to the people, "You have sinned a great sin. But now I will go up to the LORD; perhaps I can make atonement for your sin." So Moses returned to the LORD and said, "Alas, this people has sinned a great sin; they have made for themselves gods of gold. But now, if you will only forgive their sin—but if not, blot me out of the book that you have written." But the LORD said to Moses, "Whoever has sinned against me I will blot out of my book. But now go, lead the people to the place about which I have spoken to you; see, my angel shall go in front of you. Nevertheless, when the day comes for punishment, I will punish them for their sin."

Then the LORD sent a plague on the people, because they made the calf—the one that Aaron made.

. . . The LORD said to Moses, "Cut two tablets of stone like the former ones, and I will write on the tablets the words that were on the former tablets, which you broke. Be ready in the morning, and come up in the morning to Mount Sinai and present yourself there to me, on the top of the mountain. No one shall come up with you, and do not let anyone be seen throughout all the mountain; and do not let flocks or herds graze in front of that mountain." So Moses cut two tablets of stone like the former ones; and he rose early in the morning and went up on Mount Sinai, as the LORD had commanded him, and took in his hand the two tablets of stone. The LORD descended in the cloud and stood with him there, and proclaimed the name, "The LORD." The LORD passed before him, and proclaimed,

> "The LORD, the LORD,
> a God merciful and gracious,
> slow to anger,
> and abounding in steadfast love and faithfulness,
> keeping steadfast love for the thousandth generation,
> forgiving iniquity and transgression and sin,
> yet by no means clearing the guilty,
> but visiting the iniquity of the parents

upon the children
and the children's children,
to the third and the fourth generation."

And Moses quickly bowed his head toward the earth, and worshiped. He said, "If now I have found favor in your sight, O Lord, I pray, let the Lord go with us. Although this is a stiff-necked people, pardon our iniquity and our sin, and take us for your inheritance."

MOSES'S SHINING FACE

As the mediator of divine will, Moses is set apart from the masses. Indeed, the closer he gets to God, the less approachable he becomes to his own people. His holiness actually scares them. In addition to illustrating his special status as holy man, does this story also suggest a sense of loneliness? Is holiness isolating?

Michelangelo's famous sculpture of Moses with two blunt horns was inspired by this story. What is here translated as "shining face" was translated in the Latin Vulgate as "two horns." That was not a mistranslation. The Hebrew literally describes two horns coming from his forehead, but most believe that they are better understood figuratively as rays or beams of light.

EXODUS 34:29–35

Moses came down from Mount Sinai. As he came down from the mountain with the two tablets of the covenant in his hand, Moses did not know that the skin of his face shone because he had been talking with God. When Aaron and all the Israelites saw Moses, the skin of his face was shining, and they were afraid to come near him. But Moses called to them; and Aaron and all the leaders of the congregation returned to him, and Moses spoke with them. Afterward all the Israelites came near, and he gave them in commandment all that the LORD had spoken with him on Mount Sinai. When Moses had finished speaking with them, he put a veil on his face; but whenever Moses went in before the LORD to speak with him, he would take the veil off, until he came out; and when he came out, and told the Israelites what he had been commanded, the Israelites would see the face of Moses, that the skin of his face was shining; and Moses would put the veil on his face again, until he went in to speak with him.

LEVITICUS: STRANGE FIRES

Too many readers skip over the book of Leviticus, presuming it's just a bunch of irrelevant laws and rites. In fact, although most of us won't want to adhere to most of its codes, they are nonetheless strangely fascinating, as are the stories that are intertwined with them. The brief story of Aaron's sons, Nadab and Abihu, is one of the most fascinating—and disturbing.

Moses and Aaron had just completed several sacrifices, and now it was the sons' turn. What exactly was "unholy" or, as the King James Version put it, "strange," about their fire? It's left to the imagination. But the image of these enthusiastic young priests coming forward to make their offering, only to have it blow up in their faces, has inspired sympathy for them over against the powers that be. The Indigo Girls' song "Strange Fire" is a powerful example.

LEVITICUS 10:1-3

Now Aaron's sons, Nadab and Abihu, each took his censer, put fire in it, and laid incense on it; and they offered unholy fire before the LORD, such as he had not commanded them. And fire came out from the presence of the LORD and consumed them, and they died before the LORD. Then Moses said to Aaron, "This is what the LORD meant when he said,

'Through those who are near me
   I will show myself holy,

I come to you with strange
   fire, I make an offering
   of love
The incense of my soul is
   burned by the fire in my
   blood
I come with a softer answer
   to the questions that lie in
   your path
I want to harbor you from the
   anger, find a refuge from
   the wrath

This is a message of love,
   love that moves from the
   inside out
A love that never grows tired
I come to you with strange
   fire
   —Indigo Girls, "Strange Fire"

and before all the people
  I will be glorified.'"

And Aaron was silent.

SCAPEGOAT

Not only is the ritual described in Leviticus 16 the basis for the Jewish holiday of Yom Kippur, or the Day of Atonement; it is also the origin of the idea of the scapegoat. Today, "scapegoating" is not usually a ritual activity, but a social or political one: people or groups are made to carry the blame for social ills or political misdeeds for which they are not responsible. Like the poor goat in this story, moreover, contemporary scapegoats never choose this role, and they rarely get to speak for themselves.

LEVITICUS 16:1–34

The LORD spoke to Moses after the death of the two sons of Aaron, when they drew near before the LORD and died. The LORD said to Moses:

Tell your brother Aaron not to come just at any time into the sanctuary inside the curtain before the mercy seat that is upon the ark, or he will die; for I appear in the cloud upon the mercy seat. Thus shall Aaron come into the holy place: with a young bull for a sin offering and a ram for a burnt offering. He shall put on the holy linen tunic, and shall have the linen undergarments next to his body, fasten the linen sash, and wear the linen turban; these are the holy vestments. He shall bathe his body in water, and then put them on. He shall take from the congregation of the people of Israel two male goats for a sin offering, and one ram for a burnt offering.

Aaron shall offer the bull as a sin offering for himself, and shall make atonement for himself and for his house. He shall take the two goats and set them before the LORD at the entrance of the tent of meeting; and Aaron shall cast lots on the two goats, one lot for the LORD and the other lot for Azazel. Aaron shall present the goat on which the lot fell for the LORD, and offer it as a sin offering; but the goat on which the lot fell for Azazel shall be presented alive before the LORD to make atonement over it, that it may be sent away into the wilderness to Azazel.

Aaron shall present the bull as a sin offering for himself, and shall make atonement for himself and for his house; he shall slaughter the bull as a sin offering for himself. He shall take a censer full of coals of fire from the altar before the LORD, and two handfuls of crushed sweet incense, and he shall bring it inside the curtain and put the incense on the fire before the LORD, that the cloud of the incense may cover the mercy seat that is upon the covenant, or he will die. He shall take some of the blood of the bull, and sprinkle it with his finger on the front of the mercy seat, and before the mercy seat he shall sprinkle the blood with his finger seven times.

He shall slaughter the goat of the sin offering that is for the people and bring its blood inside the curtain, and do with its blood as he did with the blood of the bull, sprinkling it upon the mercy seat and before the mercy seat. Thus he shall make atonement for the sanctuary, because of the uncleannesses of the people of Israel, and because of their transgressions, all their sins; and so he shall do for the tent of meeting, which remains with them in the midst of their uncleannesses. No one shall be in the tent of meeting from the time he enters to make atonement in the sanctuary until he comes out and has made atonement for himself and for his house and for all the assembly of Israel. Then he shall go out to the altar that is before the LORD and make atonement on its behalf, and shall take some of the blood of the bull and of the blood of the goat, and put it on each of the horns of the altar. He shall sprinkle some of the blood on it with his finger seven times, and cleanse it and hallow it from the uncleannesses of the people of Israel.

When he has finished atoning for the holy place and the tent of meeting and the altar, he shall present the live goat. Then Aaron shall lay both his hands on the head of the live goat, and confess over it all the iniquities of the people of Israel, and all their transgressions, all their sins, putting them on the head of the goat, and sending it away into the wilderness by means of someone designated for the task. The goat shall bear on itself all their iniquities to a barren region; and the goat shall be set free in the wilderness.

Then Aaron shall enter the tent of meeting, and shall take off the linen vestments that he put on when he went into the holy place, and shall leave them there. He shall bathe his body in water in a holy place, and put on his vestments; then he shall come out and offer his burnt offering and the burnt offering of the people, making atonement for himself and for the people. The fat of the sin offering he shall turn into smoke on the altar. The one who sets the goat free for Azazel shall wash his clothes and bathe his body in water, and afterward may come into the camp. The bull of the sin offering and the goat of the sin offering, whose blood was brought in to make atonement in the holy place, shall be taken outside the camp; their skin and their flesh and their dung shall be consumed in fire. The one who burns them shall wash his clothes and bathe his body in water, and afterward may come into the camp.

This shall be a statute to you forever: In the seventh month, on the tenth day of the month, you shall deny yourselves, and shall do no work, neither the citizen nor the alien who resides among you. For on this day atonement shall be made for you, to cleanse you; from all your sins you shall be clean before the LORD. It is a sabbath of complete rest to you, and you shall deny yourselves; it is a statute forever. The priest who is anointed and consecrated as priest in his father's place shall make atonement, wearing the linen vestments, the holy vestments. He shall make atonement for the sanctuary, and he shall make atonement for the tent of meeting and for the altar, and he shall make atonement for the priests and for all the people of the assembly. This shall be an everlasting statute for you, to make atonement for the people of Israel once in the year for all their sins. And Moses did as the LORD had commanded him.

JUBILEE

The rich get richer while the poor get poorer. It's nothing new. What a society does about it is another question. This biblical story indicates that ancient Israelite culture understood that the accumulation of wealth, and especially the accumulation of debt, could not go unchecked.

Globalization has, of course, made problems worse. Whole countries find themselves struggling under insupportable debt that severely hinders their potential for development. In this context, the biblical concept of Jubilee has taken on a global meaning: Jubilee Debt Relief is an international organization that seeks to release the world's poorest countries from the debt that keeps them down.

On a more personal level, many people celebrate their fiftieth birthday as a Jubilee, an opportunity to release themselves from stifling expectations and debts that they have carried for too long.

We often presume that ancient societies were more "primitive" and less complex than ours. Regulations like this one suggest we might want to revise some of those presumptions.

LEVITICUS 25:8–17

You shall count off seven weeks of years, seven times seven years, so that the period of seven weeks of years gives forty-nine years. Then you shall have the trumpet sounded loud; on the tenth day of the seventh month—on the day of atonement—you shall have the trumpet sounded throughout all your land. And you shall hallow the fiftieth year and you shall proclaim liberty throughout the land to all its inhabitants. It shall be a jubilee for you: you shall return, every one of you, to your property and every one of you to your family. That fiftieth year shall be a jubilee for you: you shall not sow, or reap the aftergrowth, or harvest the unpruned vines. For it is a jubilee; it shall be holy to you: you shall eat only what the field itself produces.

> America, in this young century, proclaims liberty throughout all the world and to all the inhabitants thereof.
> —George W. Bush, Second Inaugural Address, January 20, 2005

In this year of jubilee you shall return, every one of you, to your property. When you make a sale to your neighbor or buy from your neighbor, you shall not cheat one another. When you buy from your neighbor, you shall pay only for the number of years since the jubilee; the seller shall charge you only for the remaining crop years. If the years are more, you shall increase the price, and if the years are fewer, you shall diminish the price; for it is a certain number of harvests that are being sold to you. You shall not cheat one another, but you shall fear your God; for I am the LORD your God.

THE BRONZE SERPENT

The image of a serpent wrapped around a pole (which also appears in the Greek story of the rod of Asclepius) has become a nearly universal symbol for the science of medicine. This is ironic, since such a prescription for snakebite or any other sickness would be the end of any medical doctor's career. On another level, this story from the book of Numbers seems to suggest that the source of the poison is also often the source of the cure. It's a story of vaccination, biblical style.

NUMBERS 21:4–9

From Mount Hor they set out by the way to the Red Sea, to go around the land of Edom; but the people became impatient on the way. The people spoke against God and against Moses, "Why have you brought us up out of Egypt to die in the wilderness? For there is no food and no water, and we detest this miserable food." Then the LORD sent poisonous serpents among the people, and they bit the people, so that many Israelites died. The people came to Moses and said, "We have sinned by speaking against the LORD and against you; pray to the LORD to take away the serpents from us." So Moses prayed for the people. And the LORD said to Moses, "Make a poisonous serpent, and set it on a pole; and everyone who is bitten shall look at it and live." So Moses made a serpent of bronze, and put it upon a pole; and whenever a serpent bit someone, that person would look at the serpent of bronze and live.

BALAAM'S ASS

There are only two talking animals in the Bible. The first is the serpent in Genesis 3, and the second is Balaam's donkey, or ass. Balaam is caught between two powers, a pawn in their game. Balak, king of the Moabites, wants Balaam to curse the Israelites so he can defeat them in battle. God tells Balaam to go to Balak, but *not* to do as he says.

Given that God had commanded him to go to Balak, why was he being stopped in his tracks? Was Balaam secretly planning to curse the Israelites, as he knew Balak wanted? Or did God have

a change of mind? The text doesn't say. Moreover, does Balaam seem at all surprised to hear his donkey speak? Is he used to talking with him?

NUMBERS 22:22–35

God's anger was kindled because he [Balaam] was going, and the angel of the LORD took his stand in the road as his adversary. Now he was riding on the donkey, and his two servants were with him. The donkey saw the angel of the LORD standing in the road, with a drawn sword in his hand; so the donkey turned off the road, and went into the field; and Balaam struck the donkey, to turn it back onto the road. Then the angel of the LORD stood in a narrow path between the vineyards, with a wall on either side. When the donkey saw the angel of the LORD, it scraped against the wall, and scraped Balaam's foot against the wall; so he struck it again. Then the angel of the LORD went ahead, and stood in a narrow place, where there was no way to turn either to the right or to the left. When the donkey saw the angel of the LORD, it lay down under Balaam; and Balaam's anger was kindled, and he struck the donkey with his staff. Then the LORD opened the mouth of the donkey, and it said to Balaam, "What have I done to you, that you have struck me these three times?" Balaam said to the donkey, "Because you have made a fool of me! I wish I had a sword in my hand! I would kill you right now!" But the donkey said to Balaam, "Am I not your donkey, which you have ridden all your life to this day? Have I been in the habit of treating you this way?" And he said, "No."

Then the LORD opened the eyes of Balaam, and he saw the angel of the LORD standing in the road, with his drawn sword in his hand; and he bowed down, falling on his face. The angel of the LORD said to him, "Why have you struck your donkey these three times? I have come out as an adversary, because your way is perverse before me. The donkey saw me, and turned away from me these three times. If it had not turned away from me, surely just now I would have killed you and let it live." Then Balaam said to the angel of the LORD, "I have sinned, for I did not know that you were standing in the road to oppose me. Now therefore, if it is displeasing to you, I will return home." The angel of the LORD said to Balaam, "Go with the men; but speak only what I tell you to speak." So Balaam went on with the officials of Balak.

"HEAR, O ISRAEL"

Whether or not you are familiar with the words of this biblical passage, you have probably seen it more often than any other. It is written on a little parchment scroll inside every mezuzah, that small rectangular box that you see attached to the doorframes of Jewish households around the world. The mezuzah takes literally the commandment to write "these words . . . on the doorposts of your house."

Known as the Shema, which is the first Hebrew word of the passage ("Hear"), this is the central commandment of the Hebrew Bible and the cornerstone of Judaism, and therefore of Christianity. In the most economic of terms, it proclaims the oneness of God and the single-hearted, single-minded love that this oneness demands.

DEUTERONOMY 6:4-9

Hear, O Israel: The LORD is our God, the LORD alone. You shall love the LORD your God with all your heart, and with all your soul, and with all your might. Keep these words that I am commanding you today in your heart. Recite them to your children and talk about them when you are at home and when you are away, when you lie down and when you rise. Bind them as a sign on your hand, fix them as an emblem on your forehead, and write them on the doorposts of your house and on your gates.

Historical Books

JOSHUA, JERICHO, AND RAHAB

The story of the conquest of Canaan under Moses's successor, Joshua, has fed many subsequent conquests, from the British conquest of the Maori in New Zealand, to the United States' decimation of Native Americans, to the occupation of Palestinian land by Israeli settlers. All these conquerors imagined themselves in biblical terms as a "chosen people" taking what was divinely ordained to be theirs. For this reason, many wish that these stories of conquest in Joshua, the first of the so-called Historical Books, had never found their way into the Bible. Since they did, perhaps we can develop a different, more critical way of reading them—not as inspiration for conquest, but as a mirror, reminding us of our long-standing, dangerous propensity to construe the world in nationalistic terms and see ourselves as engaged in holy war against ungodly "others."

JOSHUA 2:1-24; 6:1-25

Then Joshua son of Nun sent two men secretly from Shittim as spies, saying, "Go, view the land, especially Jericho." So they went, and entered the house of a prostitute whose name was Rahab, and spent the night there. The king of Jericho was told, "Some Israelites have come here tonight to search out the land." Then the king of Jericho sent orders to Rahab, "Bring out the men who have come to you, who entered your house, for they have come only to search out the whole land." But the woman took the two men and hid them. Then she said, "True, the men came to me, but I did not know where they came from. And when it was time to close the gate at dark, the men went out. Where the men went I do not know. Pursue them quickly, for you can overtake them." She had, however, brought them up to the roof and hidden them with the stalks of flax that she had laid out on the roof. So the men pursued them on the way to the Jordan as far as the fords. As soon as the pursuers had gone out, the gate was shut.

Before they went to sleep, she came up to them on the roof and said to the men: "I know that the LORD has given you the land, and that dread of you has fallen on us, and that all the inhabitants of the land melt in fear before you. For we have heard how the LORD dried up the water of the Red Sea before you when you came out of Egypt, and what you did to the two kings of the Amorites that were beyond the Jordan, to Sihon and Og, whom you utterly destroyed. As soon as we heard it, our hearts melted, and there was no courage left in any of us because of you. The LORD your God is indeed God in heaven above and on earth below. Now then, since I have dealt kindly with you, swear to me by the LORD that you in turn will deal kindly with my family. Give me a sign of good faith that you will spare my father and mother, my brothers and sisters, and all who belong to them, and deliver our lives from death." The men said to her, "Our life for yours! If you do not tell this business of ours, then we will deal kindly and faithfully with you when the LORD gives us the land."

Then she let them down by a rope through the window, for her house was on the outer side of the city wall and she resided within the wall itself. She said to them, "Go toward the hill country, so that the pursuers may not come upon you. Hide yourselves there three days, until the pursuers have returned; then afterward you may go your way." The men said to her, "We will be released from this oath that you have made us swear to you if we invade the land and you do not tie this crimson cord in the window through which you let us down, and you do not gather into your house your father and mother, your brothers, and all your family. If any of you go out of the doors of your house into the street, they shall be responsible for their own death, and we shall be innocent; but if a hand is laid upon any who are with you in the house, we shall bear the responsibility for their death. But if you tell this business of ours, then we shall be released from this oath that you made us swear to you." She said, "According to your words, so be it." She sent them away and they departed. Then she tied the crimson cord in the window.

They departed and went into the hill country and stayed there three days, until the pursuers returned. The pursuers had searched all along the way and found nothing. Then the two men came down again from the hill country. They crossed over, came to Joshua son of Nun, and told him all that had happened to them. They said to Joshua, "Truly the LORD has given all the land into our hands; moreover all the inhabitants of the land melt in fear before us."

. . . Now Jericho was shut up inside and out because of the Israelites; no one came out and no one went in. The LORD said to Joshua, "See, I have handed Jericho over to you, along with its king and soldiers. You shall march around the city, all the warriors circling the city once. Thus you shall do for six days, with seven priests bearing seven trumpets of rams' horns before the ark. On the seventh day you shall march around the city seven times, the priests blowing the trumpets. When they make a long blast with the ram's horn, as soon as you hear the sound of the trumpet, then all the people shall shout with a great shout; and the wall of the city will fall down flat, and all the people shall charge straight ahead." So Joshua son of Nun summoned the priests and said to them, "Take up the ark of the covenant, and have seven priests carry seven trumpets of rams' horns in front of the ark of the LORD." To the people he said, "Go forward and march around the city; have the armed men pass on before the ark of the LORD."

As Joshua had commanded the people, the seven priests carrying the seven trumpets of rams' horns before

The Twelve Tribes of Israel

Descended from Leah and Jacob:
Reuben
Simeon
Levi
Judah
Issachar
Zebulun

Descended from Bilhah and Jacob:
Dan
Naphtali

Descended from Zilpah and Jacob:
Gad
Asher

Descended from Rachel and Jacob:
Joseph (split into the two half-tribes Ephraim and Manasseh, named after Joseph's sons)
Benjamin

A QUICK HISTORY LESSON

Although our main interest is in getting to know the Hebrew Bible as literature, it's helpful to have a basic understanding of the historical contexts from which it comes. For our purposes, we may divide the history of ancient Israel into three main periods:

1. Premonarchical period: From the emergence of Israel as a coalition of tribes to the rise of the United Monarchy under King Saul and especially King David, around 1000 BCE. Historians and archaeologists question how historically reliable are different biblical accounts of this period, which includes the ancestral narratives of Genesis, the story of slavery and liberation in Exodus, the wandering in the wilderness in Numbers and Deuteronomy, the conquest of Canaan in Joshua, the time of the judges in Judges, and the story of the last judge, Samuel, in 1 Samuel.

2. Monarchical period: From the United Monarchy through the Divided Kingdom (the Northern Kingdom, usually called Israel or Samaria, and the Southern Kingdom, Judah, with Jerusalem as its capital), to the destruction of the Northern Kingdom by the Assyrians in 722 BCE and the destruction of the Temple in Jerusalem and the exile of Judeans by the Babylonians in 587 BCE. This history is narrated in the books of Samuel and Kings and then retold differently in the books of Chronicles.

3. Postmonarchical period: From the time of the Babylonian exile to the defeat of Babylon in 539 BCE by Persia under King Cyrus, the return of the Judeans to Jerusalem, and the rebuilding of the Temple. Thus begins the Second Temple period, which continued until the destruction of Jerusalem by Rome in 70 CE. Although the return from exile is formative for biblical literature,

it is important to remember that most Judeans did not return, but remained in what came to be known as the Jewish Diaspora. Esther and Daniel are biblical stories from the Jewish Diaspora.

As even this brief outline suggests, ancient Israel was never a dominant force in the ancient Near East. Caught in the traffic lane between the superpowers of Egypt to the south and Assyria and Babylon to the north, as a nation it was small, highly unstable, briefly unified, and ultimately short-lived. This socio-political reality shapes the literature of the Hebrew Bible in many ways. We see it in the glorification of underdogs and tricksters, in prophetic condemnations of injustice against the widow and the orphan, and in the central story of liberation from slavery. We'll see it in the New Testament as well.

the LORD went forward, blowing the trumpets, with the ark of the covenant of the LORD following them. And the armed men went before the priests who blew the trumpets; the rear guard came after the ark, while the trumpets blew continually. To the people Joshua gave this command: "You shall not shout or let your voice be heard, nor shall you utter a word, until the day I tell you to shout. Then you shall shout." So the ark of the LORD went around the city, circling it once; and they came into the camp, and spent the night in the camp.

Then Joshua rose early in the morning, and the priests took up the ark of the LORD. The seven priests carrying the seven trumpets of rams' horns before the ark of the LORD passed on, blowing the trumpets continually. The armed men went before them, and the rear guard came after the ark of the LORD, while the trumpets blew continually. On the second day they marched around the city once and then returned to the camp. They did this for six days.

On the seventh day they rose early, at dawn, and marched around the city in the same manner seven times. It was only on that day that they marched around the city seven times. And at the seventh time, when the priests had blown the trumpets, Joshua said to the people, "Shout! For the LORD has given you the city. The city and all that is in it shall be devoted to the LORD for destruction. Only Rahab the prostitute and all who are with her in her house shall live because she hid the messengers we sent. As for you, keep away from the things devoted to destruction, so as not to covet and take any of the devoted things and make the camp of Israel an object for destruction, bringing trouble upon it. But all silver and gold, and vessels of bronze and iron, are sacred to the LORD; they shall go into the treasury of the LORD." So the people shouted, and the trumpets were blown. As soon as the people heard the sound of the trumpets, they raised a great shout, and the wall fell down flat; so the people charged straight ahead into the city and captured it. Then they devoted to destruction by the edge of the sword all in the city, both men and women, young and old, oxen, sheep, and donkeys.

Joshua said to the two men who had spied out the land, "Go into the prostitute's house, and bring the woman out of it and all who belong to her, as you swore to her." So the young men who had been spies went in and brought Rahab out, along with her father, her mother, her brothers, and all who belonged to her—they brought all her kindred out—and set them outside the camp of Israel. They burned down the city, and everything in it; only the silver and gold, and the vessels of bronze and iron, they put into the treasury of the house of the LORD. But Rahab the prostitute, with her family and all who belonged to her, Joshua spared. Her family has lived in Israel ever since. For she hid the messengers whom Joshua sent to spy out Jericho.

JUDGE DEBORAH AND JAEL

The Hebrew Bible loves a femme fatale—so long as she's working for "us" against "them." Jael, like Rahab, finds herself in a double bind: she's a woman in a man's world and a foreigner who could easily end up on the wrong end of an Israelite spear. So she does what she needs to. She invites Commander Sisera into her tent, tucks him in, and nails his head to the ground.

This story from the book of Judges is actually told twice—first in prose (below) and then in poetry, as the "Song of Deborah," which praises Jael as "most blessed of women."

Where is the power in this story? Who has it, where do they find it, and how do they use it?

JUDGES 4:1-22

The Israelites again did what was evil in the sight of the LORD, after Ehud died. So the LORD sold them into the hand of King Jabin of Canaan, who reigned in Hazor; the commander of his army was Sisera, who lived in Harosheth-ha-goiim. Then the Israelites cried out to the LORD for help; for he had nine hundred chariots of iron, and had oppressed the Israelites cruelly twenty years.

At that time Deborah, a prophetess, wife of Lappidoth, was judging Israel. She used to sit under the palm of Deborah between Ramah and Bethel in the hill country of Ephraim; and the Israelites came up to her for judgment. She sent and summoned Barak son of Abinoam

> Lappidoth means "flames" in Hebrew. Deborah could as easily be a "woman of flames" as the wife of some guy named Lappidoth.

from Kedesh in Naphtali, and said to him, "The LORD, the God of Israel, commands you, 'Go, take position at Mount Tabor, bringing ten thousand from the tribe of Naphtali and the tribe of Zebulun. I will draw out Sisera, the general of Jabin's army, to meet you by the Wadi Kishon with his chariots and his troops; and I will give him into your hand.'" Barak said to her, "If you will go with me, I will go; but if you will not go with me, I will not go." And she said, "I will surely go with you; nevertheless, the road on which you are going will not lead to your glory, for the LORD will sell Sisera into the hand of a woman." Then Deborah got up and went with Barak to Kedesh. Barak summoned Zebulun and Naphtali to Kedesh; and ten thousand warriors went up behind him; and Deborah went up with him.

Now Heber the Kenite had separated from the other Kenites, that is, the descendants of Hobab the father-in-law of Moses, and had encamped as far away as Elon-bezaanannim, which is near Kedesh.

When Sisera was told that Barak son of Abinoam had gone up to Mount Tabor, Sisera called out all his chariots, nine hundred chariots of iron, and all the troops who were with him, from Harosheth-ha-goiim to the Wadi Kishon. Then Deborah said to Barak, "Up! For this is the day on which the LORD has given Sisera into your hand. The LORD is indeed going out before you." So Barak went down from Mount Tabor with ten thousand warriors following him. And the LORD threw Sisera and all his chariots and all his army into a panic before Barak; Sisera got down from his chariot and fled away on foot, while Barak pursued the chariots and the army to Harosheth-ha-goiim. All the army of Sisera fell by the sword; no one was left.

Now Sisera had fled away on foot to the tent of Jael wife of Heber the Kenite; for there was peace between King Jabin of Hazor and the clan of Heber the Kenite. Jael came out to meet Sisera, and said to him, "Turn aside, my lord, turn aside to me; have no fear." So he turned aside to her into the tent, and she covered him with a rug. Then he said to her, "Please give me a little water to drink; for I am thirsty." So she opened a skin of milk and gave him a drink and covered him. He said to her, "Stand at the entrance of the tent, and if anybody comes and asks you, 'Is anyone here?' say, 'No.'" But Jael wife of Heber took a tent peg, and took a hammer in her hand, and went softly to him and drove the peg into his temple, until it went down into the ground—he was lying fast asleep from weariness— and he died. Then, as Barak came in pursuit of Sisera, Jael went out to meet him, and said to him, "Come, and I will show you the man whom you are seeking." So he went into her tent; and there was Sisera lying dead, with the tent peg in his temple.

JEPHTHAH'S DAUGHTER

Women and children have always been the most unjust victims of war. Although this brief story of Jephthah's daughter is not a realistic illustration of that fact, it does highlight how such victims often fall prey to the rashness of leaders as much as to the violence of warriors.

For many, like Byron, Jephthah's daughter is lauded as a heroine of wartime self-sacrifice—to the neglect of the unlawful vow that called for her sacrifice. For many others, however, it is a story of stupid death.

Pay close attention to the details of the story. Is it significant that the "spirit of the LORD" came upon Jephthah right before he made his vow? Does that mean it was inspired? Assuming not,

why was there no divine intervention, as in the near sacrifice of Isaac by Abraham?

Then the spirit of the LORD came upon Jephthah, and he passed through Gilead and Manasseh. He passed on to Mizpah of Gilead, and from Mizpah of Gilead he passed on to the Ammonites. And Jephthah made a vow to the LORD, and said, "If you will give the Ammonites into my hand, then whoever comes out of the doors of my house to meet me, when I return victorious from the Ammonites, shall be the LORD's, to be offered up by me as a burnt offering." So Jephthah crossed over to the Ammonites to fight against them; and the LORD gave them into his hand. He inflicted a massive defeat on them from Aroer to the neighborhood of Minnith, twenty towns, and as far as Abel-keramim. So the Ammonites were subdued before the people of Israel.

Then Jephthah came to his home at Mizpah; and there was his daughter coming out to meet him with timbrels and with dancing. She was his only child; he had no son or daughter except her. When he saw her, he tore his clothes, and said, "Alas, my daughter! You have brought me very low; you have become the cause of great trouble to me. For I have opened my mouth to the LORD, and I cannot take back my vow." She said to him, "My father, if you have opened your mouth to the LORD, do to me according to what has gone out of your mouth, now that the LORD has given you vengeance against your enemies, the Ammonites." And she said to her father, "Let this thing be done for me: Grant me two months, so that I may go and wander on the mountains, and bewail my virginity, my companions and I." "Go," he said and sent her away for two months. So she departed, she and her companions, and bewailed her virginity on the mountains. At the end of

> I have won the great battle for thee,
> And my Father and Country are free!
> When this blood of thy giving hath gushed,
> When the voice that thou lovest is hushed,
> Let my memory still be thy pride,
> And forget not I smiled as I died!
>
> —Lord Byron, "Jephtha's Daughter"

two months, she returned to her father, who did with her according to the vow he had made. She had never slept with a man. So there arose an Israelite custom that for four days every year the daughters of Israel would go out to lament the daughter of Jephthah the Gileadite.

SHIBBOLETH

Here is a story about minding your P's and Q's—or, in Hebrew, your *shins* ("sh" sound) and *sins* ("s" sound). Jephthah's men identify and kill their enemies—members of another Israelite tribe—by the way they pronounce the word shibboleth/sibboleth. In modern English, "shibboleth" has come to refer to any practice that identifies someone with a particular geographical region or ethnic group. In the world of digital networking, Shibboleth is a working group whose goal is developing authentication systems for sharing resources between different organizations.

JUDGES 12:1-6

The men of Ephraim were called to arms, and they crossed to Zaphon and said to Jephthah, "Why did you cross over to fight against the Ammonites, and did not call us to go with you? We will burn your house down over you!" Jephthah said to them, "My people and I were engaged in conflict with the Ammonites who oppressed us severely. But when I called you, you did not deliver me from their hand. When I saw that you would not deliver me, I took my life in my hand, and crossed over against the Ammonites, and the LORD gave them into my hand. Why then have you come up to me this day, to fight against me?" Then Jephthah gathered all the men of Gilead and fought with Ephraim; and the men of Gilead defeated Ephraim, because they said, "You are fugitives from Ephraim, you Gileadites—in the heart of Ephraim and Manasseh." Then the Gileadites took the fords of the Jordan against the Ephraimites. Whenever one of the fugitives of Ephraim said, "Let me go over," the men of Gilead would say to him, "Are you an Ephraimite?" When he said, "No," they said to him, "Then say Shibboleth," and he said, "Sibboleth," for he could not pronounce it right. Then they seized him and killed him at the fords of the Jordan. Forty-two thousand of the Ephraimites fell at that time.

SAMSON

The mere name Samson conjures an image of the strong man brought low by the love of a woman. But his story is not so simple. Indeed, Samson sometimes seems hell-bent on destruction without anyone's help. And he sure was a nightmare of a son-in-law. He lived hard and died hard, burning out rather than fading away.

Inspired by Samson's derogatory reference to the "uncircumcised Philistines" who dominated Israel at the time, the nineteenth-century cultural critic Matthew Arnold invented the term "uncultured Philistines" to denigrate modern society's uneducated enemies of high culture. This is ironic, since Samson would probably have taken sides with them against Arnold!

Speaking of "low culture," the long, flowing hair worn by so many professional wrestlers and strong men is signature Samsonite. No wonder that, in the 2007 "Hair vs. Hair" match between business magnate Donald Trump and Vince McMahon, wrestling celebrity and chairman of World Wrestling Entertainment (WWE), the loser had his head shaved bald in public.

With four chapters devoted to him, Samson is the most complexly developed character in the book of Judges. Yet here, as in other biblical stories, few windows on his inner life are given. Many have read love between the lines. What details of the story invite such romantic readings?

JUDGES 14:1–16:31

Once Samson went down to Timnah, and at Timnah he saw a Philistine woman. Then he came up, and told his father and mother, "I saw a Philistine woman at Timnah; now get her for me as my wife." But his father and mother said to him, "Is there not a woman among your kin, or among all our people, that you must go to take a wife from the uncircumcised Philistines?" But Samson said to his father, "Get her for me, because she pleases me." His father and mother did not know that this was from the LORD; for he was seeking a pretext to act against the Philistines. At that time the Philistines had dominion over Israel.

Then Samson went down with his father and mother to Timnah. When he came to the vineyards of Timnah, suddenly a young lion roared at him. The spirit of the LORD rushed on him, and he tore the lion apart barehanded as one might tear apart a kid. But he did not tell his father or his mother what he had done. Then he went down and talked with the woman, and she pleased Samson. After a while he returned to marry her, and he turned aside to see the carcass of the lion, and there was a swarm of bees in the body of the lion, and honey. He scraped it out into his hands, and went on, eating as he went. When he came to his father and mother, he gave some to them, and they ate it. But he did not tell them that he had taken the honey from the carcass of the lion.

His father went down to the woman, and Samson made a feast there as the young men were accustomed to do. When the people saw him, they brought thirty companions to be with him. Samson said to them, "Let me now put a riddle to you. If you can explain it to me within the seven days of the feast, and find it out, then I will give you thirty linen garments and thirty festal garments. But if you cannot explain it to me, then you shall give me thirty linen garments and thirty festal garments." So they said to him, "Ask your riddle; let us hear it." He said to them,

"Out of the eater came something to eat.
Out of the strong came something sweet."

But for three days they could not explain the riddle.

On the fourth day they said to Samson's wife, "Coax your husband to explain the riddle to us, or we will burn you and your father's house with fire. Have you invited us here to impoverish us?" So Samson's wife wept before him, saying, "You hate me; you do not really love me. You have asked a riddle of my people, but you have not explained it to me." He said to her, "Look, I have not told my father or my mother. Why should I tell you?" She wept before him the seven days that their feast lasted; and because she nagged him, on the seventh day he told her. Then she explained the riddle to her people. The men of the town said to him on the seventh day before the sun went down,

"What is sweeter than honey?
What is stronger than a lion?"

And he said to them,

"If you had not plowed with my heifer,
you would not have found out my riddle."

Then the spirit of the LORD rushed on him, and he went down to Ashkelon. He killed thirty men of the town, took their spoil, and gave the festal garments to those who had explained the riddle. In hot anger he went back to his father's house. And Samson's wife was given to his companion, who had been his best man.

After a while, at the time of the wheat harvest, Samson went to visit his wife, bringing along a kid. He said, "I want to go into my wife's room." But her father would not allow him to go in. Her father said, "I was sure that you had rejected her; so I gave her to your companion. Is not her younger sister prettier than she? Why not take her instead?" Samson said to them, "This time, when I do mischief to the Philistines, I will be without blame." So Samson went and caught three hundred foxes, and took some torches; and he turned the foxes tail to tail, and put a torch between each pair of tails. When he had set fire to the torches, he let the foxes go into the standing grain of the Philistines, and burned up the shocks and the standing grain, as well as the vineyards and olive groves. Then the Philistines asked, "Who has done this?" And they said, "Samson, the son-in-law of the Timnite, because he has taken Samson's wife and given her to his companion." So the Philistines came up, and burned her and her father. Samson said to them, "If this is what you do, I swear I will not stop until I have taken revenge on you." He struck them down hip and thigh with great slaughter; and he went down and stayed in the cleft of the rock of Etam.

Then the Philistines came up and encamped in Judah, and made a raid on Lehi. The men of Judah said, "Why have you come up against us?" They said, "We have come up to bind Samson, to do to him as he did to us." Then three thousand men of Judah went down to the cleft of the rock of Etam, and they said to Samson, "Do you not know that the Philistines are rulers over us? What then have you done to us?" He replied, "As they did to me, so I have done to them." They said to him, "We have come down to bind you, so that we may give you into the hands of the Philistines." Samson answered them, "Swear to me that you yourselves will not attack me." They said to him, "No, we will only bind you and give you into their hands; we will not kill you." So they bound him with two new ropes, and brought him up from the rock.

When he came to Lehi, the Philistines came shouting to meet him; and the spirit of the LORD rushed on him, and the ropes that were on his arms became like flax that has caught fire, and his bonds melted off his hands. Then he found a fresh jawbone of a donkey, reached down and took it, and with it he killed a thousand men. And Samson said,

"With the jawbone of a donkey,
    heaps upon heaps,
with the jawbone of a donkey
    I have slain a thousand men."

When he had finished speaking, he threw away the jawbone; and that place was called Ramath-lehi.

By then he was very thirsty, and he called on the LORD, saying, "You have granted this great victory by the hand of your servant. Am I now to die of thirst, and fall into the hands of the uncircumcised?" So God split open the hollow place that is at Lehi, and water came from it. When he drank, his spirit returned, and he revived. Therefore it was named En-hakkore, which is at Lehi to this day. And he judged Israel in the days of the Philistines twenty years.

Once Samson went to Gaza, where he saw a prostitute and went in to her. The Gazites were told, "Samson has come here." So they circled around and lay in wait for him all night at the city gate. They kept quiet all night, thinking, "Let us wait until the light of the morning; then we will kill him." But Samson lay only until midnight. Then at midnight he rose up, took hold of the doors of the city gate and the two posts, pulled them up, bar and all, put them on his shoulders, and carried them to the top of the hill that is in front of Hebron.

After this he fell in love with a woman in the valley of Sorek, whose name was Delilah. The lords of the Philistines came to her and said to her, "Coax him, and find out what makes his strength so great, and how we may overpower him, so that we may bind him in order to subdue him; and we will each give you eleven hundred pieces of silver." So Delilah said to Samson, "Please tell me what makes your strength so great, and how you could be bound, so that one could subdue you." Samson said to her, "If they bind me with seven fresh bowstrings that are not dried out, then I shall become weak, and be like anyone else." Then the lords of the Philistines brought her seven fresh bowstrings that had not dried out, and she bound him with them. While men were lying in wait in an inner chamber, she said to him, "The Philistines are upon you, Samson!" But he snapped the bowstrings, as a strand of fiber snaps when it touches the fire. So the secret of his strength was not known.

Then Delilah said to Samson, "You have mocked me and told me lies; please tell me how you could be bound." He said to her, "If they bind me with new ropes that have not been used, then I shall become weak, and be like anyone else." So Delilah took new ropes and bound him with them, and said to him, "The Philistines are upon you, Samson!" (The men lying in wait were in an inner chamber.) But he snapped the ropes off his arms like a thread.

Then Delilah said to Samson, "Until now you have mocked me and told me lies; tell me how you could be bound." He said to her, "If you weave the seven locks of my head with the web and make it tight with the pin, then I shall become weak, and be like anyone else." So while he slept, Delilah took the seven locks of his head and wove them into the web, and made them tight with the pin. Then she said to him, "The Philistines are upon you, Samson!" But he awoke from his sleep, and pulled away the pin, the loom, and the web.

Then she said to him, "How can you say, 'I love you,' when your heart is not with me? You have mocked me three times now and have not told me what makes your strength so great." Finally, after she had nagged him with her words day after day, and pestered him, he was tired to death. So he told her his whole secret, and said to her, "A razor has never come upon my head; for I have been a nazirite to God from my mother's womb. If my head were shaved, then my strength would leave me; I would become weak, and be like anyone else."

When Delilah realized that he had told her his whole secret, she sent and called the lords of the Philistines, saying, "This time come up, for he has told his whole secret to me." Then the lords of the Philistines came up to her, and brought the money in their hands. She let him fall asleep on her lap; and she called a man, and had him shave off the seven locks of his head. He began to weaken, and his strength left him. Then she said, "The

Philistines are upon you, Samson!" When he awoke from his sleep, he thought, "I will go out as at other times, and shake myself free." But he did not know that the LORD had left him. So the Philistines seized him and gouged out his eyes. They brought him down to Gaza and bound him with bronze shackles; and he ground at the mill in the prison. But the hair of his head began to grow again after it had been shaved.

Now the lords of the Philistines gathered to offer a great sacrifice to their god Dagon, and to rejoice; for they said, "Our god has given Samson our enemy into our hand." When the people saw him, they praised their god; for they said, "Our god has given our enemy into our hand, the ravager of our country, who has killed many of us." And when their hearts were merry, they said, "Call Samson, and let him entertain us." So they called Samson out of the prison, and he performed for them. They made him stand between the pillars; and Samson said to the attendant who held him by the hand, "Let me feel the pillars on which the house rests, so that I may lean against them." Now the house was full of men and women; all the lords of the Philistines were there, and on the roof there were about three thousand men and women, who looked on while Samson performed.

> **Blues legend Blind Willie Johnson was once arrested for inciting a riot outside a New Orleans city building by singing "If I Had My Way I'd Tear the Building Down," based on the Samson story.**

Then Samson called to the LORD and said, "LORD GOD, remember me and strengthen me only this once, O God, so that with this one act of revenge I may pay back the Philistines for my two eyes." And Samson grasped the two middle pillars on which the house rested, and he leaned his weight against them, his right hand on the one and his left hand on the other. Then Samson said, "Let me die with the Philistines." He strained with all his might; and the house fell on the lords and all the people who were in it. So those he killed at his death were more than those he had killed during his life. Then his brothers and all his family came down and took him and brought him up and buried him between Zorah and Eshtaol in the tomb of his father Manoah. He had judged Israel twenty years.

RUTH: A GREAT-GRANDMOTHER

In many families, the juiciest stories are about grandparents. So it is with King David's great-grandmother Ruth. It is a story of two widowed women, an Israelite named Naomi and her Moabite daughter-in-law Ruth, trying to survive and thrive against all odds. Ultimately they succeed by taking matters into their own hands while making the men around them feel as though it was their own doing.

The Hollywood blockbuster *The Story of Ruth* (1960) and numerous romance novels have celebrated the relationship between Ruth and her future husband, Boaz, as a timeless love story. Love is never mentioned in the biblical text, but the famous "threshing floor scene" is certainly charged with sexuality, as Ruth sidles up and uncovers Boaz's feet. It seems an odd thing to do, until one realizes that the Hebrew word for feet is often a euphemism for male genitalia.

As you read, consider what sort of bind Ruth and Naomi each face as unmarried, widowed women in a patriarchal world. What are their options? Also pay attention to details in the text that give expression to the nature of their relationship.

"Where You Go, I Will Go"

RUTH 1:6–17

Then she [Naomi] started to return with her daughters-in-law from the country of Moab, for she had heard in the country of Moab that the LORD had considered his people and given them food. So she set out from the place where she had been living, she and her two daughters-in-law, and they went on their way to go back to the land of Judah. But Naomi said to her two daughters-in-law, "Go back each of you to your mother's house. May the LORD deal kindly with you, as you have dealt with the dead and with me. The LORD grant that you may find security, each of you in the house of your husband." Then she kissed them, and they wept aloud. They said to her, "No, we will return with you to your people." But Naomi said, "Turn back, my daughters, why will you go with me? Do I still have sons in my womb that they may become your husbands? Turn back, my daughters, go your way, for I am too old to have a husband. Even if I thought there was hope for me, even if I should have a husband tonight and bear sons, would you then wait until they were grown?

Would you then refrain from marrying? No, my daughters, it has been far more bitter for me than for you, because the hand of the LORD has turned against me." Then they wept aloud again. Orpah kissed her mother-in-law, but Ruth clung to her.

So she said, "See, your sister-in-law has gone back to her people and to her gods; return after your sister-in-law." But Ruth said,

Ironically, Ruth's poetic vow to stay with her mother-in-law is frequently recited in wedding ceremonies—to the spouse, not the new mother-in-law.

"Do not press me to leave you
    or to turn back from following you!
Where you go, I will go;
    where you lodge, I will lodge;
your people shall be my people,
    and your God my God.
Where you die, I will die—
    there will I be buried.
May the LORD do thus and so to me,
    and more as well,
if even death parts me from you!"

On the Threshing Floor

RUTH 3:1-13

Naomi her mother-in-law said to her, "My daughter, I need to seek some security for you, so that it may be well with you. Now here is our kinsman Boaz, with whose young women you have been working. See, he is winnowing barley tonight at the threshing floor. Now wash and anoint yourself, and put on your best clothes and go down to the threshing floor;

but do not make yourself known to the man until he has finished eating and drinking. When he lies down, observe the place where he lies; then, go and uncover his feet and lie down; and he will tell you what to do." She said to her, "All that you tell me I will do."

So she went down to the threshing floor and did just as her mother-in-law had instructed her. When Boaz had eaten and drunk, and he was in a contented mood, he went to lie down at the end of the heap of grain. Then she came stealthily and uncovered his feet, and lay down. At midnight the man was startled, and turned over, and there, lying at his feet, was a woman! He said, "Who are you?" And she answered, "I am Ruth, your servant; spread your cloak over your servant, for you are next-of-kin." He said, "May you be blessed by the LORD, my daughter; this last instance of your loyalty is better than the first; you have not gone after young men, whether poor or rich. And now, my daughter, do not be afraid, I will do for you all that you ask, for all the assembly of my people know that you are a worthy woman. But now, though it is true that I am a near kinsman, there is another kinsman more closely related than I. Remain this night, and in the morning, if he will act as next-of-kin for you, good; let him do it. If he is not willing to act as next-of-kin for you, then, as the LORD lives, I will act as next-of-kin for you. Lie down until the morning."

"A KING . . . LIKE OTHER NATIONS"

The Bible often argues with itself. Its final form incorporates different perspectives on key issues and questions. So it is with kingship. Although most passages embrace the idea, and the biblical tradition ultimately celebrates David and Solomon as the great kings of the United Monarchy, other stories, like this one in the first book of Samuel, see it as a failure, the result of the Israelite people's insecurity and lack of faith.

This scathing critique of Israel's desire to have a government "like other nations" influenced debates over the Constitution of the United States as the young nation defined itself over against existing European monarchies.

Take note of Samuel's gloomy predictions. Many of them will come true only too soon, under Solomon.

ARE JEWISH AND CHRISTIAN BIBLES THE SAME?

The books in Jewish and Christian versions of the Hebrew Bible are the same. They are based on translations of the same ancient Hebrew manuscripts. And yet, beginning with Ruth, the order in which they appear is different. Why?

Jewish versions divide the books into three main sections: Torah ("law" or "instruction"), which includes the first five books, from Genesis to Deuteronomy; Nevi'im ("prophets"), which includes the "former prophets," Joshua, Judges, Samuel, and Kings, as well as those books that we normally associate with biblical prophecy, Isaiah, Jeremiah, Amos, and so on; and Ketuvim ("writings"), which includes everything that doesn't fit into the first two categories. The first letters of these three main sections give us the consonants of Tanak, which is the traditional Jewish name for the Hebrew Bible.

The order of books in Christian versions follows that of the ancient Greek translation of Jewish Scriptures known as the Septuagint ("Seventy," referring to the legend that seventy different rabbis translated it independently and ended up with the exact same thing). Like the Tanak, this order begins with the Torah, here called the Pentateuch (*pentateuchos*, "five books"), but the remaining books are organized differently. Ruth, for example, is not included in the Ketuvim, but is inserted between Judges and 1–2 Samuel—thus putting the story of how Ruth became the great-grandmother of King David in its proper chronological place.

To complicate matters, the Septuagint included several other early Jewish texts along with significantly different versions of and additions to the books of Esther and Daniel. These additional books are collectively known as the Apocrypha and are part of the Greek and Slavonic Orthodox canons. Jerome, whose translation formed the basis for the Latin Vulgate Bible, which came to define the Roman Catholic canon in the Middle Ages, had excluded those books, because they did not appear in his Hebrew manuscripts. After his death, however, seven of these texts, along with the additions to Esther and Daniel, were added back into the Vulgate Bible. They are the books of Tobit, Judith, the Wisdom of Solomon, Ecclesiasticus (Sirach), Baruch, and 1–2 Maccabees, and they remain part of the Roman Catholic canon as its Apocrypha. Protestants exclude them, for the same reason Jerome had.

1 SAMUEL 8:1–22

When Samuel became old, he made his sons judges over Israel. The name of his firstborn son was Joel, and the name of his second, Abijah; they were judges in Beer-sheba. Yet his sons did not follow in his ways, but turned aside after gain; they took bribes and perverted justice.

Then all the elders of Israel gathered together and came to Samuel at Ramah, and said to him, "You are old and your sons do not follow in your ways; appoint for us, then, a king to govern us, like other nations." But the thing displeased Samuel when they said, "Give us a king to govern us." Samuel prayed to the LORD, and the LORD said to Samuel, "Listen to the voice of the people in all that they say to you; for they have not rejected you, but they have rejected me from being king over them. Just as they have done to me, from the day I brought them up out of Egypt to this day, forsaking me and serving other gods, so also they are doing to you. Now then, listen to their voice; only—you shall solemnly warn them, and show them the ways of the king who shall reign over them."

So Samuel reported all the words of the LORD to the people who were asking him for a king. He said, "These will be the ways of the king who will reign over you: he will take your sons and appoint them to his chariots and to be his horsemen, and to run before his chariots; and he will appoint for himself commanders of thousands and commanders of fifties, and some to plow his ground and to reap his harvest, and to make his implements of war and the equipment of his chariots. He will take your daughters to be perfumers and cooks and bakers. He will take the best of your fields and vineyards and olive orchards and give them to his courtiers. He will take one-tenth of your grain and of your vineyards and give it to his officers and his courtiers. He will take your male and female slaves, and the best of your cattle and donkeys, and put them to his work. He will take one-tenth of your flocks, and you shall be his slaves. And in that day you will cry out because of your king, whom you have chosen for yourselves; but the LORD will not answer you in that day."

But the people refused to listen to the voice of Samuel; they said, "No! but we are determined to have a king over us, so that we also may be like other nations, and that our king may govern us and go out before us and fight our battles." When Samuel had heard all the words of the people, he repeated them in the ears of the LORD. The LORD said to Samuel, "Listen to their voice and set a king over them." Samuel then said to the people of Israel, "Each of you return home."

DAVID: THE ORIGINAL POLITICAL ICON

Long before magazine and television "infotainment" began turning presidential candidates into pop stars, long before celebrity charisma was a prerequisite for political success, there was David. He is the biblical prototype for today's political icons: good-looking, brave, patriotic, pious, honorable, humble. Or so he seems. And he can really play that harp. But as with today's pop stars, political and otherwise, there are dark sides to his character that only gradually emerge.

Is he really so loyal to King Saul? So humble, so selfless? Is he capable of love for others? Is it divine providence or cool calculation that allows him to rise to the top while those around him fall? Indeed, just as his national position is secured, his private family life begins to fall apart—first with Bathsheba, then with his children.

No doubt this vexing complexity is what makes him so fascinating to us. He seems to be the original Teflon king; nothing seems to stick to him. But what are we seeing that those around him cannot?

Soothing Notes

1 SAMUEL 16:14-23

Now the spirit of the LORD departed from Saul, and an evil spirit from the LORD tormented him. And Saul's servants said to him, "See now, an evil spirit from God is tormenting you. Let our lord now command the servants who attend you to look for someone who is skillful in playing the lyre; and when the evil spirit from God is upon you, he will play it, and you will feel better." So Saul said to his servants, "Provide for me someone who can play well, and bring him to me." One of the young men answered, "I have seen a son of Jesse the Bethlehemite who is skillful in playing, a man of valor, a warrior, prudent in speech, and a man of good presence; and the LORD is with him." So Saul sent messengers to Jesse, and said, "Send me your son David who is with the sheep." Jesse took a donkey loaded with bread, a skin of wine, and a kid, and sent them by his son David to Saul. And David came to Saul, and entered his service. Saul loved him greatly, and he became his armor-bearer. Saul sent to Jesse, saying, "Let David remain in my service, for he has found favor in my sight." And whenever the evil spirit from God came upon Saul, David took the lyre and played it with his hand, and Saul would be relieved and feel better, and the evil spirit would depart from him.

Israel's first king, Saul, seems fated to fail from the start. While he still reigns, God has Samuel anoint Jesse's youngest son, David, as king. From this point on, David's inevitable rise correlates with Saul's inevitable fall. This brief episode is the source of the now iconic image of David as a harpist, which in turn feeds the tradition that he wrote many of the Psalms.

David and Goliath

1 SAMUEL 17:1-58

Now the Philistines gathered their armies for battle; they were gathered at Socoh, which belongs to Judah, and encamped between Socoh and Azekah, in Ephes-dammim. Saul and the Israelites gathered and encamped in the valley of Elah, and formed ranks against the Philistines. The Philistines stood on the mountain on the one side, and Israel stood on the mountain on the other side, with a valley between them. And there came out from the camp of the Philistines a champion named Goliath, of Gath, whose height was six cubits and a span. He had a helmet of bronze on his head, and he was armed with a coat of mail; the weight of the coat was five thousand shekels of bronze. He had greaves of bronze on his legs and a javelin of bronze slung between his shoulders. The shaft of his spear was like a weaver's beam, and his spear's head weighed six hundred shekels of iron; and his shield-bearer went before him. He stood and shouted to the ranks of Israel, "Why have you come out to draw up for battle? Am I not a Philistine, and are you not servants of Saul? Choose a man for yourselves, and let him come down to me. If he is able to fight with me and kill me, then we will be your servants; but if I prevail against him and kill him, then you shall be our servants and serve us." And the Philistine said, "Today I defy the ranks of Israel! Give me a man, that we may fight together." When Saul and all Israel heard these words of the Philistine, they were dismayed and greatly afraid.

Now David was the son of an Ephrathite of Bethlehem in Judah, named Jesse, who had eight sons. In the days of Saul the man was already old and advanced in years. The three eldest sons of Jesse had followed Saul to the battle; the names of his three sons who went to the battle were Eliab the firstborn, and next to him Abinadab, and the third Shammah. David was the youngest; the three eldest followed Saul, but David went back and forth from Saul to feed his father's sheep at Bethlehem. For forty days the Philistine came forward and took his stand, morning and evening.

Jesse said to his son David, "Take for your brothers an ephah of this parched grain and these ten loaves, and carry them quickly to the camp to your brothers; also take these ten cheeses to the commander of their thousand. See how your brothers fare, and bring some token from them."

Now Saul, and they, and all the men of Israel, were in the valley of Elah, fighting with the Philistines. David rose early in the morning, left the sheep with a keeper, took the provisions, and went as Jesse had commanded him. He came to the encampment as the army was going forth to the battle line, shouting the war cry. Israel and the Philistines drew up for battle, army against army. David left the things in charge of the keeper of the baggage, ran to the ranks, and went and greeted his brothers. As he talked with them, the champion, the Philistine of Gath, Goliath by name, came up out of the ranks of the Philistines, and spoke the same words as before. And David heard him.

All the Israelites, when they saw the man, fled from him and were very much afraid. The Israelites said, "Have you seen this man who has come up? Surely he has come up to defy Israel. The king will greatly enrich the man who kills him, and will give him his daughter and make his family free in Israel." David said to the men who stood by him, "What shall be done for the man who kills this Philistine, and takes away the reproach from Israel? For who is this uncircumcised Philistine that he should defy the armies of the living God?" The people answered him in the same way, "So shall it be done for the man who kills him."

David's defeat of Goliath has inspired countless artistic depictions, the most famous of which is Michelangelo's sculpture in Florence. That David is quite muscular and masculine, in contrast to the effeminate interpretation by Michelangelo's predecessor Donatello. The wide range of visual representations of David in art reflects the spectrum of ways we can interpret the complex character of David in the biblical narrative.

His eldest brother Eliab heard him talking to the men; and Eliab's anger was kindled against David. He said, "Why have you come down? With whom have you left those few sheep in the wilderness? I know your presumption and the evil of your heart; for you have come down just to see the battle." David said, "What have I done now? It was only a question." He turned away from him toward another and spoke in the same way; and the people answered him again as before.

When the words that David spoke were heard, they repeated them before Saul; and he sent for him. David said to Saul, "Let no one's heart fail because of him; your servant will go and fight with this Philistine." Saul said to David, "You are not able to go against this Philistine to fight with him; for you are just a boy, and he has been a warrior from his youth." But David said to Saul, "Your servant used to keep sheep for his father; and whenever a lion or a bear came, and took a lamb from the flock, I went after it and struck it down, rescuing the lamb from its mouth; and if it turned against me, I would catch it by the jaw, strike it down, and kill it. Your servant has killed both lions and bears; and this uncircumcised Philistine shall be like one of them, since he has defied the armies of the living God." David said, "The LORD, who saved me from the paw of the lion and from the paw of the bear, will save me from the hand of this Philistine." So Saul said to David, "Go, and may the LORD be with you!"

> Tonight, we are making sure America understands that sometimes one small smooth stone is even more effective than a whole lot of armor.
>
> —Republican presidential hopeful Mike Huckabee, after unexpected wins in the Super Tuesday primaries, February 5, 2008

Saul clothed David with his armor; he put a bronze helmet on his head and clothed him with a coat of mail. David strapped Saul's sword over the armor, and he tried in vain to walk, for he was not used to them. Then David said to Saul, "I cannot walk with these; for I am not used to them." So David removed them. Then he took his staff in his hand, and chose five smooth stones from the wadi, and put them in his shepherd's bag, in the pouch; his sling was in his hand, and he drew near to the Philistine.

The Philistine came on and drew near to David, with his shield-bearer in front of him. When the Philistine looked and saw David, he disdained him, for he was only a youth, ruddy and handsome in appearance. The Philistine said to David, "Am I a dog, that you come to me with sticks?" And the Philistine cursed David by his gods. The Philistine said to David, "Come to me, and I will give your flesh to the birds of the air and to the wild animals of the field." But David said to the Philistine, "You come to me with sword and spear and javelin; but I come to you in the name of the LORD of hosts, the God of the armies of Israel, whom you have defied. This very day the LORD will deliver you into my hand, and I will strike you down and cut off your head; and I will give the dead bodies of the Philistine army this very day to the birds of the air and to the wild animals of the earth, so that all the earth may know that there is a God in Israel, and that all this assembly may know that the LORD does not save by sword and spear; for the battle is the LORD's and he will give you into our hand."

When the Philistine drew nearer to meet David, David ran quickly toward the battle line to meet the Philistine. David put his hand in his bag, took out a stone, slung it, and struck the Philistine on his forehead; the stone sank into his forehead, and he fell face down on the ground.

So David prevailed over the Philistine with a sling and a stone, striking down the Philistine and killing him; there was no sword in David's hand. Then David ran and stood over the Philistine; he grasped his sword, drew it out of its sheath, and killed him; then he cut off his head with it.

When the Philistines saw that their champion was dead, they fled. The troops of Israel and Judah rose up with a shout and pursued the Philistines as far as Gath and the gates of Ekron, so that the wounded Philistines fell on the way from Shaaraim as far as Gath and Ekron. The Israelites came back from chasing the Philistines, and they plundered their camp. David took the head of the Philistine and brought it to Jerusalem; but he put his armor in his tent.

When Saul saw David go out against the Philistine, he said to Abner, the commander of the army, "Abner, whose son is this young man?" Abner said, "As your soul lives, O king, I do not know." The king said, "Inquire whose son the stripling is." On David's return from killing the Philistine, Abner took him and brought him before Saul, with the head of the Philistine in his hand. Saul said to him, "Whose son are you, young man?" And David answered, "I am the son of your servant Jesse the Bethlehemite."

Rising Star

1 SAMUEL 18:1-16

When David had finished speaking to Saul, the soul of Jonathan was bound to the soul of David, and Jonathan loved him as his own soul.

Saul took him that day and would not let him return to his father's house. Then Jonathan made a covenant with David, because he loved him as his own soul. Jonathan stripped himself of the robe that he was wearing, and gave it to David, and his armor, and even his sword and his bow and his belt. David went out and was successful wherever Saul sent him; as a result, Saul set him over the army. And all the people, even the servants of Saul, approved.

As they were coming home, when David returned from killing the Philistine, the women came out of all the towns of Israel, singing and dancing, to meet King Saul, with tambourines, with songs of joy, and with musical instruments. And the women sang to one another as they made merry,

> "Saul has killed his thousands,
>   and David his ten thousands."

Saul was very angry, for this saying displeased him. He said, "They have ascribed to David ten thousands, and to me they have ascribed thousands; what more can he have but the kingdom?" So Saul eyed David from that day on.

The next day an evil spirit from God rushed upon Saul, and he raved within his house, while David was playing the lyre, as he did day by day. Saul had his spear in his hand; and Saul threw the spear, for he thought, "I will pin David to the wall." But David eluded him twice.

Saul was afraid of David, because the LORD was with him but had departed from Saul. So Saul removed him from his presence, and made him a commander of a thousand; and David marched out and came in, leading the army. David had success in all his undertakings; for the LORD was with him. When Saul saw that he had great success, he stood in awe of him. But all Israel and Judah loved David; for it was he who marched out and came in leading them.

"How the Mighty Have Fallen"

2 SAMUEL 1:1-27

After the death of Saul, when David had returned from defeating the Amalekites, David remained two days in Ziklag. On the third day, a man came from Saul's camp, with his clothes torn and dirt on his head. When he came to David, he fell to the ground and did obeisance. David said to him, "Where have you come from?" He said to him, "I have escaped from the camp of Israel." David said to him, "How did things go? Tell me!" He answered, "The army fled from the battle, but also many of the army fell and died; and Saul and his son Jonathan also died." Then David asked the young man who was reporting to him, "How do you know that Saul and his son Jonathan died?" The young man reporting to him said, "I happened to be on Mount Gilboa; and there was Saul leaning on his spear, while the chariots and the horsemen drew close to him. When he looked behind him, he saw me, and called to me. I answered, 'Here sir.' And he said to me, 'Who are you?' I answered him, 'I am an Amalekite.' He said to me, 'Come, stand over me and kill me; for convulsions have seized me, and yet my life still lingers.' So I stood over him, and killed him, for I knew that he could not live after he had fallen. I took the crown that was on his head and the armlet that was on his arm, and I have brought them here to my lord."

Then David took hold of his clothes and tore them; and all the men who were with him did the same. They mourned and wept, and fasted until evening for Saul and for his son Jonathan, and for the army of the Lord and for the house of Israel, because they had fallen by the sword. David said to the young man who had reported to him, "Where do you come from?" He answered, "I am the son of a resident alien, an Amalekite." David said to him, "Were you not afraid to lift your hand to destroy the Lord's anointed?" Then David called one of the young men and said, "Come here and strike him down." So he struck him down and he died. David said to him, "Your blood be on your head; for your own mouth has testified against you, saying, 'I have killed the Lord's anointed.'"

David intoned this lamentation over Saul and his son Jonathan. (He ordered that The Song of the Bow be taught to the people of Judah; it is written in the Book of Jashar.) He said:

Your glory, O Israel, lies slain upon your high places!
  How the mighty have fallen!
Tell it not in Gath,
  proclaim it not in the streets of Ashkelon;
or the daughters of the Philistines will rejoice,
  the daughters of the uncircumcised will exult.

You mountains of Gilboa,
    let there be no dew or rain upon you,
    nor bounteous fields!
For there the shield of the mighty was defiled,
    the shield of Saul, anointed with oil no more.
From the blood of the slain,
    from the fat of the mighty,
the bow of Jonathan did not turn back,
    nor the sword of Saul return empty.
Saul and Jonathan, beloved and lovely!
    In life and in death they were not divided;
they were swifter than eagles,
    they were stronger than lions.
O daughters of Israel, weep over Saul,
    who clothed you with crimson, in luxury,
    who put ornaments of gold on your apparel.
How the mighty have fallen
    in the midst of the battle!
Jonathan lies slain upon your high places.
    I am distressed for you, my brother Jonathan;
greatly beloved were you to me;
    your love to me was wonderful,
    passing the love of women.
How the mighty have fallen,
    and the weapons of war perished!

David and Bathsheba

2 SAMUEL 11:1–27

In the spring of the year, the time when kings go out to battle, David sent Joab with his officers and all Israel with him; they ravaged the Ammonites, and besieged Rabbah. But David remained at Jerusalem.

It happened, late one afternoon, when David rose from his couch and was walking about on the roof of the king's house, that he saw from the roof a woman bathing; the woman was very beautiful. David sent someone to inquire about the woman. It was reported, "This is Bathsheba daughter of Eliam, the wife of Uriah the Hittite." So David sent messengers to get her, and she came to him, and he lay with her. (Now she was purifying herself after her period.) Then she returned to her house. The woman conceived; and she sent and told David, "I am pregnant."

So David sent word to Joab, "Send me Uriah the Hittite." And Joab sent Uriah to David. When Uriah came to him, David asked how Joab and the people fared, and how the war was going. Then David said to Uriah, "Go down to your house, and wash your feet." Uriah went out of the king's house, and there followed him a present from

In Nathaniel Hawthorne's *The Scarlet Letter,* the widow gives the austere Mr. Dimmesdale a room whose walls are decorated with tapestries depicting episodes of this story "which made the fair woman of the scene almost as grimly picturesque as the woe-denouncing seer."

the king. But Uriah slept at the entrance of the king's house with all the servants of his lord, and did not go down to his house. When they told David, "Uriah did not go down to his house," David said to Uriah, "You have just come from a journey. Why did you not go down to your house?" Uriah said to David, "The ark and Israel and Judah remain in booths; and my lord Joab and the servants of my lord are camping in the open field; shall I then go to my house, to eat and to drink, and to lie with my wife? As you live, and as your soul lives, I will not do such a thing." Then David said to Uriah, "Remain here today also, and tomorrow I will send you back." So Uriah remained in Jerusalem that day. On the next day, David invited him to eat and drink in his presence and made him drunk; and in the evening he went out to lie on his couch with the servants of his lord, but he did not go down to his house.

In the morning David wrote a letter to Joab, and sent it by the hand of Uriah. In the letter he wrote, "Set Uriah in the forefront of the hardest fighting, and then draw back from him, so that he may be struck down and die." As Joab was besieging the city, he assigned Uriah to the place where he knew there were valiant warriors. The men of the city came out and fought with Joab; and some of the servants of David among the people fell. Uriah the Hittite was killed as well. Then Joab sent and told David all the news about the fighting; and he instructed the messenger,

"When you have finished telling the king all the news about the fighting, then, if the king's anger rises, and if he says to you, 'Why did you go so near the city to fight? Did you not know that they would shoot from the wall? Who killed Abimelech son of Jerubbaal? Did not a woman throw an upper millstone on him from the wall, so that he died at Thebez? Why did you go so near the wall?' then you shall say, 'Your servant Uriah the Hittite is dead too.'"

So the messenger went, and came and told David all that Joab had sent him to tell. The messenger said to David, "The men gained an advantage over us, and came out against us in the field; but we drove them back to the entrance of the gate. Then the archers shot at your servants from the wall; some of the king's servants are dead; and your servant Uriah the Hittite is dead also." David said to the messenger, "Thus you shall say to Joab, 'Do not let this matter trouble you, for the sword devours now one and now another; press your attack on the city, and overthrow it.' And encourage him."

When the wife of Uriah heard that her husband was dead, she made lamentation for him. When the mourning was over, David sent and brought her to his house, and she became his wife, and bore him a son. But the thing that David had done displeased the LORD.

Absalom, Absalom!

2 SAMUEL 18:1-33

Then David mustered the men who were with him, and set over them commanders of thousands and commanders of hundreds. And David divided the army into three groups: one third under the command of Joab, one third under the command of Abishai son of Zeruiah, Joab's brother, and one third under the command of Ittai the Gittite. The king said to the men, "I myself will also go out with you." But the men said, "You shall not go out. For if we flee, they will not care about us. If half of us die, they will not care about us. But you are worth ten thousand of us; therefore it is better that you send us help from the city." The king said to them, "Whatever seems best to you I will do." So the king stood at the side of the gate, while all the army marched out by hundreds and by thousands. The king ordered Joab and Abishai and Ittai, saying, "Deal gently for my sake with the young man Absalom." And all the people heard when the king gave orders to all the commanders concerning Absalom.

So the army went out into the field against Israel; and the battle was fought in the forest of Ephraim. The men of Israel were defeated there by the servants of David, and the slaughter there was great on that day, twenty thousand men. The battle spread over the face of all the country; and the forest claimed more victims that day than the sword.

Absalom happened to meet the servants of David. Absalom was riding on his mule, and the mule went under the thick branches of a great oak. His head caught fast in the oak, and he was left hanging between heaven and earth, while the mule that was under him went on. A man saw it, and told Joab, "I saw Absalom hanging in an oak." Joab said to the man who told him, "What, you saw him! Why then did you not strike him there to the ground? I would have been glad to give you ten pieces of silver and a belt." But the man said to Joab, "Even if I felt in my hand the weight of a thousand pieces of silver, I would not raise my hand against the king's son; for in our hearing the king commanded you and Abishai

> David's daughter Tamar is raped by his son and her half brother Amnon. Enraged, her full brother Absalom has Amnon murdered and then flees. He returns to lead an insurrection against David, at one point even taking control of Jerusalem. William Faulkner's novel *Absalom, Absalom!* offers a parallel taking place in the American South, in which Thomas Sutpen's family falls apart as one son, Henry, kills another son, Charles Bon (Henry's half brother), to keep him from marrying Judith, Henry's sister and Charles's half sister.

and Ittai, saying: For my sake protect the young man Absalom! On the other hand, if I had dealt treacherously against his life (and there is nothing hidden from the king), then you yourself would have stood aloof." Joab said, "I will not waste time like this with you." He took three spears in his hand, and thrust them into the heart of Absalom, while he was still alive in the oak. And ten young men, Joab's armor-bearers, surrounded Absalom and struck him, and killed him.

Then Joab sounded the trumpet, and the troops came back from pursuing Israel, for Joab restrained the troops. They took Absalom, threw him into a great pit in the forest, and raised over him a very great heap of stones. Meanwhile all the Israelites fled to their homes. Now Absalom in his lifetime had taken and set up for himself a pillar that is in the King's Valley, for he said, "I have no son to keep my name in remembrance"; he called the pillar by his own name. It is called Absalom's Monument to this day.

Then Ahimaaz son of Zadok said, "Let me run, and carry tidings to the king that the LORD has delivered him from the power of his enemies." Joab said to him, "You are not to carry tidings today; you may carry tidings another day, but today you shall not do so, because the king's son is dead." Then Joab said to a Cushite, "Go, tell the king what you have seen." The Cushite bowed before Joab, and ran. Then Ahimaaz son of Zadok said again to Joab, "Come what may, let me also run after the Cushite." And Joab said, "Why will you run, my son, seeing that you have no reward for the tidings?" "Come what may," he said, "I will run." So he said to him, "Run." Then Ahimaaz ran by the way of the Plain, and outran the Cushite.

Now David was sitting between the two gates. The sentinel went up to the roof of the gate by the wall, and when he looked up, he saw a man running alone. The sentinel shouted and told the king. The king said, "If he is alone, there are tidings in his mouth." He kept coming, and drew near. Then the sentinel saw another man running; and the sentinel called to the gatekeeper and said, "See, another man running alone!" The king said, "He also is bringing tidings." The sentinel said, "I think the running of the first one is like the running of Ahimaaz son of Zadok." The king said, "He is a good man, and comes with good tidings."

Then Ahimaaz cried out to the king, "All is well!" He prostrated himself before the king with his face to the ground, and said, "Blessed be the LORD your God, who has delivered up the men who raised their hand against my lord the king." The king said, "Is it well with the young man Absalom?" Ahimaaz answered, "When Joab sent your servant, I saw a great tumult, but I do not know what it was." The king said, "Turn aside, and stand here." So he turned aside, and stood still.

Then the Cushite came; and the Cushite said, "Good tidings for my lord the king! For the LORD has vindicated you this day, delivering you from the power of all who rose up against you." The king said to the Cushite, "Is it well with the young man Absalom?" The Cushite answered, "May the enemies of my lord the king, and all who rise up to do you harm, be like that young man."

The king was deeply moved, and went up to the chamber over the gate, and wept; and as he went, he said, "O my son Absalom, my son, my son Absalom! Would I had died instead of you, O Absalom, my son, my son!"

KING SOLOMON

Solomon, like his father, is a mixed bag. Celebrated for his wisdom, his wealth, and especially for building the Jerusalem Temple, he also exploited his own people, built houses of worship for the gods of his hundreds (yes, hundreds) of foreign wives, and worshiped those gods himself. After his reign, his servant Jeroboam led the ten northern tribes to split from the two southern tribes, which remained under his son Rehoboam. So begins the period of the Divided Kingdom.

These days, Solomon's failings are remembered less well than his wisdom and especially his wealth, thanks to the popular Victorian novel *King Solomon's Mines,* by Sir H. Rider Haggard (1885), which was made into two blockbuster movies (1950, 1985). In this original "lost world" story, Allan Quatermain discovers King Solomon's mines of gold, diamonds, and ivory in a supposedly unexplored part of Africa.

Dividing the Baby

1 KINGS 3:16-28

Later, two women who were prostitutes came to the king and stood before him. The one woman said, "Please, my lord, this woman and I live in the same house; and I gave birth while she was in the house. Then on the third day after I gave birth, this woman also gave birth. We were together; there was no one else with us in the house, only the two of us were in the house. Then this woman's son died in the night, because she lay on him.

She got up in the middle of the night and took my son from beside me while your servant slept. She laid him at her breast, and laid her dead son at my breast. When I rose in the morning to nurse my son, I saw that he was dead; but when I looked at him closely in the morning, clearly it was not the son I had borne." But the other woman said, "No, the living son is mine, and the dead son is yours." The first said, "No, the dead son is yours, and the living son is mine." So they argued before the king.

> In politics, this story is often recalled to oppose a compromise between two sides that destroys the whole. For example, those against splitting Jerusalem between Israel and Palestine call such plans "dividing the baby."

Then the king said, "The one says, 'This is my son that is alive, and your son is dead'; while the other says, 'Not so! Your son is dead, and my son is the living one.'" So the king said, "Bring me a sword," and they brought a sword before the king. The king said, "Divide the living boy in two; then give half to the one, and half to the other." But the woman whose son was alive said to the king—because compassion for her son burned within her—"Please, my lord, give her the living boy; certainly do not kill him!" The other said, "It shall be neither mine nor yours; divide it." Then the king responded: "Give the first woman the living boy; do not kill him. She is his mother." All Israel heard of the judgment that the king had rendered; and they stood in awe of the king, because they perceived that the wisdom of God was in him, to execute justice.

The Wisdom of Solomon

1 KINGS 4:29-34

God gave Solomon very great wisdom, discernment, and breadth of understanding as vast as the sand on the seashore, so that Solomon's wisdom surpassed the wisdom of all the people of the east, and all the wisdom of Egypt. He was wiser than anyone else, wiser than Ethan the Ezrahite, and Heman, Calcol, and Darda, children of Mahol; his fame spread throughout all the surrounding nations. He composed three thousand proverbs, and his songs numbered a thousand and five. He would speak of trees, from the cedar that is in the Lebanon to the hyssop that grows in the wall; he would speak of animals, and birds, and reptiles, and fish. People came from all the nations to hear the wisdom of Solomon; they came from all the kings of the earth who had heard of his wisdom.

A Visit from the Queen of Sheba

1 KINGS 10:1-9

When the queen of Sheba heard of the fame of Solomon (fame due to the name of the LORD), she came to test him with hard questions. She came to Jerusalem with a very great retinue, with camels bearing spices, and very much gold, and precious stones; and when she came to Solomon, she told him all that was on her mind. Solomon answered all her questions; there was nothing hidden from the king that he could not explain to her. When the queen of Sheba had observed all the wisdom of Solomon, the house that he had built, the food of his table, the seating of his officials, and the attendance of his servants, their clothing, his valets, and his burnt offerings that he offered at the house of the LORD, there was no more spirit in her.

> When I see what you know, what you have read, and seen, and thought, I feel what a nothing I am! I'm like the poor Queen of Sheba who lives in the Bible. There is no more spirit in me.
> —Tess to Angel Clare, in Thomas Hardy's *Tess of the d'Urbervilles*

So she said to the king, "The report was true that I heard in my own land of your accomplishments and of your wisdom, but I did not believe the reports until I came and my own eyes had seen it. Not even half had been told me; your wisdom and prosperity far surpass the report that I had heard. Happy are your wives! Happy are these your servants, who continually attend you and hear your wisdom! Blessed be the LORD your God, who has delighted in you

> In *King Solomon's Mines,* Allan Quatermain and his team of explorers climb a peak in a mountain range called "Sheba's Breasts."

and set you on the throne of Israel! Because the LORD loved Israel forever, he has made you king to execute justice and righteousness."

Solomon's Wives and Gods

1 KINGS 11:1–8

King Solomon loved many foreign women along with the daughter of Pharaoh: Moabite, Ammonite, Edomite, Sidonian, and Hittite women, from the nations concerning which the LORD had said to the Israelites, "You shall not enter into marriage with them, neither shall they with you; for they will surely incline your heart to follow their gods"; Solomon clung to these in love. Among his wives were seven hundred princesses and three hundred concubines; and his wives turned away his heart. For when Solomon was old, his wives turned away his heart after other gods; and his heart was not true to the LORD his God, as was the heart of his father David. For Solomon followed Astarte the goddess of the Sidonians, and Milcom the abomination of the Ammonites. So Solomon did what was evil in the sight of the LORD, and did not completely follow the LORD, as his father David had done. Then Solomon built a high place for Chemosh the abomination of Moab, and for Molech the abomination of the Ammonites, on the mountain east of Jerusalem. He did the same for all his foreign wives, who offered incense and sacrificed to their gods.

ELIJAH AND JEZEBEL

Jezebel has gotten a very bad rap. In popular culture, her name has become a pejorative term for any woman who uses her sexual power to dominate men, often destroying many other lives in the process—for instance, the headstrong Southern belle in the scandalous red dress played by Bette Davis in *Jezebel* (1938). Yet the biblical story says nothing of Jezebel's sexuality. Her power is strictly political, set against the foil of her weak, insecure husband, Ahab. These days the name Jezebel is also sometimes used as a denigrating nickname for a powerful woman who allegedly wields too much influence over her husband, whether he is king or president or prime minister.

Elijah, on the other hand, is the prototypical lonely prophet, isolated for confronting the powers that be with a truth that he alone can see. It is this image that captured the imagination of science fiction writer Philip K. Dick (whose works form the basis for the films *Blade Runner, Total Recall,* and *Minority Report,* among others). He once claimed that the spirit of Elijah had possessed him.

What details in Elijah's story have made him such a powerfully suggestive figure? What allows him to live beyond his own story? Also, are he and Jezebel opposites? Or mirror images?

Troubler of Israel

1 KINGS 18:17–46

When Ahab saw Elijah, Ahab said to him, "Is it you, you troubler of Israel?" He answered, "I have not troubled Israel; but you have, and your father's house, because you have forsaken the commandments of the LORD and followed the Baals. Now therefore have all Israel assemble for me at Mount Carmel, with the four hundred fifty prophets of Baal and the four hundred prophets of Asherah, who eat at Jezebel's table."

So Ahab sent to all the Israelites, and assembled the prophets at Mount Carmel. Elijah then came near to all the people, and said, "How long will you go limping with two different opinions? If the LORD is God, follow him; but if Baal, then follow him." The people did not answer him a word. Then Elijah said to the people, "I, even I only, am left a prophet of the LORD; but Baal's prophets number four hundred fifty. Let two bulls be given to us; let them choose one bull for themselves, cut it in pieces, and lay it on the wood, but put no fire to it; I will prepare the other bull and lay it on the wood, but put no fire to it. Then you call on the name of your god and I will call on the name of the LORD; the god who answers by fire is indeed God." All the people answered, "Well spoken!" Then Elijah said to the prophets of Baal, "Choose for yourselves one bull and prepare it first, for you are many; then call on the name of your god, but put no fire to it." So they took the bull that was given them, prepared it, and called on the name of Baal from morning until noon, crying, "O Baal, answer us!" But there was no voice, and no answer. They limped about the altar that they had made. At noon Elijah mocked them, saying, "Cry aloud! Surely he is a god; either he is meditating, or he has wandered away, or he is on a journey, or perhaps he is asleep and must be awakened." Then they cried aloud and, as was their custom, they cut themselves with swords and lances until the blood gushed out over them. As midday passed, they raved on until the time of the offering of the oblation, but there was no voice, no answer, and no response.

Then Elijah said to all the people, "Come closer to me"; and all the people came closer to him. First he repaired the altar of the LORD that had been thrown down; Elijah took twelve stones, according to the number of the tribes of the sons of Jacob, to whom the word of the LORD came, saying, "Israel shall be your name"; with the stones he built an altar in the name of the LORD. Then he made a trench around the altar, large enough to contain two measures of seed. Next he put the wood in order, cut the bull in pieces, and laid it on the wood. He said, "Fill four jars with water and pour it on the burnt offering and on the wood." Then he said, "Do it a second time"; and they did it a second time. Again he said, "Do it a third time"; and they did it a third time, so that the water ran all around the altar, and filled the trench also with water.

At the time of the offering of the oblation, the prophet Elijah came near and said, "O LORD, God of Abraham, Isaac, and Israel, let it be known this day that you are God in Israel, that I am your servant, and that I have done all these things at your bidding. Answer me, O LORD, answer me, so that this people may know that you, O LORD, are God, and that you have turned their hearts back." Then the fire of the LORD fell and consumed the burnt offering, the wood, the stones, and the dust, and even licked up the water that was in the trench. When all the people saw it, they fell on their faces and said, "The LORD indeed is God; the LORD indeed is God." Elijah said to them, "Seize the prophets of Baal; do not let one of them escape." Then they seized them; and Elijah brought them down to the Wadi Kishon, and killed them there.

Elijah said to Ahab, "Go up, eat and drink; for there is a sound of rushing rain." So Ahab went up to eat and to drink. Elijah went up to the top of Carmel; there he bowed himself down upon the earth and put his face between his knees. He said to his servant, "Go up now, look toward the sea." He went up and looked, and said, "There is nothing." Then he said, "Go again seven times." At the seventh time he said, "Look, a little cloud no bigger than a person's hand is rising out of the sea." Then he said, "Go say to Ahab, 'Harness your chariot and go down before the rain stops you.'" In a little while the heavens grew black with clouds and wind; there was a heavy rain. Ahab rode off and went to Jezreel. But the hand of the LORD was on Elijah; he girded up his loins and ran in front of Ahab to the entrance of Jezreel.

"A Still Small Voice"

1 KINGS 19:1-18

Ahab told Jezebel all that Elijah had done, and how he had killed all the prophets with the sword. Then Jezebel sent a messenger to Elijah, saying, "So may the gods do to me, and more also, if I do not make your life like the life of one of them by this time tomorrow." Then he was afraid; he got up and fled for his life, and came to Beer-sheba, which belongs to Judah; he left his servant there.

But he himself went a day's journey into the wilderness, and came and sat down under a solitary broom tree. He asked that he might die: "It is enough; now, O LORD, take away my life, for I am no better than my ancestors." Then he lay down under the broom tree and fell asleep. Suddenly an angel touched him and said to him, "Get up and eat." He looked, and there at his head was a cake baked on hot stones, and a jar of water. He ate and drank, and lay down again. The angel of the LORD came a second time, touched him, and said, "Get up and eat, otherwise the journey will be too much for you." He got up, and ate and drank; then he went in the strength of that food forty days and forty nights to Horeb the mount of God. At that place he came to a cave, and spent the night there.

Then the word of the LORD came to him, saying, "What are you doing here, Elijah?" He answered, "I have been very zealous for the LORD, the God of hosts; for the Israelites have forsaken your covenant, thrown down your altars, and killed your prophets with the sword. I alone am left, and they are seeking my life, to take it away."

He said, "Go out and stand on the mountain before the LORD, for the LORD is about to pass by." Now there was a great wind, so strong that it was splitting mountains and breaking rocks in pieces before the LORD, but the LORD was not in the wind; and after the wind an earthquake, but the LORD was not in the earthquake; and after the earthquake a fire, but the LORD was not in the fire; and after the fire a sound of sheer silence. When Elijah heard it, he wrapped his face in his mantle and went out and stood at the entrance of the cave. Then there came a voice to him that said, "What are you doing here, Elijah?" He answered, "I have been very zealous for the LORD, the God of hosts; for the Israelites have forsaken your covenant, thrown down your altars, and killed your prophets with the sword. I alone am left, and they are seeking my life, to take it away." Then the LORD said to him, "Go, return on your way to the wilderness of Damascus; when you arrive, you shall anoint Hazael as king over Aram. Also you shall anoint Jehu son of Nimshi as king over Israel; and you shall anoint Elisha son of Shaphat of Abel-meholah as prophet in your place. Whoever escapes from the sword of Hazael, Jehu shall kill; and whoever escapes from the sword of Jehu, Elisha shall kill. Yet I will leave seven thousand in Israel, all the knees that have not bowed to Baal, and every mouth that has not kissed him."

> The phrase translated here as the "sound of sheer silence" is better known as the "still small voice" of the King James Version.

Chariot of Fire

2 KINGS 2:1-14

Now when the LORD was about to take Elijah up to heaven by a whirlwind, Elijah and Elisha were on their way from Gilgal. Elijah said to Elisha, "Stay here; for the LORD has sent me as far as Bethel." But Elisha said, "As the LORD lives, and as you yourself live, I will not leave you." So they went down to Bethel. The company of prophets who were in Bethel came out to Elisha, and said to him, "Do you know that today the LORD will take your master away from you?" And he said, "Yes, I know; keep silent."

Elijah said to him, "Elisha, stay here; for the LORD has sent me to Jericho." But he said, "As the LORD lives, and as you yourself live, I will not leave you." So they came to Jericho. The company of prophets who were at Jericho drew near to Elisha, and said to him, "Do you know that today the LORD will take your master away from you?" And he answered, "Yes, I know; be silent."

Then Elijah said to him, "Stay here; for the LORD has sent me to the Jordan." But he said, "As the LORD lives, and as you yourself live, I will not leave you." So the two of them went on. Fifty men of the company of prophets also went, and stood at some distance from them, as they both were standing by the Jordan. Then Elijah took his mantle and rolled it up, and struck the water; the water was parted to the one side and to the other, until the two of them crossed on dry ground.

When they had crossed, Elijah said to Elisha, "Tell me what I may do for you, before I am taken from you." Elisha said, "Please let me inherit a double share of your spirit." He responded, "You have asked a hard thing; yet, if you see me as I am being taken from you, it will be granted you; if not, it will not." As they continued walking and talking, a chariot of fire and horses of fire separated the two of them, and Elijah ascended in a whirlwind into heaven. Elisha kept watching and crying out, "Father, father! The chariots of Israel and its horsemen!" But when he could no longer see him, he grasped his own clothes and tore them in two pieces.

He picked up the mantle of Elijah that had fallen from him, and went back and stood on the bank of the Jordan. He took the mantle of Elijah that had fallen from him, and struck the water, saying, "Where is the LORD, the God of Elijah?" When he had struck the water, the water was parted to the one side and to the other, and Elisha went over.

The title for the Academy Award–winning film *Chariots of Fire* derives from a line in the British hymn "Jerusalem," whose text was taken from William Blake's biblically inspired poem about his own prophetic mentor, Milton:

Bring me my bow of burning gold:
Bring me my arrows of desire:
Bring me my spear: O clouds, unfold!
Bring me my chariot of fire!

ESTHER: A BOOK OF HIDING

In Hebrew, the name Esther can mean "I am hiding." The deceptively simple story of Esther is one of hidden identities and masked motives. Even the question of divine presence is a matter of debate, for God is never explicitly mentioned. Is it an entirely secular story of survival by means of a messy mix of chance and strategy? Or is it one of subtle providence?

Ambiguity runs deep in the book of Esther, but so does a sense of carnival and play. The ancient rabbis understood this when they said you should get so drunk on Purim, the holiday celebrating the story, that you can't tell the difference between the words "Blessed be Mordecai," referring to one of the Jewish heroes of the story, and "Cursed be Haman," referring to the anti-Jewish archenemy.

Watch for parallels between characters. What do the king and Haman have in common? What about Vashti and Esther? Vashti and Mordecai? Also watch for reversals and inversions of expectations. What drives them? Accident? Providence? Strategy? All of the above?

Queen Vashti

ESTHER 1:1–2:18

This happened in the days of Ahasuerus, the same Ahasuerus who ruled over one hundred twenty-seven provinces from India to Ethiopia. In those days when King Ahasuerus sat on his royal throne in the citadel of Susa, in the third year of his reign, he gave a banquet for all his officials and ministers. The army of Persia and Media and the nobles and governors of the provinces were present, while he displayed the great wealth of his kingdom and the splendor and pomp of his majesty for many days, one hundred eighty days in all.

When these days were completed, the king gave for all the people present in the citadel of Susa, both great and small, a banquet lasting for seven days, in the court of the garden of the king's palace. There were white cotton curtains and blue hangings tied with cords of fine linen and purple to silver rings and marble pillars. There were couches of gold and silver on a mosaic pavement of porphyry, marble, mother-of-pearl, and colored stones. Drinks were served in golden goblets, goblets of different kinds, and the royal wine was lavished according to the bounty of the king. Drinking was by flagons, without restraint; for the king had given orders to all the officials of his palace to do as each one desired. Furthermore, Queen Vashti gave a banquet for the women in the palace of King Ahasuerus.

On the seventh day, when the king was merry with wine, he commanded Mehuman, Biztha, Harbona, Bigtha and Abagtha, Zethar and Carkas, the seven eunuchs who attended him, to bring Queen Vashti before the king, wearing the royal crown, in order to show the peoples and the officials her beauty; for she was fair to behold. But Queen Vashti refused to come at the king's command conveyed by the eunuchs. At this the king was enraged, and his anger burned within him.

Then the king consulted the sages who knew the laws (for this was the king's procedure toward all who were versed in law and custom, and those next to him were Carshena, Shethar, Admatha, Tarshish, Meres, Marsena, and Memucan, the seven officials of Persia and Media, who had access to the king, and sat first in the kingdom): "According to the law, what is to be done to Queen Vashti because she has not performed the command of King Ahasuerus conveyed by the eunuchs?" Then Memucan said in the presence of the king and the officials, "Not only has Queen Vashti done wrong to the king, but also to all the officials and all the peoples who are in all the provinces of King Ahasuerus. For this deed of the queen will be made known to all women, causing them to look with contempt on their husbands, since they will say, 'King Ahasuerus commanded Queen Vashti to be brought before him, and she did not come.' This very day the noble ladies of Persia and Media who have heard of the queen's behavior will rebel against the king's officials, and there will be no end of contempt and wrath! If it pleases the king, let a royal order go out from him, and let it be written among the laws of the Persians and the Medes so that it may not be altered, that Vashti is never again to come before King Ahasuerus; and let the king give her royal position to another who is better than she. So when the decree made by the king is proclaimed throughout all his kingdom, vast as it is, all women will give honor to their husbands, high and low alike."

This advice pleased the king and the officials, and the king did as Memucan proposed; he sent letters to all the royal provinces, to every province in its own script and to every people in its own language, declaring that every man should be master in his own house.

After these things, when the anger of King Ahasuerus had abated, he remembered Vashti and what she had done and what had been decreed against her. Then the king's servants who attended him said, "Let beautiful young virgins be sought out for the king. And let the king appoint commissioners in all the provinces of his kingdom to gather all the beautiful young virgins to the harem in the citadel of Susa under custody of Hegai, the king's eunuch, who is in charge of the women; let their cosmetic treatments be given them. And let the girl who pleases the king be queen instead of Vashti." This pleased the king, and he did so.

Now there was a Jew in the citadel of Susa whose name was Mordecai son of Jair son of Shimei son of Kish, a Benjaminite. Kish had been carried away from Jerusalem among the captives carried away with King Jeconiah of Judah, whom King Nebuchadnezzar of Babylon had carried away. Mordecai had brought up Hadassah, that is Esther, his cousin, for she had neither father nor mother; the girl was fair and beautiful, and when her father and her mother died, Mordecai adopted her as his own daughter. So when the king's order and his edict were proclaimed, and when many young women were gathered in the citadel of Susa in custody of Hegai, Esther also was taken into the king's palace and put in custody of Hegai, who had charge of the women. The girl pleased him and won his favor, and he quickly provided her with her cosmetic treatments and her portion of food, and with seven chosen maids from the king's palace, and advanced her and her maids to the best place in

---

She heard again the King's
    command,
And left her high estate;
Strong in her earnest
    womanhood,
She calmly met her fate,

And left the palace of the
    King,
Proud of her spotless name—
A woman who could bend to
    grief
But would not bend to
    shame.
    —Frances E. W. Harper,
    "Vashti"

---

the harem. Esther did not reveal her people or kindred, for Mordecai had charged her not to tell. Every day Mordecai would walk around in front of the court of the harem, to learn how Esther was and how she fared.

The turn came for each girl to go in to King Ahasuerus, after being twelve months under the regulations for the women, since this was the regular period of their cosmetic treatment, six months with oil of myrrh and six months with perfumes and cosmetics for women. When the girl went in to the king she was given whatever she asked for to take with her from the harem to the king's palace. In the evening she went in; then in the morning she came back to the second harem in custody of Shaashgaz, the king's eunuch, who was in charge of the concubines; she did not go in to the king again, unless the king delighted in her and she was summoned by name.

When the turn came for Esther daughter of Abihail the uncle of Mordecai, who had adopted her as his own daughter, to go in to the king, she asked for nothing except what Hegai the king's eunuch, who had charge of the women, advised. Now Esther was admired by all who saw her. When Esther was taken to King Ahasuerus in his royal palace in the tenth month, which is the month of Tebeth, in the seventh year of his reign, the king loved Esther more than all the other women; of all the virgins she won his favor and devotion, so that he set the royal crown on her head and made her queen instead of Vashti. Then the king gave a great banquet to all his officials and ministers—"Esther's banquet." He also granted a holiday to the provinces, and gave gifts with royal liberality.

Mordecai and Haman

ESTHER 3:1–15

After these things King Ahasuerus promoted Haman son of Hammedatha the Agagite, and advanced him and set his seat above all the officials who were with him. And all the king's servants who were at the king's gate bowed down and did obeisance to Haman; for the king had so commanded concerning him. But Mordecai did not bow down or do obeisance. Then the king's servants who were at the king's gate said to Mordecai, "Why do you disobey the king's command?" When they spoke to him day after day and he would not listen to them, they told Haman, in order to see whether Mordecai's words would avail; for he had told them that he was a Jew. When Haman saw that Mordecai did not bow down or do obeisance to him, Haman was infuriated. But he thought it beneath him to lay hands on Mordecai alone. So, having been told who Mordecai's people were, Haman plotted to destroy all the Jews, the people of Mordecai, throughout the whole kingdom of Ahasuerus.

In the first month, which is the month of Nisan, in the twelfth year of King Ahasuerus, they cast Pur—which means "the lot"—before Haman for the day and for the month, and the lot fell on the thirteenth day of the twelfth month, which is the month of Adar. Then Haman said to King Ahasuerus, "There is a certain people scattered and separated among the peoples in all the provinces of your kingdom; their laws are different from those of every other people, and they do not keep the king's laws, so that it is not appropriate for the king to tolerate them. If it pleases the king, let a decree be issued for their destruction, and I will pay ten thousand talents of silver into the hands of those who have charge of the king's business, so that they may put it into the king's treasuries." So the king took his signet ring from his hand and gave it to Haman son of Hammedatha the Agagite, the enemy of the Jews. The king said to Haman, "The money is given to you, and the people as well, to do with them as it seems good to you."

In an episode from the hit television comedy *Seinfeld* ("The Library"), George Costanza is something of a modern-day Mordecai, recalling how his nemesis from high school, Coach Heyman (pronounced just like Haman), had nicknamed him "Can't-Standja" and encouraged the other boys to give him "atomic wedgies." At the end of the episode, George finds Heyman, crazed and homeless, on the library steps. In a classic Seinfeldian twist on the reversal-of-fortunes theme in Esther, this fallen nemesis still succeeds in giving George one last atomic wedgie.

Then the king's secretaries were summoned on the thirteenth day of the first month, and an edict, according to all that Haman commanded, was written to the king's satraps and to the governors over all the provinces and to the officials of all the peoples, to every province in its own script and every people in its own language; it was written in the name of King Ahasuerus and sealed with the king's ring. Letters were sent by couriers to all the king's provinces, giving orders to destroy, to kill, and to annihilate all Jews, young and old, women and children, in one day, the thirteenth day of the twelfth month, which is the month of Adar, and to plunder their goods. A copy of the document was to be issued as a decree in every province by proclamation, calling on all the peoples to be ready for that day. The couriers went quickly by order of the king, and the decree was issued in the citadel of Susa. The king and Haman sat down to drink; but the city of Susa was thrown into confusion.

Esther Takes Charge

ESTHER 4:1-17

When Mordecai learned all that had been done, Mordecai tore his clothes and put on sackcloth and ashes, and went through the city, wailing with a loud and bitter cry; he went up to the entrance of the king's gate, for no one might enter the king's gate clothed with sackcloth. In every province, wherever the king's command and his decree came, there was great mourning among the Jews, with fasting and weeping and lamenting, and most of them lay in sackcloth and ashes.

When Esther's maids and her eunuchs came and told her, the queen was deeply distressed; she sent garments to clothe Mordecai, so that he might take off his sackcloth; but he would not accept them. Then Esther called for Hathach, one of the king's eunuchs, who had been appointed to attend her, and ordered him to go to Mordecai to learn what was happening and why. Hathach went out to Mordecai in the open square of the city in front of the king's gate, and Mordecai told him all that had happened to him, and the exact sum of money that Haman had promised to pay into the king's treasuries for the destruction of the Jews. Mordecai also gave him a copy of the written decree issued in Susa for their destruction, that he might show it to Esther, explain it to her, and charge her to go to the king to make supplication to him and entreat him for her people.

Hathach went and told Esther what Mordecai had said. Then Esther spoke to Hathach and gave him a message for Mordecai, saying, "All the king's servants and the people of the king's provinces know that if any man or woman goes to the king inside the inner court without being called, there is but one law—all alike are to be put to death. Only if the king holds out the golden scepter to someone, may that person live. I myself have not been called to come in to the king for thirty days." When they told Mordecai what Esther had said, Mordecai told them to reply to Esther, "Do not think that in the king's palace you will escape any more than all the other Jews. For if you keep silence at such a time as this, relief and deliverance will rise for the Jews from another quarter, but you and your father's family will perish. Who knows? Perhaps you have come to royal dignity for just such a time as this." Then Esther said in reply to Mordecai, "Go, gather all the Jews to be found in Susa, and hold a fast on my behalf, and neither eat nor drink for three days, night or day. I and my maids will also fast as you do. After that I will go to the king, though it is against the law; and if I perish, I perish." Mordecai then went away and did everything as Esther had ordered him.

> **Mordecai's warning that if Esther refuses to act on behalf of the Jews, deliverance will come from "another quarter" is often interpreted as a reference to God. In fact, in Jewish tradition, the word here translated "quarter" (*maqom*) is a name for God. In the context of this story, however, because Esther does act, God does not need to.**

Reversal of Fortunes

ESTHER 7:1-10

So the king and Haman went in to feast with Queen Esther. On the second day, as they were drinking wine, the king again said to Esther, "What is your petition, Queen Esther? It shall be granted you. And what is your request? Even to the half of my kingdom, it shall be fulfilled." Then Queen Esther answered, "If I have won your favor, O king, and if it pleases the king, let my life be given me—that is my petition—and the lives of my people—that is my request. For we have been sold, I and my people, to be destroyed, to be killed, and to be annihilated. If we had been sold merely as slaves, men and women, I would have held my peace; but no enemy can compensate for this damage to the king." Then King Ahasuerus said to Queen Esther, "Who is he, and where is he, who has presumed to do this?" Esther said, "A foe and enemy, this wicked Haman!" Then Haman was terrified before the king and the queen. The king rose from the feast in wrath and went into the palace garden, but Haman stayed to beg his life from Queen Esther, for he saw that the king had determined to destroy him. When the king returned from the palace garden to the banquet hall, Haman had thrown himself on the couch where Esther was reclining; and the king said, "Will he even assault the queen in my presence, in my own house?" As the words left the mouth of the king, they covered Haman's face. Then Harbona, one of the eunuchs in attendance on the king, said, "Look, the very gallows that Haman has prepared for Mordecai, whose word saved the king, stands at Haman's house, fifty cubits high." And the king said, "Hang him on that." So they hanged Haman on the gallows that he had prepared for Mordecai. Then the anger of the king abated.

> **I imagine Purim without the miracle of Purim. And I know everything.**
>
> —The minstrel Avrémel, in Elie Wiesel's *The Trial of God*

Poetry and Wisdom

JOB AND THE VOICE OF SUFFERING

Have you ever avoided acknowledging that your life is going well for fear that, as soon as you draw attention to it, everything will go bad? That's essentially what happens to Job. His life is golden. His great prosperity is matched only by his perfect piety. Until, that is, God takes special notice and makes him the subject of a divine experiment. How righteous would he be if everything were taken from him—his property, his children, even his health?

Faith is a crutch, some say. Not in Job. Here, faith is the problem. As Job's world falls apart, he plumbs some of life's most profound questions. Is this a moral universe? Is life fair? Is God fair? Is it okay, or even necessary, to question divine justice? Without religious faith, none of these problems need arise.

The story begins and ends with brief, straightforward narrative. But between these prose bookends is some of the most compelling and intensely provocative poetry in the Hebrew Bible, as Job contends with his friends over the meaning, or meaninglessness, of his suffering. Ultimately, their argument draws God into the fray. But even that "voice from the whirlwind" brings no real resolution.

It is because this story refuses to whitewash the problem of pain with pious answers that it continues to have such profound influence in contemporary culture. In addition to famous retellings by Carl Jung, Archibald MacLeish, and Robert Frost, among many others, one can hear echoes of Job's voice in C. S. Lewis's well-known spiritual crisis as he confronted the suffering and death of his wife from cancer—a story powerfully told in his *A Grief Observed* and the film *Shadowlands,* starring Anthony Hopkins.

Jerome, who translated the Bible into Latin in the Vulgate, said that the book of Job is like a slippery eel: the harder you try to grasp it, the more it wriggles loose. Keep that in mind as you read these selections. Hold the words loosely. Let them trouble the waters.

"Skin for Skin"

JOB 1:1-2:13

There was once a man in the land of Uz whose name was Job. That man was blameless and upright, one who feared God and turned away from evil. There were born to him seven sons and three daughters. He had seven thousand sheep, three thousand camels, five hundred yoke of oxen, five hundred donkeys, and very many servants; so that this man was the greatest of all the people of the east. His sons used to go and hold feasts in one another's houses in turn; and they would send and invite their three sisters to eat and drink with them. And when the feast days had run their course, Job would send and sanctify them, and he would rise early in the morning and offer burnt offerings according to the number of them all; for Job said, "It may be that my children have sinned, and cursed God in their hearts." This is what Job always did.

One day the heavenly beings came to present themselves before the LORD, and Satan ["the accuser"] also came among them. The LORD said to Satan, "Where have you

As one of the "heavenly beings" (literally, "sons of God"), the character here called "Satan" is not the Satan of later Jewish and Christian theology. In fact, the Hebrew word *satan* is a noun meaning "opponent" or "accuser." Here it appears with a definite article in the Hebrew, *ha-satan,* "the accuser," clearly indicating that it is not a proper name. Think of him, therefore, as something closer to the prosecuting attorney in the divine court.

come from?" Satan answered the LORD, "From going to and fro on the earth, and from walking up and down on it." The LORD said to Satan, "Have you considered my servant Job? There is no one like him on the earth, a blameless and upright man who fears God and turns away from evil." Then Satan answered the LORD, "Does Job fear God for nothing? Have you not put a fence around him and his house and all that he has, on every side? You have blessed the work of his hands, and his possessions have increased in the land. But stretch out your hand now, and touch all that he has, and he will curse you to your face." The LORD said to Satan, "Very well, all that he has is in your power; only do not stretch out your hand against him!" So Satan went out from the presence of the LORD.

One day when his sons and daughters were eating and drinking wine in the eldest brother's house, a messenger came to Job and said, "The oxen were plowing and the donkeys were feeding beside them, and the Sabeans fell on them and carried them off, and killed the servants with the edge of the sword; I alone have escaped to tell you." While he was still speaking, another

> Throughout this prologue, the word translated "curse" is the Hebrew word for "bless." The assumption of translators is that the Hebrew scribes used that word in place of one for "curse," because even to talk about cursing God would be blasphemy. Not all agree. In any case, it's interesting to note that some in the southern United States use "bless" euphemistically for "curse," as in "She sure gave him a good blessin' out."

came and said, "The fire of God fell from heaven and burned up the sheep and the servants, and consumed them; I alone have escaped to tell you." While he was still speaking, another came and said, "The Chaldeans formed three columns, made a raid on the camels and carried them off, and killed the servants with the edge of the sword; I alone have escaped to tell you." While he was still speaking, another came and said, "Your sons and daughters were eating and drinking wine in their eldest brother's house, and suddenly a great wind came across the desert, struck the four corners of the house, and it fell on the young people, and they are dead; I alone have escaped to tell you."

Then Job arose, tore his robe, shaved his head, and fell on the ground and worshiped. He said, "Naked I came from my mother's womb, and naked shall I return there; the LORD gave, and the LORD has taken away; blessed be the name of the LORD."

In all this Job did not sin or charge God with wrongdoing.

One day the heavenly beings came to present themselves before the LORD, and Satan also came among them to present himself before the LORD. The LORD said to Satan, "Where have you come from?" Satan answered the LORD, "From going to and fro on the earth, and from walking up and down on it." The LORD said to Satan, "Have you considered my servant Job? There is no one like him on the earth, a blameless and upright man who fears God and turns away from evil. He still persists in his integrity, although you incited me against him, to destroy him for no reason." Then Satan answered the LORD, "Skin for skin! All that people have they will give to save their lives. But stretch out your hand now and touch his bone and his flesh, and he will curse you to your face." The LORD said to Satan, "Very well, he is in your power; only spare his life."

So Satan went out from the presence of the LORD, and inflicted loathsome sores on Job from the sole of his foot to the crown of his head. Job took a potsherd with which to scrape himself, and sat among the ashes.

Then his wife said to him, "Do you still persist in your integrity? Curse God, and die." But he said to her, "You speak as any foolish woman would speak. Shall we receive the good at the hand of God, and not receive the bad?" In all this Job did not sin with his lips.

Now when Job's three friends heard of all these troubles that had come upon him, each of them set out from his home—Eliphaz the Temanite, Bildad the Shuhite, and Zophar the Naamathite. They met together to go and console and comfort him. When they saw him from a distance, they did not recognize him, and they raised their voices and wept aloud; they tore their robes and threw dust in the air upon their heads. They sat with him on the ground seven days and seven nights, and no one spoke a word to him, for they saw that his suffering was very great.

Let There Be Darkness

JOB 3:1-26

After this Job opened his mouth and cursed the day of his birth. Job said:

"Let the day perish in which I was born,
　　and the night that said,
　　'A man-child is conceived.'
Let that day be darkness!
　　May God above not seek it,
　　or light shine on it.
Let gloom and deep darkness
　　claim it.
　　Let clouds settle upon it;
　　let the blackness of the day
　　terrify it.
That night—let thick darkness
　　seize it!
　　let it not rejoice among the
　　days of the year;
　　let it not come into the
　　number of the months.
Yes, let that night be barren;
　　let no joyful cry be heard in it.
Let those curse it who curse.
　　the Sea,
　　those who are skilled to rouse
　　up Leviathan.
Let the stars of its dawn be dark;
　　let it hope for light, but have none;
　　may it not see the eyelids of the morning—
because it did not shut the doors of my mother's womb,
　　and hide trouble from my eyes.

"Why did I not die at birth,
　　come forth from the womb and expire?

In this powerful lament, born of pain, Job curses the day of his birth. In a sense, he also curses creation itself, insofar as much of his language calls for the reversal of the created order: "Let that day be darkness," for example, is very close in Hebrew to "Let there be light" in Genesis 1, and sea monsters like Leviathan are elsewhere in the Bible represented as forces of primordial chaos that threaten the divine order of creation. Personal chaos becomes cosmic chaos.

Why were there knees to receive me,
    or breasts for me to suck?
Now I would be lying down and quiet;
    I would be asleep; then I would be at rest
with kings and counselors of the earth
    who rebuild ruins for themselves,
or with princes who have gold,
    who fill their houses with silver.
Or why was I not buried like a stillborn child,
    like an infant that never sees the light?
There the wicked cease from troubling,
    and there the weary are at rest.
There the prisoners are at ease together;
    they do not hear the voice of the taskmaster.
The small and the great are there,
    and the slaves are free from their masters.

"Why is light given to one in misery,
    and life to the bitter in soul,
who long for death, but it does not come,
    and dig for it more than for hidden treasures;
who rejoice exceedingly,
    and are glad when they find the grave?
Why is light given to one who cannot see the way,
    whom God has fenced in?
For my sighing comes like my bread,
    and my groanings are poured out like water.
Truly the thing that I fear comes upon me,
    and what I dread befalls me.
I am not at ease, nor am I quiet;
    I have no rest; but trouble comes."

Arguing with "Friends"

JOB 18:1–19:29

Then Bildad the Shuhite answered:

"How long will you hunt for words?
  Consider, and then we shall speak.
Why are we counted as cattle?
  Why are we stupid in your
  sight?
You who tear yourself in your
  anger—
  shall the earth be forsaken
  because of you,
  or the rock be removed out of
  its place?

"Surely the light of the wicked is
  put out,
  and the flame of their fire does
  not shine.
The light is dark in their tent,
  and the lamp above them is
  put out.
Their strong steps are shortened,
  and their own schemes throw
  them down.
For they are thrust into a net by
  their own feet,
  and they walk into a pitfall.
A trap seizes them by the heel;
  a snare lays hold of them.
A rope is hid for them in the ground,
  a trap for them in the path.
Terrors frighten them on every side,
  and chase them at their heels.

Most of the book of Job consists of an argument between Job and his friends, who insist on defending God against Job's challenges and accusations. Their basic worldview is that God has created a moral universe in which the good are blessed and the wicked are cursed. We, of course, know that such is not the case with Job. As the argument progresses, the friends seem increasingly willing to sacrifice Job's particular case to their worldview.

Their strength is consumed by hunger,
    and calamity is ready for their stumbling.
By disease their skin is consumed,
    the firstborn of Death consumes their limbs.
They are torn from the tent in which they trusted,
    and are brought to the king of terrors.
In their tents nothing remains;
    sulfur is scattered upon their habitations.
Their roots dry up beneath,
    and their branches wither above.
Their memory perishes from the earth,
    and they have no name in the street.
They are thrust from light into darkness,
    and driven out of the world.
They have no offspring or descendant among their people,
    and no survivor where they used to live.
They of the west are appalled at their fate,
    and horror seizes those of the east.
Surely such are the dwellings of the ungodly,
    such is the place of those who do not know God."

Then Job answered:

"How long will you torment me,
    and break me in pieces with words?
These ten times you have cast reproach upon me;
    are you not ashamed to wrong me?
And even if it is true that I have erred,
    my error remains with me.
If indeed you magnify yourselves against me,
    and make my humiliation an argument against me,
know then that God has put me in the wrong,
    and closed his net around me.
Even when I cry out, 'Violence!' I am not answered;
    I call aloud, but there is no justice.
He has walled up my way so that I cannot pass,
    and he has set darkness upon my paths.

He has stripped my glory from me,
  and taken the crown from my head.
He breaks me down on every side, and I am gone,
  he has uprooted my hope like a tree.
He has kindled his wrath against me,
  and counts me as his adversary.
His troops come on together;
  they have thrown up siegeworks against me,
  and encamp around my tent.

"He has put my family far from me,
  and my acquaintances are wholly estranged from me.
My relatives and my close friends have failed me;
  the guests in my house have forgotten me;
my serving girls count me as a stranger;
  I have become an alien in their eyes.
I call to my servant, but he gives me no answer;
  I must myself plead with him.
My breath is repulsive to my wife;
  I am loathsome to my own family.
Even young children despise me;
  when I rise, they talk against me.
All my intimate friends abhor me,
  and those whom I loved have turned against me.
My bones cling to my skin and to my flesh,
  and I have escaped by the skin of my teeth.
Have pity on me, have pity on me, O you my friends,
  for the hand of God has touched me!
Why do you, like God, pursue me,
  never satisfied with my flesh?

"O that my words were written down!
  O that they were inscribed in a book!
O that with an iron pen and with lead
  they were engraved on a rock forever!
For I know that my Redeemer lives,
  and that at the last he will stand upon the earth;

and after my skin has been thus destroyed,
  then in my flesh I shall see God,
whom I shall see on my side,
  and my eyes shall behold, and not another.
  My heart faints within me!
If you say, 'How we will persecute him!'
  and, 'The root of the matter is found in him';
be afraid of the sword,
  for wrath brings the punishment of the sword,
  so that you may know there is a judgment."

Out of the Whirlwind

JOB 38:1-21; 40:1-42:6

Then the LORD answered Job out of the whirlwind:

"Who is this that darkens
  counsel by words without
  knowledge?
Gird up your loins like a man,
  I will question you, and you
  shall declare to me.

"Where were you when I laid the
  foundation of the earth?
  Tell me, if you have
  understanding.
Who determined its
  measurements—surely you
  know!
  Or who stretched the line upon it?
On what were its bases sunk,
  or who laid its cornerstone
when the morning stars sang together
  and all the heavenly beings shouted for joy?

Eventually, God joins the fray, silencing Job and his friends. Although this voice from the whirlwind overwhelms Job with power, even monstrous power, it's fair to ask whether it answers Job's questions or responds to his charges.

"Or who shut in the sea with doors
    when it burst out from the womb?—
when I made the clouds its garment,
    and thick darkness its swaddling band,
and prescribed bounds for it,
    and set bars and doors,
and said, 'Thus far shall you come, and no farther,
    and here shall your proud waves be stopped'?

"Have you commanded the morning since your days began,
    and caused the dawn to know its place,
so that it might take hold of the skirts of the earth,
    and the wicked be shaken out of it?
It is changed like clay under the seal,
    and it is dyed like a garment.
Light is withheld from the wicked,
    and their uplifted arm is broken.

"Have you entered into the springs of the sea,
    or walked in the recesses of the deep?
Have the gates of death been revealed to you,
    or have you seen the gates of deep darkness?
Have you comprehended the expanse of the earth?
    Declare, if you know all this.
Where is the way to the dwelling of light,
    and where is the place of darkness,
that you may take it to its territory
    and that you may discern the paths to its home?
Surely you know, for you were born then,
    and the number of your days is great!"

. . . And the LORD said to Job:

"Shall a faultfinder contend with the Almighty?
    Anyone who argues with God must respond."

Then Job answered the LORD:

"See, I am of small account; what shall I answer you?
    I lay my hand on my mouth.

I have spoken once, and I will not answer;
   twice, but will proceed no further."

Then the LORD answered Job out of the whirlwind:

"Gird up your loins like a man;
   I will question you, and you declare to me.
Will you even put me in the wrong?
   Will you condemn me that you may be justified?
Have you an arm like God,
   and can you thunder with a voice like his?

"Deck yourself with majesty and dignity;
   clothe yourself with glory and splendor.
Pour out the overflowings of your anger,
   and look on all who are proud, and abase them.
Look on all who are proud, and bring them low;
   tread down the wicked where they stand.
Hide them all in the dust together;
   bind their faces in the world below.
Then I will also acknowledge to you
   that your own right hand can give you victory.

"Look at Behemoth,
   which I made just as I made you;
   it eats grass like an ox.
Its strength is in its loins,
   and its power in the muscles of its belly.
It makes its tail stiff like a cedar;
   the sinews of its thighs are knit together.
Its bones are tubes of bronze,
   its limbs like bars of iron.

"It is the first of the great acts of God—
   only its Maker can approach it with the sword.
For the mountains yield food for it
   where all the wild animals play.
Under the lotus plants it lies,
   in the covert of the reeds and in the marsh.

The lotus trees cover it for shade;
  the willows of the wadi surround it.
Even if the river is turbulent, it is not frightened;
  it is confident though Jordan rushes against its mouth.
Can one take it with hooks
  or pierce its nose with a snare?

"Can you draw out Leviathan with a fishhook,
  or press down its tongue with a cord?
Can you put a rope in its nose,
  or pierce its jaw with a hook?
Will it make many supplications to you?
  Will it speak soft words to you?
Will it make a covenant with you
  to be taken as your servant forever?
Will you play with it as with a bird,
  or will you put it on leash for your girls?
Will traders bargain over it?
  Will they divide it up among the merchants?
Can you fill its skin with harpoons,
  or its head with fishing spears?
Lay hands on it;
  think of the battle; you will not do it again!
Any hope of capturing it will be disappointed;
  were not even the gods overwhelmed at the sight of it?
No one is so fierce as to dare to stir it up.
  Who can stand before it?
Who can confront it and be safe?
  —under the whole heaven, who?

"I will not keep silence concerning its limbs,
  or its mighty strength, or its splendid frame.
Who can strip off its outer garment?
  Who can penetrate its double coat of mail?
Who can open the doors of its face?
  There is terror all around its teeth.
Its back is made of shields in rows,
  shut up closely as with a seal.

One is so near to another
   that no air can come between them.
They are joined one to another;
   they clasp each other and cannot be separated.
Its sneezes flash forth light,
   and its eyes are like the eyelids of the dawn.
From its mouth go flaming torches;
   sparks of fire leap out.
Out of its nostrils comes smoke,
   as from a boiling pot and burning rushes.
Its breath kindles coals,
   and a flame comes out of its mouth.
In its neck abides strength,
   and terror dances before it.
The folds of its flesh cling
   together;
   it is firmly cast and
   immovable.
Its heart is as hard as stone,
   as hard as the lower millstone.
When it raises itself up the gods
   are afraid;
   at the crashing they are beside
   themselves.
Though the sword reaches it, it
   does not avail,
   nor does the spear, the dart, or
   the javelin.
It counts iron as straw,
   and bronze as rotten wood.
The arrow cannot make it flee;
   slingstones, for it, are turned
   to chaff.
Clubs are counted as chaff;
   it laughs at the rattle of
   javelins.

Whereas many have seen in this depiction of Leviathan something primordially monstrous, Thomas Hobbes famously made it a figure of state order in his political treatise *Leviathan* (1651): "Hitherto I have set forth the nature of Man (whose Pride and other Passions have compelled him to submit himselfe to Government;) together with the great power of his Governour, whom I compare to Leviathan, taking that comparison out of the two last verses of the one and fourtieth of Job; where God having set forth the great power of Leviathan, calleth him King of the Proud."

Its underparts are like sharp potsherds;
    it spreads itself like a threshing sledge on the mire.
It makes the deep boil like a pot;
    it makes the sea like a pot of ointment.
It leaves a shining wake behind it;
    one would think the deep to be white-haired.
On earth it has no equal,
    a creature without fear.
It surveys everything that is lofty;
    it is king over all that are proud."

Then Job answered the LORD:

"I know that you can do all things,
    and that no purpose of yours can be thwarted.
'Who is this that hides counsel without knowledge?'
Therefore I have uttered what I did not understand,
    things too wonderful for me, which I did not know.
'Hear, and I will speak;
    I will question you, and you declare to me.'
I had heard of you by the hearing of the ear,
    but now my eye sees you;
therefore I despise myself,
    and repent in dust and ashes."

A Happy Ending?

JOB 42:7-17

After the LORD had spoken these words to Job, the LORD said to Eliphaz the Temanite: "My wrath is kindled against you and against your two friends; for you have not spoken of me what is right, as my servant Job has. Now therefore take seven bulls and seven rams, and go to my servant Job, and offer up for

After overpowering Job, God expresses anger at Job's friends because they, unlike Job, have not "spoken of me what is right." Yet they have been God's defenders against Job's challenges from the beginning! So, what does it mean to speak rightly to or about God?

READING BIBLICAL POETRY

Most cultures have poetry—some form of elevated speech and writing set apart from everyday language and prose. But the way it is elevated differs from culture to culture. In some ways, Hebrew biblical poetry is similar to English poetry. It looks about the same on a printed page, with short lines of about the same length, and it is rich with similes, analogies, and metaphors. But other aspects of this poetry are very different from what we are used to. The most distinctive is its use of parallelism, that is, the division of lines into two or three equal and parallel parts. Knowing a little bit about this feature of Hebrew biblical poetry will help you appreciate it more fully.

There are three types of parallelism. The first and most common is called *synonymous* parallelism. It has two parts, usually printed as two lines, with the second closely mirroring the first. A good example is Psalm 51:10:

Create in me a clean heart, O God,
and put a new and right spirit within me.

Note how each part of the first half has a parallel in the second:

| create | in me | a clean | heart |
| put | within me | a new and right | spirit |

The effect is more than simple reiteration. The second part intensifies the first. At the same time, insofar as there is no such thing as a pure synonym, the slight differences in the second part create tensions that add poetic depth.

The second kind of parallelism is called *antithetical,* because the second part strengthens and amplifies the first by articulating its antithesis. A good example is Isaiah 40:4, well known to most hearers from its use in Handel's *Messiah:*

Every valley shall be lifted up,
and every mountain and hill be made low.

Note how the raising of that which is low in the first part parallels the lowering of that which is high in the second, evoking a vision in which the way things have always been gets turned upside down:

| every valley | lifted up |
| every mountain and hill | made low |

The third kind of parallelism is called *synthetic,* because the second part completes the first in some way. Psalm 23:4 is a good example:

for you are with me;
your rod and your staff—
they comfort me.

The second and third divisions of this line are roughly equal to the first, but they don't parallel it in content. Rather, they fill it out with a metaphor (a shepherd's staff) and a feeling (comfort).

As you read Hebrew biblical poetry, watch for these different kinds of parallelism, always asking what effect they have. Often, you'll find different forms of parallelism employed from one line to the next. Sometimes you'll find lines that don't easily fit into one of these three categories. The categories are, after all, scholarly abstractions. The poets of the Hebrew Bible didn't learn them in creative writing workshops, nor were they required to adhere to them. In fact, as we know from contemporary literature, good poetry often plays between careful adherence to and intentional breaking of familiar conventions. Watch, then, not only for easily identifiable forms, but also for creative mixing and altering of those forms.

yourselves a burnt offering; and my servant Job shall pray for you, for I will accept his prayer not to deal with you according to your folly; for you have not spoken of me what is right, as my servant Job has done." So Eliphaz the Temanite and Bildad the Shuhite and Zophar the Naamathite went and did what the LORD had told them; and the LORD accepted Job's prayer.

And the LORD restored the fortunes of Job when he had prayed for his friends; and the LORD gave Job twice as much as he had before. Then there came to him all his brothers and sisters and all who had known him before, and they ate bread with him in his house; they showed him sympathy and comforted him for all the evil that the LORD had brought upon him; and each of them gave him a piece of money and a gold ring. The LORD blessed the latter days of Job more than his beginning; and he had fourteen thousand sheep, six thousand camels, a thousand yoke of oxen, and a thousand donkeys. He also had seven sons and three daughters. He named the first Jemimah, the second Keziah, and the third Keren-happuch. In all the land there were no women so beautiful as Job's daughters; and their father gave them an inheritance along with their brothers. After this Job lived one hundred and forty years, and saw his children, and his children's children, four generations. And Job died, old and full of days.

PSALMS: THE BIBLICAL SONGBOOK

Most record albums and songbooks include a range of styles and themes, tones and moods. None have a wider range than the biblical songbook we call the Psalms. The Psalms give voice to the tremendous depth and breadth of human experience, from upbeat exuberance, to insecure longing, to godforsaken loneliness and everything in between.

Many of the Psalms' most evocative poetic expressions and images continue to resonate today, especially in times of trouble. The "valley of the shadow of death" (Psalm 23) has given expression to the feeling of many soldiers in many battles. The image of the Israelite exiles lamenting "by the rivers of Babylon" (Psalm 137) captured the experience of Jamaicans and many others whose ancestors had been carried into captivity and slavery. And when President Clinton made a public apology for his affair with Monica Lewinsky, he borrowed much of his language from Psalm 51, traditionally believed to be King David's confession for the Bathsheba affair. In ten short minutes, he referred to the psalm's image of a "broken spirit" three times, and his last request that "the words of my mouth and the meditations of my heart" be accepted came from Psalm 19.

There is no right way to read these poems. There is no single point or perspective to discover. In some, you might find a voice that speaks to your own story and experience. In others, you might meet another voice whose imagination and view of the world are far different from your own. As you read, allow your imagination to dwell in the rich, figurative language of these poems. Ask what meanings and ideas their metaphorical language opens up in your imagination that would be closed off by flatter vocabularies.

"Why Have You Forsaken Me?"

PSALM 22:1-31

My God, my God, why have you forsaken me?
    Why are you so far from helping me, from the words of my
    groaning?
O my God, I cry by day, but you do not answer;
    and by night, but find no rest.

Yet you are holy,
    enthroned on the praises of Israel.
In you our ancestors trusted;
    they trusted, and you delivered them.
To you they cried, and were saved;
    in you they trusted, and were not put to shame.

But I am a worm, and not human;
    scorned by others, and despised by the people.
All who see me mock at me;
    they make mouths at me, they shake their heads;
"Commit your cause to the LORD; let him deliver—
    let him rescue the one in whom he delights!"

Yet it was you who took me from the womb;
　　you kept me safe on my mother's breast.
On you I was cast from my birth,
　　and since my mother bore me you have been my God.
Do not be far from me,
　　for trouble is near
　　and there is no one to help.

Many bulls encircle me,
　　strong bulls of Bashan surround me;
they open wide their mouths at me,
　　like a ravening and roaring lion.

I am poured out like water,
　　and all my bones are out of joint;
my heart is like wax;
　　it is melted within my breast;
my mouth is dried up like a potsherd,
　　and my tongue sticks to my jaws;
　　you lay me in the dust of death.

For dogs are all around me;
　　a company of evildoers encircles me.
My hands and feet have shriveled;
I can count all my bones.
They stare and gloat over me;
they divide my clothes among themselves,
　　and for my clothing they cast lots.

But you, O LORD, do not be far away!
　　O my help, come quickly to my aid!
Deliver my soul from the sword,
　　my life from the power of the dog!
　　Save me from the mouth of the lion!

From the horns of the wild oxen you have rescued me.
I will tell of your name to my brothers and sisters;
　　in the midst of the congregation I will praise you:
You who fear the LORD, praise him!

All you offspring of Jacob, glorify him;
    stand in awe of him, all you offspring of Israel!
For he did not despise or abhor
    the affliction of the afflicted;
he did not hide his face from me,
    but heard when I cried to him.

From you comes my praise in the great congregation;
    my vows I will pay before those who fear him.
The poor shall eat and be satisfied;
    those who seek him shall praise the LORD.
    May your hearts live forever!

All the ends of the earth shall remember
    and turn to the LORD;
and all the families of the nations
    shall worship before him.
For dominion belongs to the LORD,
    and he rules over the nations.

To him, indeed, shall all who sleep in the earth bow down;
    before him shall bow all who go down to the dust,
    and I shall live for him.
Posterity will serve him;
    future generations will be told about the LORD,
and proclaim his deliverance to a people yet unborn,
    saying that he has done it.

"The Lord Is My Shepherd"

PSALM 23:1-6

The LORD is my shepherd, I shall not want.
    He makes me lie down in green pastures;
he leads me beside still waters;
    he restores my soul.
He leads me in right paths
    for his name's sake.

Even though I walk through the darkest valley,
    I fear no evil;
for you are with me;
    your rod and your staff—
    they comfort me.
You prepare a table before me
    in the presence of my enemies;
you anoint my head with oil;
    my cup overflows.
Surely goodness and mercy shall
    follow me
    all the days of my life,
and I shall dwell in the house of
    the LORD
    my whole life long.

"A Broken and Contrite Heart"

PSALM 51:1-19

Have mercy on me, O God,
    according to your steadfast
    love;
according to your abundant
    mercy
    blot out my transgressions.
Wash me thoroughly from my iniquity,
    and cleanse me from my sin.

For I know my transgressions,
    and my sin is ever before me.
Against you, you alone, have I sinned,
    and done what is evil in your sight,
so that you are justified in your sentence
    and blameless when you pass judgment.
Indeed, I was born guilty,
    a sinner when my mother conceived me.

The King James Version's "valley of the shadow of death" (here translated "the darkest valley") has often served as an apt metaphor for modern war, as in Nobel laureate John Galsworthy's psalm "Valley of the Shadow" (1915):

God, I am travelling out to
    death's sea,
    I, who exulted in sunshine
    and laughter,
Dreamed not of dying—death
    is such waste of me!
    Grant me one comfort:
    Leave not the hereafter
Of mankind to war, as though
    I had died not—

You desire truth in the inward being;
 therefore teach me wisdom in my secret heart.
Purge me with hyssop, and I shall be clean;
 wash me, and I shall be whiter than snow.
Let me hear joy and gladness;
 let the bones that you have crushed rejoice.
Hide your face from my sins,
 and blot out all my iniquities.

Create in me a clean heart, O God,
 and put a new and right spirit within me.
Do not cast me away from your
    presence,
 and do not take your holy
 spirit from me.
Restore to me the joy of your
 salvation,
 and sustain in me a willing
 spirit.

Then I will teach transgressors
 your ways,
 and sinners will return to you.
Deliver me from bloodshed,
 O God,
 O God of my salvation,
 and my tongue will sing aloud
 of your deliverance.

And if my repentance is genuine and sustained, and if I can maintain both a broken spirit and a strong heart, then good can come of this for our country as well as for me and my family. . . . I ask that God give me a clean heart, let me walk by faith and not sight.

—President Bill Clinton, speaking at a White House prayer breakfast, following in the wake of his affair with Monica Lewinsky, September 11, 1998

O Lord, open my lips,
 and my mouth will declare your praise.
For you have no delight in sacrifice;
 if I were to give a burnt offering, you would not be pleased.
The sacrifice acceptable to God is a broken spirit;
 a broken and contrite heart, O God, you will not despise.

Do good to Zion in your good pleasure;
 rebuild the walls of Jerusalem,
then you will delight in right sacrifices,

in burnt offerings and whole burnt offerings;
  then bulls will be offered on your altar.

"My Soul Is Full of Troubles"

PSALM 88:1-18

O LORD, God of my salvation,
  when, at night, I cry out in your presence,
let my prayer come before you;
  incline your ear to my cry.

For my soul is full of troubles,
  and my life draws near to Sheol.
I am counted among those who go down to the Pit;
  I am like those who have no help,
like those forsaken among the dead,
  like the slain that lie in the grave,
like those whom you remember no more,
  for they are cut off from your hand.
You have put me in the depths of the Pit,
  in the regions dark and deep.
Your wrath lies heavy upon me,
  and you overwhelm me with all your waves. *Selah*

You have caused my companions to shun me;
  you have made me a thing of horror to them.
I am shut in so that I cannot escape;
  my eye grows dim through sorrow.
Every day I call on you, O LORD;
  I spread out my hands to you.
Do you work wonders for the dead?
  Do the shades rise up to praise you? *Selah*
Is your steadfast love declared in the grave,
  or your faithfulness in Abaddon?
Are your wonders known in the darkness,
  or your saving help in the land of forgetfulness?

But I, O LORD, cry out to you;
    in the morning my prayer comes before you.
O LORD, why do you cast me off?
    Why do you hide your face from me?
Wretched and close to death from my youth up,
    I suffer your terrors; I am desperate.
Your wrath has swept over me;
    your dread assaults destroy me.
They surround me like a flood all day long;
    from all sides they close in on me.
You have caused friend and neighbor to shun me;
    my companions are in darkness.

"Like a Child with Its Mother"

PSALM 131:1-3

O LORD, my heart is not lifted up,
    my eyes are not raised too high;
I do not occupy myself with things
    too great and too marvelous for me.
But I have calmed and quieted my soul,
    like a weaned child with its mother;
    my soul is like the weaned child that is with me.

O Israel, hope in the LORD
    from this time on and forevermore.

"By the Rivers of Babylon"

PSALM 137:1-9

By the rivers of Babylon—
    there we sat down and there we wept
    when we remembered Zion.
On the willows there
    we hung up our harps.

For there our captors
    asked us for songs,
and our tormentors asked for mirth, saying,
    "Sing us one of the songs of Zion!"

How could we sing the LORD's song
    in a foreign land?
If I forget you, O Jerusalem,
    let my right hand wither!
Let my tongue cling to the roof
    of my mouth,
    if I do not remember you,
if I do not set Jerusalem
    above my highest joy.

Remember, O LORD, against the
    Edomites
    the day of Jerusalem's fall,
how they said, "Tear it down!
    Tear it down!
    Down to its foundations!"
O daughter Babylon, you
    devastator!
    Happy shall they be who pay you back
    what you have done to us!
Happy shall they be who take your little ones
    and dash them against the rock!

The Rastafarian song "Rivers of Babylon," first recorded in 1970 by the Melodians, is an adaptation of this psalm, whose poignant expression of displacement and loss resonates with the experiences of many more recent exiles. Mercifully, the Melodians stopped short of quoting the shockingly violent revenge fantasy that concludes the psalm.

THE WISDOM OF PROVERBS

If you know one verse from the book of Proverbs, it's probably "Spare the rod and spoil the child," the popular paraphrase of Proverbs 13:24 first coined by Samuel Butler in 1662. Indeed, many children have felt this verse before ever hearing it! Too bad their parents didn't know, as most scholars now argue, that the "rod" in this verse was not for spanking, but for guiding—like a shepherd's staff.

As you read these selections, you'll probably find that you're familiar with a great deal more than the "spanking verse." Indeed, Western traditions of parenting and moral education are steeped in the lessons of Proverbs.

Note how often its kernels are drawn from familiar experience and observation of the everyday world. Note too their use of commonplace imagery and metaphors. At the same time, you can't miss the fact that most of them are gendered. Although not a story per se, this collection of wisdom sayings is framed as practical advice given by a father to his son. How does this patriarchal framework shape your reading experience?

Familiar Proverbs

Say to wisdom, "You are my sister,"
    and call insight your intimate friend. (7:4)

A scoffer who is rebuked will only hate you;
    the wise, when rebuked, will love you. (9:8)

A slack hand causes poverty,
    but the hand of the diligent makes rich. (10:4)

Hatred stirs up strife,
    but love covers all offenses. (10:12)

When pride comes, then comes disgrace;
    but wisdom is with the humble. (11:2)

The righteousness of the upright saves them,
    but the treacherous are taken captive by their schemes. (11:6)

Whoever loves discipline loves knowledge,
    but those who hate to be rebuked are stupid. (12:1)

Fools think their own way is right,
    but the wise listen to advice. (12:15)

One who is clever conceals knowledge,
   but the mind of a fool broadcasts folly. (12:23)

Those who guard their mouths preserve their lives;
   those who open wide their lips come to ruin. (13:3)

Those who spare the rod hate their children,
   but those who love them are diligent to discipline them. (13:24)

Those who oppress the poor insult their Maker,
   but those who are kind to the needy honor him. (14:31))

A soft answer turns away wrath,
   but a harsh word stirs up anger. (15:1)

Better is a little with righteousness
   than large income with
   injustice. (16:8)

Gray hair is a crown of glory;
   it is gained in a righteous life.
   (16:31)

Better is a dry morsel with quiet
   than a house full of feasting
   with strife. (17:1)

Grandchildren are the crown of
   the aged,
   and the glory of children is their parents. (17:6)

> **If Matrimony and Hanging go
> By Dest'ny, why not
>   Whipping too?
> What Med'cine else can cure
>   the Fits
> Of Lovers, when they lose
>   their Wits?
> Love is a Boy, by Poets stil'd,
> Then Spare the Rod, and
>   spoil the Child.**
>
> —Samuel Butler, *Hudibras*

One who forgives an affront fosters friendship,
   but one who dwells on disputes will alienate a friend. (17:9)

A fool takes no pleasure in understanding,
   but only in expressing personal opinion. (18:2)

An ally offended is stronger than a city;
   such quarreling is like the bars of a castle. (18:19)

Death and life are in the power of the tongue,
   and those who love it will eat its fruits. (18:21)

A gossip reveals secrets;
    therefore do not associate with a babbler. (20:19)

The glory of youths is their strength,
    but the beauty of the aged is their gray hair. (20:29)

The getting of treasures by a lying tongue
    is a fleeting vapor and a snare of death. (21:6)

If you close your ear to the cry of the poor,
    you will cry out and not be heard. (21:13)

Train children in the right way,
    and when old, they will not stray. (22:6)

Do not speak in the hearing of a fool,
    who will only despise the wisdom of your words. (23:9)

Listen to your father who begot you,
    and do not despise your mother when she is old. (23:22)

Let your foot be seldom in your neighbor's house,
    otherwise the neighbor will become weary of you and hate you.
    (25:17)

Do not answer fools according to their folly,
    or you will be a fool yourself. (26:4)

As a door turns on its hinges,
    so does a lazy person in bed. (26:14)

Do not boast about tomorrow,
    for you do not know what a day may bring. (27:1)

Whoever gives to the poor will lack nothing,
    but one who turns a blind eye will get many a curse. (28:27)

Wisdom Personified

PROVERBS 8:22-36

"The LORD created me at the beginning of his work,
    the first of his acts of long ago.

Ages ago I was set up,
    at the first, before the
    beginning of the earth.
When there were no depths I was
    brought forth,
    when there were no springs
    abounding with water.
Before the mountains had been
    shaped,
    before the hills, I was brought
    forth—
when he had not yet made earth
    and fields,
    or the world's first bits of soil.
When he established the heavens,
    I was there,
    when he drew a circle on the
    face of the deep,
when he made firm the skies above,
    when he established the fountains of the deep,
when he assigned to the sea its limit,
    so that the waters might not transgress his command,
when he marked out the foundations of the earth,
    then I was beside him, like a master worker;
and I was daily his delight,
    rejoicing before him always,
rejoicing in his inhabited world
    and delighting in the human race.

"And now, my children, listen to me:
    happy are those who keep my ways.
Hear instruction and be wise,
    and do not neglect it.
Happy is the one who listens to me,
    watching daily at my gates,
    waiting beside my doors.

In this fascinating poem within the book of Proverbs, Wisdom (*Hokmah*) is personified as a divine consort who was present at the creation, "before the beginning of the earth." In later Jewish philosophy and in the Gospel of John, she is identified also with the divine Logos, or "Word."

For whoever finds me finds life
   and obtains favor from the Lord;
but those who miss me injure themselves;
   all who hate me love death."

"Her Works Praise Her"

PROVERBS 31:10-31

A capable wife who can find?
   She is far more precious than jewels.
The heart of her husband trusts
   in her,
   and he will have no lack of
   gain.
She does him good, and not
   harm,
   all the days of her life.
She seeks wool and flax,
   and works with willing hands.
She is like the ships of the
   merchant,
   she brings her food from far
   away.
She rises while it is still night
   and provides food for her
   household
   and tasks for her servant-girls.
She considers a field and buys it;
   with the fruit of her hands she
   plants a vineyard.
She girds herself with strength,
   and makes her arms strong.
She perceives that her
   merchandise is profitable.

This well-known poem in praise of a virtuous wife, sometimes called the "Proverbs 31 Woman," is quoted (from the King James Version) as an epigraph in Kaye Gibbon's novel *A Virtuous Woman,* the story of Ruby Pitt Woodrow, a cultured young woman damaged by an abusive relationship. Ruby finds love and healing in a relationship with an older, homely bachelor named Blinking Jack Stokes, who expects nothing from her, but thinks the world of her. The poem itself makes clear what we've seen elsewhere in Proverbs, namely, that it assumes male readers.

Her lamp does not go out at night.
She puts her hands to the distaff,
   and her hands hold the spindle.
She opens her hand to the poor,
   and reaches out her hands to the needy.
She is not afraid for her household when it snows,
   for all her household are clothed in crimson.
She makes herself coverings;
   her clothing is fine linen and purple.
Her husband is known in the city gates,
   taking his seat among the elders of the land.
She makes linen garments and sells them;
   she supplies the merchant with sashes.
Strength and dignity are her clothing,
   and she laughs at the time to come.
She opens her mouth with wisdom,
   and the teaching of kindness is on her tongue.
She looks well to the ways of her household,
   and does not eat the bread of idleness.
Her children rise up and call her happy;
   her husband too, and he praises her:
"Many women have done excellently,
   but you surpass them all."
Charm is deceitful, and beauty is vain,
   but a woman who fears the LORD is to be praised.
Give her a share in the fruit of her hands,
    and let her works praise her in the city gates.

ECCLESIASTES: IS IT ALL IN VAIN?

What if, in the end, all our striving after wisdom and understanding is in vain, nothing more than a chasing after the wind? That's precisely what the teacher in the book of Ecclesiastes comes to believe. His is a countervoice to the one we hear in the wisdom tradition of Proverbs. How ironic, then, that his proclamation of futility was transformed into the anthem of hope "Turn! Turn! Turn!" by the Byrds. How was that possible? Is there something about this teacher's honest admission of the vanity of it all that opens up, in the aftermath of cynicism, a new hope? Maybe. Or maybe it's just too hard to believe that that's all there is.

"Vanity of Vanities"

ECCLESIASTES 1:2–18

Vanity of vanities, says the Teacher,
    vanity of vanities! All is vanity.
What do people gain from all the toil
    at which they toil under the sun?
A generation goes, and a generation comes,
    but the earth remains forever.
The sun rises and the sun goes down,
    and hurries to the place where it rises.
The wind blows to the south,
    and goes around to the north;
round and round goes the wind,
    and on its circuits the wind returns.
All streams run to the sea,
    but the sea is not full;
to the place where the streams flow,
    there they continue to flow.
All things are wearisome;
    more than one can express;
the eye is not satisfied with seeing,
    or the ear filled with hearing.
What has been is what will be,
    and what has been done is what will be done;
    there is nothing new under the sun.
Is there a thing of which it is said,
    "See, this is new"?
It has already been,
    in the ages before us.
The people of long ago are not remembered,
    nor will there be any remembrance

of people yet to come
    by those who come after them.

I, the Teacher, when king over Israel in Jerusalem, applied my mind to seek and to search out by wisdom all that is done under heaven; it is an unhappy business that God has given to human beings to be busy with. I saw all the deeds that are done under the sun; and see, all is vanity and a chasing after wind.

What is crooked cannot be made straight,
    and what is lacking cannot be counted.

I said to myself, "I have acquired great wisdom, surpassing all who were over Jerusalem before me; and my mind has had great experience of wisdom and knowledge." And I applied my mind to know wisdom and to know madness and folly. I perceived that this also is but a chasing after wind.

For in much wisdom is much vexation,
    and those who increase knowledge increase sorrow.

Turn! Turn! Turn!

ECCLESIASTES 3:1-8

For everything there is a season, and a time for every matter under heaven:

    a time to be born, and a time to die;
    a time to plant, and a time to pluck up what is planted;
    a time to kill, and a time to heal;
    a time to break down, and a time to build up;
    a time to weep, and a time to laugh;
    a time to mourn, and a time to dance;
    a time to throw away stones, and a time to gather stones together;
    a time to embrace, and a time to refrain from embracing;
    a time to seek, and a time to lose;

a time to keep, and a time to
    throw away;
a time to tear, and a time to sew;
a time to keep silence, and a
    time to speak;
a time to love, and a time to
    hate;
a time for war, and a time for
    peace.

LOVE, SEX, AND THE SONG OF SONGS

Parents wanting biblical backup for a conservative stance on sexuality will do well to avoid the Song of Songs. Also known as the Song of Solomon, this collection of erotic love poetry is presented as a dialogue between an unmarried young woman and her beloved. Longing intensifies as fulfillment is postponed. It's the original teenage love song and the biblical prototype for everything from *Romeo and Juliet* to today's romance novels. The desire that overflows its lines is enough to make even contemporary readers blush.

As you read, consider how the poetry piles metaphor upon metaphor. What feelings do they evoke? How does this literally excessive language combine with the experience of postponement and frustration to deepen desire?

Originally written by Pete Seeger in the 1950s, "Turn! Turn! Turn!" quotes directly from the King James Version of this passage—but with two major additions: the repetition of the refrain "Turn! Turn! Turn!" summoning change to come, and the climactic response, "I swear it's not too late," immediately following "a time for peace." Rereleased by the Byrds in 1965, the song soon became a popular antiwar anthem.

"A Lily of the Valleys"

SONG OF SONGS 1:2–2:7

Let him kiss me with the kisses of his mouth!
For your love is better than wine,
    your anointing oils are fragrant,

your name is perfume poured out;
    therefore the maidens love you.
Draw me after you, let us make haste.
    The king has brought me into his chambers.
We will exult and rejoice in you;
    we will extol your love more than wine;
    rightly do they love you.

I am black and beautiful,
    O daughters of Jerusalem,
like the tents of Kedar,
    like the curtains of Solomon.
Do not gaze at me because I am dark,
    because the sun has gazed on me.
My mother's sons were angry with me;
    they made me keeper of the vineyards,
    but my own vineyard I have not kept!
Tell me, you whom my soul loves,
    where you pasture your flock,
    where you make it lie down at noon;
for why should I be like one who is veiled
    beside the flocks of your companions?

If you do not know,
    O fairest among women,
follow the tracks of the flock,
    and pasture your kids
    beside the shepherds' tents.

I compare you, my love,
    to a mare among Pharaoh's chariots.
Your cheeks are comely with ornaments,
    your neck with strings of jewels.
We will make you ornaments of gold,
    studded with silver.

While the king was on his couch,
    my nard gave forth its fragrance.
My beloved is to me a bag of myrrh
    that lies between my breasts.

My beloved is to me a cluster of henna blossoms
    in the vineyards of En-gedi.

Ah, you are beautiful, my love;
    ah, you are beautiful;
    your eyes are doves.
Ah, you are beautiful, my beloved,
    truly lovely.
Our couch is green;
    the beams of our house are cedar,
    our rafters are pine.

I am a rose of Sharon,
    a lily of the valleys.
As a lily among brambles,
    so is my love among maidens.

As an apple tree among the trees of the wood,
    so is my beloved among young men.
With great delight I sat in his shadow,
    and his fruit was sweet to my taste.
He brought me to the banqueting house,
    and his intention toward me was love.
Sustain me with raisins,
    refresh me with apples;
    for I am faint with love.
O that his left hand were under my head,
    and that his right hand embraced me!
I adjure you, O daughters of Jerusalem,
    by the gazelles or the wild does:
do not stir up or awaken love
    until it is ready!

"Faint with Love"

SONG OF SONGS 5:2–8

I slept, but my heart was awake.
Listen! my beloved is knocking.

"Open to me, my sister, my love,
    my dove, my perfect one;
for my head is wet with dew,
    my locks with the drops of the night."
I had put off my garment;
    how could I put it on again?
I had bathed my feet;
    how could I soil them?
My beloved thrust his hand into the opening,
    and my inmost being yearned for him.
I arose to open to my beloved,
    and my hands dripped with myrrh,
my fingers with liquid myrrh,
    upon the handles of the bolt.
I opened to my beloved,
    but my beloved had turned and was gone.
My soul failed me when he spoke.
I sought him, but did not find him;
    I called him, but he gave no answer.
Making their rounds in the city
    the sentinels found me;
they beat me, they wounded me,
    they took away my mantle,
    those sentinels of the walls.
I adjure you, O daughters of Jerusalem,
    if you find my beloved,
tell him this:
    I am faint with love.

"An Ivory Tower"

SONG OF SONGS 7:1-5

How graceful are your feet in sandals,
    O queenly maiden!
Your rounded thighs are like jewels,
    the work of a master hand.

Your navel is a rounded bowl
    that never lacks mixed wine.
Your belly is a heap of wheat,
    encircled with lilies.
Your two breasts are like two fawns,
    twins of a gazelle.
Your neck is like an ivory tower.
Your eyes are pools in Heshbon,
    by the gate of Bath-rabbim.
Your nose is like a tower of Lebanon,
    overlooking Damascus.
Your head crowns you like Carmel,
    and your flowing locks are like
    purple;
    a king is held captive in the tresses.

Early biblical interpreters sometimes saw the "ivory tower" of the young woman's neck in this passage as a symbol of the church, its whiteness representing the purity and wisdom of its priesthood. From there came the image of the ivory tower as the university—a far cry indeed from a lover's gorgeous neck!

"Love Is Strong as Death"

SONG OF SONGS 8:6-7

Set me as a seal upon your heart,
    as a seal upon your arm;
for love is strong as death,
    passion fierce as the grave.
Its flashes are flashes of fire,
    a raging flame.
Many waters cannot quench love,
    neither can floods drown it.
If one offered for love
    all the wealth of one's house,
    it would be utterly scorned.

Prophets

ISAIAH: LOOK AGAIN

Despite what we see in the tabloids and on television, the biblical prophets were not ancient Nostradamuses predicting the future. Sure, they spoke about the future, but also about the past, and especially about the present. What set them apart and made their words so compelling was that they offered an alternative way of seeing. Does it look like all is right with the world? That our nation is on the right track? Look again. Does it look like all hope is lost? That we are alone and abandoned? Look again.

The book of Isaiah is actually a collection of prophetic sayings from different social and political situations across almost two centuries. In it we find many searing judgments against injustice and national hubris. What has jumped off the page over the centuries, however, are its exuberant words of hope for a new day soon to come. It is this voice that rings through Handel's *Messiah* oratorio and resonates in Yevgeny Vuchetich's iconic sculpture "Let Us Beat Swords into Plowshares," which stands outside the United Nations headquarters in New York.

Part of what makes this text's alternative way of seeing so compelling is the power of its imagery. What images does it evoke for you as you read? Also, how does its use of parallel verses intensify certain meanings and invert expectations?

"Swords into Plowshares"

ISAIAH 2:2-4

In days to come
 the mountain of the Lord's
 house
shall be established as the highest
 of the mountains,
 and shall be raised above the
 hills;
all the nations shall stream to it.
 Many peoples shall come
 and say,
"Come, let us go up to the
 mountain of the Lord,
 to the house of the God of Jacob;
that he may teach us his ways
 and that we may walk in his paths."
For out of Zion shall go forth instruction,
 and the word of the Lord from Jerusalem.
He shall judge between the nations,
 and shall arbitrate for many peoples;
they shall beat their swords into plowshares,
 and their spears into pruning hooks;
nation shall not lift up sword against nation,
 neither shall they learn war any more.

Across the street from the United Nations headquarters and Yevgeny Vuchetich's statue, in Ralph Bunche Park, is the Isaiah Wall, which displays all four lines of Isaiah 2:4 (beginning "They shall beat their swords into plowshares").

"Wonderful Counselor"

ISAIAH 9:2-7

The people who walked in darkness
 have seen a great light;
those who lived in a land of deep darkness—
 on them light has shined.
You have multiplied the nation,
 you have increased its joy;

they rejoice before you
    as with joy at the harvest,
    as people exult when dividing plunder.
For the yoke of their burden,
    and the bar across their
    shoulders,
    the rod of their oppressor,
    you have broken as on the day
    of Midian.
For all the boots of the tramping
    warriors
    and all the garments rolled in
    blood
    shall be burned as fuel for the
    fire.
For a child has been born for us,
    a son given to us;
authority rests upon his shoulders;
    and he is named
Wonderful Counselor, Mighty God,
    Everlasting Father, Prince of Peace.
His authority shall grow continually,
    and there shall be endless peace
for the throne of David and his kingdom.
    He will establish and uphold it
with justice and with righteousness
    from this time onward and forevermore.
The zeal of the LORD of hosts will do this.

> The libretto (text) for Handel's *Messiah* oratorio was done by his colleague Charles Jennens and draws from many different biblical passages. He used the King James Version except when quoting from the Psalms, which he took from the Anglican *Book of Common Prayer.*

"The Wolf Shall Live with the Lamb"

ISAIAH 11:1–9

A shoot shall come out from the stump of Jesse,
    and a branch shall grow out of his roots.
The spirit of the LORD shall rest on him,
    the spirit of wisdom and understanding,

the spirit of counsel and might,
   the spirit of knowledge and the fear of the LORD.
His delight shall be in the fear of the LORD.

He shall not judge by what his eyes see,
   or decide by what his ears hear;
but with righteousness he shall judge the poor,
   and decide with equity for the meek of the earth;
he shall strike the earth with the rod of his mouth,
   and with the breath of his lips he shall kill the wicked.
Righteousness shall be the belt around his waist,
   and faithfulness the belt around his loins.

The wolf shall live with the lamb,
   the leopard shall lie down with the kid,
the calf and the lion and the fatling together,
   and a little child shall lead them.
The cow and the bear shall graze,
   their young shall lie down together;
   and the lion shall eat straw like the ox.
The nursing child shall play over the hole of the asp,
   and the weaned child shall put its hand on the adder's den.
They will not hurt or destroy
   on all my holy mountain;
for the earth will be full of the knowledge of the LORD
   as the waters cover the sea.

Comfort Ye My People

ISAIAH 40:1-11

Comfort, O comfort my people,
   says your God.
Speak tenderly to Jerusalem,
   and cry to her
that she has served her term,
   that her penalty is paid,

that she has received from the Lord's hand
    double for all her sins.

A voice cries out:
"In the wilderness prepare the way of the Lord,
    make straight in the desert a highway for our God.
Every valley shall be lifted up,
    and every mountain and hill be made low;
the uneven ground shall become level,
    and the rough places a plain.
Then the glory of the Lord shall be revealed,
    and all people shall see it together,
    for the mouth of the Lord has spoken."

A voice says, "Cry out!"
    And I said, "What shall I cry?"
All people are grass,
    their constancy is like the flower of the field.
The grass withers, the flower fades,
    when the breath of the Lord blows upon it;
    surely the people are grass.
The grass withers, the flower fades;
    but the word of our God will stand forever.
Get you up to a high mountain,
    O Zion, herald of good tidings;
lift up your voice with strength,
    O Jerusalem, herald of good tidings,
    lift it up, do not fear;
say to the cities of Judah,
    "Here is your God!"
See, the Lord God comes with might,
    and his arm rules for him;
his reward is with him,
    and his recompense before him.
He will feed his flock like a shepherd;
    he will gather the lambs in his arms,
and carry them in his bosom,
    and gently lead the mother sheep.

THE PROPHETS

A defining feature of biblical prophets is that they are called, compelled to deliver messages from God to the people. Most often, these messages are not predictions about the distant future; rather, they offer a radically different perspective on the present. Their vision tends to run counter to the dominant, mainstream perspective. In boom times, they see the corruption of the powerful, the abuse of the poor and marginal, divine wrath, and imminent disaster. In times of suffering and exile, they see hope for healing, divine compassion, and a coming restoration.

Ancient prophets were speakers, not writers. The prophetic books are collections of sayings that were probably compiled into larger compositions and edited generations later by the prophets' disciples. Sometimes, these collections also include stories about the prophets themselves.

Some prophets, like Isaiah, operated in the halls of power and had the ear of kings and priests. Others, like Jeremiah and Amos, spoke truth to power from the margins of society and often found themselves in trouble with the law.

"Arise, Shine"

ISAIAH 60:1-3

Arise, shine; for your light has come,
  and the glory of the LORD has risen upon you.
For darkness shall cover the earth,
  and thick darkness the peoples;
but the LORD will arise upon you,
  and his glory will appear over you.
Nations shall come to your light,
  and kings to the brightness of your dawn.

JEREMIAH'S JEREMIAD

Being chosen can be as much a curse as a blessing. That was the experience of Jeremiah, who is known as the "weeping prophet." Some of his most memorable passages are poignant laments over being called to prophesy.

Faithfulness to his calling meant marginalization and persecution. His harsh criticisms of the Southern Kingdom of Judah made him very unpopular. Indeed, he is the prototype for the faithfully unpatriotic prophet. So much so that the jeremiad, a literary genre of social critique, got its name from him.

It's easy enough in retrospect to criticize the people of Judah for not heeding Jeremiah's own jeremiad. But are we today any better? Do we make space for similarly provocative, even unpatriotic prophetic voices in our society?

Prophet of Tears

JEREMIAH 4:19-28

My anguish, my anguish! I writhe in pain!
　Oh, the walls of my heart!
My heart is beating wildly;
　I cannot keep silent;
for I hear the sound of the trumpet,
　the alarm of war.
Disaster overtakes disaster,
　the whole land is laid waste.
Suddenly my tents are destroyed,
　my curtains in a moment.
How long must I see the standard,
　and hear the sound of the trumpet?
"For my people are foolish,
　they do not know me;
they are stupid children,
　they have no understanding.
They are skilled in doing evil,
　but do not know how to do good."

I looked on the earth, and lo, it was waste and void;
    and to the heavens, and they had no light.
I looked on the mountains, and lo, they were quaking,
    and all the hills moved to
    and fro.
I looked, and lo, there was no one
    at all,
    and all the birds of the air had
    fled.
I looked, and lo, the fruitful land
    was a desert,
    and all its cities were laid in
    ruins
before the LORD, before his fierce anger.

> **This vision of waste and void, with no light in the heavens, recalls the primordial chaos before creation in Genesis 1. Like Job's opening lament, this is a poem of "un-creation."**

For thus says the LORD: The whole land shall be a desolation; yet I will not make a full end.

Because of this the earth shall mourn,
    and the heavens above grow black;
for I have spoken, I have purposed;
    I have not relented nor will I turn back.

Prophetic Imagination

JEREMIAH 32:1–15

The word that came to Jeremiah from the LORD in the tenth year of King Zedekiah of Judah, which was the eighteenth year of Nebuchadrezzar. At that time the army of the king of Babylon was besieging Jerusalem, and the prophet Jeremiah was confined in the court of the guard that was in the palace of the king of Judah, where King Zedekiah of Judah had confined him. Zedekiah had said, "Why do you prophesy and say: Thus says the LORD: I am going to give this city into the hand of the king of Babylon, and he shall take it; King Zedekiah of Judah shall not escape out of the hands of the Chaldeans, but shall surely be given into the hands of the king of Babylon, and shall speak with him face to face and see him eye to eye; and he shall take Zedekiah to Babylon, and there he shall remain until I attend to him, says the LORD; though you fight against the Chaldeans, you shall not succeed?"

Jeremiah said, The word of the LORD came to me: Hanamel son of your uncle Shallum is going to come to you and say, "Buy my field that is at Anathoth, for the right of redemption by purchase is yours." Then my cousin Hanamel came to me in the court of the guard, in accordance with the word of the LORD, and said to me, "Buy my field that is at Anathoth in the land of Benjamin, for the right of possession and redemption is yours; buy it for yourself." Then I knew that this was the word of the LORD.

And I bought the field at Anathoth from my cousin Hanamel, and weighed out the money to him, seventeen shekels of silver. I signed the deed, sealed it, got witnesses, and weighed the money on scales. Then I took the sealed deed of purchase, containing the terms and conditions, and the open copy; and I gave the deed of purchase to Baruch son of Neriah son of Mahseiah, in the presence of my cousin Hanamel, in the presence of the witnesses who signed the deed of purchase, and in the presence of all the Judeans who were sitting in the court of the guard. In their presence I charged Baruch, saying, Thus says the LORD of hosts, the God of Israel: Take these deeds, both this sealed deed of purchase and this open deed, and put them in an earthenware jar, in order that they may last for a long time. For thus says the LORD of hosts, the God of Israel: Houses and fields and vineyards shall again be bought in this land.

EZEKIEL: STRANGE DREAMER

When it comes to strange dreams, the apple doesn't usually fall far from the tree. Many think that if the prophet Ezekiel were alive today, he would have been diagnosed with a psychiatric ailment and given a prescription that might have made his dreams a little more mainstream.

Ezekiel's strange visions have inspired many others to dream likewise. Texas preacher Burrell Cannon was inspired by his vision of flying wheels to build an airplane, "Ezekiel's Airship," which purportedly took to the air in 1902, a year before the Wright Flyer. And it's no accident that the most commonly beheld UFO is a flying saucer or wheel, like the one recently sighted in the film *Knowing* (2009), in which this passage figures prominently. Ezekiel's vision of a valley of dry bones coming back to life has inspired many others to hope for new life where there seems to be none.

Wheels Within Wheels

EZEKIEL 1:4–28

As I looked, a stormy wind came out of the north: a great cloud with brightness around it and fire flashing forth continually, and in the middle of the fire, something like gleaming amber. In the middle of it was something like four living creatures. This was their appearance: they were of human form. Each had four faces, and each of them had four wings. Their legs were straight, and the soles of their feet were like the sole of a calf's foot; and they sparkled like burnished bronze. Under their wings on their four sides they had human hands. And the four had their faces and their wings thus: their wings touched one another; each of them moved straight ahead, without turning as they moved. As for the appearance of their faces: the four had the face of a human being, the face of a lion on the right side, the face of an ox on the left side, and the face of an eagle; such were their faces. Their wings were spread out above; each creature had two wings, each of which touched the wing of another, while two covered their bodies. Each moved straight ahead; wherever the spirit would go, they went, without turning as they went. In the middle of the living creatures there was something that looked like burning coals of fire, like torches moving to and fro among the living creatures; the fire was bright, and lightning issued from the fire. The living creatures darted to and fro, like a flash of lightning.

As I looked at the living creatures, I saw a wheel on the earth beside the living creatures, one for each of the four of them. As for the appearance of the wheels and their construction: their appearance was like the gleaming of beryl; and the four had the same form, their construction being something like a wheel within a wheel. When they moved, they moved in any of the four directions without veering as they moved. Their rims were tall and awesome, for the rims of all four were full of eyes all around. When the living creatures moved, the wheels moved beside them; and when the living creatures rose from the earth, the wheels rose. Wherever the spirit would go, they went, and the wheels rose along with them; for the spirit of the living creatures was in the wheels. When they moved, the others moved; when they stopped, the others stopped; and when they rose from the earth, the wheels rose along with them; for the spirit of the living creatures was in the wheels.

Over the heads of the living creatures there was something like a dome, shining like crystal, spread out above their heads. Under the dome their wings were stretched out straight, one toward another; and each of the creatures had two wings covering its body. When they moved, I heard the sound of their wings like the sound of mighty waters, like the thunder of the Almighty, a sound of tumult like the sound of an army; when they stopped, they let down their wings. And there came a voice from above the dome over their heads; when they stopped, they let down their wings.

And above the dome over their heads there was something like a throne, in appearance like sapphire; and seated above the likeness of a throne was something that seemed like a human form. Upward from what appeared like the loins I saw something like gleaming amber, something that looked like fire enclosed all around; and downward from what looked like the loins I saw something that looked like fire, and there was a splendor all around. Like the bow in a cloud on a rainy day, such was the appearance of the splendor all around. This was the appearance of the likeness of the glory of the Lord.

When I saw it, I fell on my face, and I heard the voice of someone speaking.

The Valley of Dry Bones

EZEKIEL 37:1-14

The hand of the Lord came upon me, and he brought me out by the spirit of the Lord and set me down in the middle of a valley; it was full of bones. He led me all around them; there were very many lying in the valley, and they were very dry. He said to me, "Mortal, can these bones live?" I answered, "O Lord God, you know." Then he said to me,

"Prophesy to these bones, and say to them: O dry bones, hear the word of the LORD. Thus says the LORD GOD to these bones: I will cause breath to enter you, and you shall live. I will lay sinews on you, and will cause flesh to come upon you, and cover you with skin, and put breath in you, and you shall live; and you shall know that I am the LORD."

So I prophesied as I had been commanded; and as I prophesied, suddenly there was a noise, a rattling, and the bones came together, bone to its bone. I looked, and there were sinews on them, and flesh had come upon them, and skin had covered them; but there was no breath in them. Then he said to me, "Prophesy to the breath, prophesy, mortal, and say to the breath: Thus says the LORD GOD: Come from the four winds, O breath, and breathe upon these slain, that they may live." I prophesied as he commanded me, and the breath came into them, and they lived, and stood on their feet, a vast multitude.

Then he said to me, "Mortal, these bones are the whole house of Israel. They say, 'Our bones are dried up, and our hope is lost; we are cut off completely.' Therefore prophesy, and say to them, Thus says the LORD GOD: I am going to open your graves, and bring you up from your graves, O my people; and I will bring you back to the land of Israel. And you shall know that I am the LORD, when I open your graves, and bring you up from your graves, O my people. I will put my spirit within you, and you shall live, and I will place you on your own soil; then you shall know that I, the LORD, have spoken and will act, says the LORD."

DANIEL: FIERY FURNACES THEN AND NOW

Stories of survival in the face of injustice not only can encourage others who suffer likewise, but also can expose the absurdity of the system and the foolishness of its authorities. Eventually everyone, including the ruler himself, can see the "writing on the wall."

The heroes in the book of Daniel are strangers in a strange land, trying to keep the faith and remain true to themselves within a society whose rules are as absurd as they are unjust. Their stories have spoken powerfully to many others, including African Americans who have had to survive and thrive in the more recent lions' dens and fiery furnaces of slavery and racism. Louis Armstrong's performance of "Shadrach, Meshach, and Abednego" in the classic film noir *The Strip* (1951) is superficially lighthearted, but, for those with ears to hear, it may also be heard as a social critique of racism and segregation in post-World War II America.

As you read, notice how the cool, wise faithfulness of the oppressed heroes is contrasted with the pompous buffoonery of their "superiors." What do these stories imply about the relationship between power and authority?

Shadrach, Meshach, and Abednego

DANIEL 3:1–31

King Nebuchadnezzar made a golden statue whose height was sixty cubits and whose width was six cubits; he set it up on the plain of Dura in the province of Babylon. Then King Nebuchadnezzar sent for the satraps, the prefects, and the governors, the counselors, the treasurers, the justices, the magistrates, and all the officials of the provinces, to assemble and come to the dedication of the statue that King Nebuchadnezzar had set up. So the satraps, the prefects, and the governors, the counselors, the treasurers, the justices, the magistrates, and all the officials of the provinces, assembled for the dedication of the statue that King Nebuchadnezzar had set up. When they were standing before the statue that Nebuchadnezzar had set up, the herald proclaimed aloud, "You are commanded, O peoples, nations, and languages, that when you hear the sound of the horn, pipe, lyre, trigon, harp, drum, and entire musical ensemble, you are to fall down and worship the golden statue that King Nebuchadnezzar has set up. Whoever does not fall down and worship shall immediately be thrown into a furnace of blazing fire." Therefore, as soon as all the peoples heard the sound of the horn, pipe, lyre, trigon, harp, drum, and entire musical ensemble, all the peoples, nations, and languages fell down and worshiped the golden statue that King Nebuchadnezzar had set up.

Accordingly, at this time certain Chaldeans came forward and denounced the Jews. They said to King Nebuchadnezzar, "O king, live forever! You, O king, have made a decree, that everyone who hears the

sound of the horn, pipe, lyre, trigon, harp, drum, and entire musical ensemble, shall fall down and worship the golden statue, and whoever does
not fall down and worship shall be thrown into a furnace of blazing fire.
There are certain Jews whom you have appointed over the affairs of the
province of Babylon: Shadrach, Meshach, and Abednego. These pay no
heed to you, O king. They do not serve your gods and they do not worship the golden statue that you have set up."

Then Nebuchadnezzar in furious rage commanded that Shadrach,
Meshach, and Abednego be brought in; so they brought those men
before the king. Nebuchadnezzar said to them, "Is it true, O Shadrach,
Meshach, and Abednego, that you do not serve my gods and you do not
worship the golden statue that I have set up? Now if you are ready when
you hear the sound of the horn, pipe, lyre, trigon, harp, drum, and entire
musical ensemble to fall down and worship the statue that I have made,
well and good. But if you do not worship, you shall immediately be
thrown into a furnace of blazing fire, and who is the god that will deliver
you out of my hands?"

Shadrach, Meshach, and Abednego answered the king, "O Nebuchadnezzar, we have no need to present a defense to you in this matter. If our
God whom we serve is able to deliver us from the furnace of blazing fire
and out of your hand, O king, let him deliver us. But if not, be it known
to you, O king, that we will not serve your gods and we will not worship the golden statue that you have set up."

Then Nebuchadnezzar was so filled with rage against Shadrach, Meshach, and Abednego that his face was distorted. He ordered the furnace heated up seven times more than was customary, and ordered some of the strongest guards in his army to bind Shadrach, Meshach, and Abednego to throw them into the furnace of blazing fire. So the men were bound, still wearing their tunics, their trousers, their hats, and their other garments, and they were thrown into the furnace of blazing fire. Because the king's command was urgent and the furnace was so overheated, the raging flames killed

> **Too much all-fired belief and
> we'd be back
> Down burning skeptics in the
> cellar furnace
> Like Shadrach, Meshach, and
> Abednego.**
> —Robert Frost, *A Masque of
> Mercy*

the men who lifted Shadrach, Meshach, and Abednego. But the three men, Shadrach, Meshach, and Abednego, fell down, bound, into the furnace of blazing fire.

Then King Nebuchadnezzar was astonished and rose up quickly. He said to his counselors, "Was it not three men that we threw bound into the fire?" They answered the king, "True, O king." He replied, "But I see four men unbound, walking in the middle of the fire, and they are not hurt; and the fourth has the appearance of a god." Nebuchadnezzar then approached the door of the furnace of blazing fire and said, "Shadrach, Meshach, and Abednego, servants of the Most High God, come out! Come here!" So Shadrach, Meshach, and Abednego came out from the fire. And the satraps, the prefects, the governors, and the king's counselors gathered together and saw that the fire had not had any power over the bodies of those men; the hair of their heads was not singed, their tunics were not harmed, and not even the smell of fire came from them. Nebuchadnezzar said, "Blessed be the God of Shadrach, Meshach, and Abednego, who has sent his angel and delivered his servants who trusted in him. They disobeyed the king's command and yielded up their bodies rather than serve and worship any god except their own God. Therefore I make a decree: Any people, nation, or language that utters blasphemy against the God of Shadrach, Meshach, and Abednego shall be torn limb from limb, and their houses laid in ruins; for there is no other god who is able to deliver in this way." Then the king promoted Shadrach, Meshach, and Abednego in the province of Babylon.

The Writing on the Wall

DANIEL 5:1-30

King Belshazzar made a great festival for a thousand of his lords, and he was drinking wine in the presence of the thousand.

Under the influence of the wine, Belshazzar commanded that they bring in the vessels of gold and silver that his father Nebuchadnezzar had taken out of the temple in Jerusalem, so that the king and his lords, his wives, and his concubines might drink from them. So they brought in the vessels of gold and silver that had been taken out of the temple, the house of God in Jerusalem, and the king and his lords, his wives, and his concubines drank from them. They drank the wine and praised the gods of gold and silver, bronze, iron, wood, and stone.

Immediately the fingers of a human hand appeared and began writing on the plaster of the wall of the royal palace, next to the lampstand. The king was watching the hand as it wrote. Then the king's face turned pale, and his thoughts terrified him. His limbs gave way, and his knees knocked together. The king cried aloud to bring in the enchanters, the Chaldeans, and the diviners; and the king said to the wise men of Babylon, "Whoever can read this writing and tell me its interpretation shall be clothed in purple, have a chain of gold around his neck, and rank third in the kingdom." Then all the king's wise men came in, but they could not read the writing or tell the king the interpretation. Then King Belshazzar became greatly terrified and his face turned pale, and his lords were perplexed.

The queen, when she heard the discussion of the king and his lords, came into the banqueting hall. The queen said, "O king, live forever! Do not let your thoughts terrify you or your face grow pale. There is a man in your kingdom who is endowed with a spirit of the holy gods. In the days of your father he was found to have enlightenment, understanding, and wisdom like the wisdom of the gods. Your father, King Nebuchadnezzar, made him chief of the magicians, enchanters, Chaldeans, and diviners, because an excellent spirit, knowledge, and understanding to interpret dreams, explain riddles, and solve problems were found in this Daniel, whom the king named Belteshazzar. Now let Daniel be called, and he will give the interpretation."

Then Daniel was brought in before the king. The king said to Daniel, "So you are Daniel, one of the exiles of Judah, whom my father the king brought from Judah? I have heard of you that a spirit of the gods is in you, and that enlightenment, understanding, and excellent wisdom are found in you. Now the wise men, the enchanters, have been brought in before me to read this writing and tell me its interpretation, but they were not able to give the interpretation of the matter. But I have heard that you can give interpretations and solve problems. Now if you are able to read the writing and tell me its interpretation, you shall be clothed in purple, have a chain of gold around your neck, and rank third in the kingdom."

Then Daniel answered in the presence of the king, "Let your gifts be for yourself, or give your rewards to someone else! Nevertheless I will read the writing to the king and let him know the interpretation. O king, the Most High God gave your father Nebuchadnezzar kingship, greatness, glory, and majesty. And because of the greatness that he gave him, all peoples, nations, and languages trembled and feared before him. He killed those he wanted to kill, kept alive those he wanted to keep alive, honored those he wanted to honor, and degraded those he wanted to degrade. But when his heart was lifted up and his spirit was hardened so that he acted proudly, he was deposed from his kingly throne, and his glory was stripped from him. He was driven from human society, and his mind was made like that of an animal. His dwelling was with the wild asses, he was fed grass like oxen, and his body was bathed with the dew of heaven, until he learned that the Most High God has sovereignty over the kingdom of mortals, and sets over it whomever he will. And you, Belshazzar his son, have not humbled your heart, even though you knew all this! You have exalted yourself against the Lord of heaven! The vessels of his temple have been brought in before you, and you and your lords, your wives and your concubines have been drinking wine from them. You have praised the gods of silver and gold, of bronze, iron, wood, and stone, which do not see or hear or know; but the God in whose power is your very breath, and to whom belong all your ways, you have not honored.

"So from his presence the hand was sent and this writing was inscribed. And this is the writing that was inscribed: Mene, Mene, Tekel, and Parsin. This is the interpretation of the matter: Mene, God has numbered the days of your kingdom and brought it to an end; Tekel, you have been weighed on the scales and found wanting; Peres, your kingdom is divided and given to the Medes and Persians."

Then Belshazzar gave the command, and Daniel was clothed in purple, a chain of gold was put around his neck, and a proclamation was made concerning him that he should rank third in the kingdom.

That very night Belshazzar, the Chaldean king, was killed. And Darius the Mede received the kingdom, being about sixty-two years old.

Daniel in the Lions' Den

DANIEL 6:1-24

It pleased Darius to set over the kingdom one hundred twenty satraps, stationed throughout the whole kingdom, and over them three presidents, including Daniel; to these the satraps gave account, so that the king might suffer no loss. Soon Daniel distinguished himself above all the other presidents and satraps because an excellent spirit was in him, and the king planned to appoint him over the whole kingdom. So the presidents and the satraps tried to find grounds for complaint against Daniel in connection with the kingdom. But they could find no grounds for complaint or any corruption, because he was faithful, and no negligence or corruption could be found in him. The men said, "We shall not find any ground for complaint against this Daniel unless we find it in connection with the law of his God."

So the presidents and satraps conspired and came to the king and said to him, "O King Darius, live forever! All the presidents of the kingdom, the prefects and the satraps, the counselors and the governors are agreed that the king should establish an ordinance and enforce an interdict, that whoever prays to anyone, divine or human, for thirty days, except to you, O king, shall be thrown into a den of lions. Now, O king, establish the interdict and sign the document, so that it cannot be changed, according to the law of the Medes and the Persians, which cannot be revoked." Therefore King Darius signed the document and interdict.

Although Daniel knew that the document had been signed, he continued to go to his house, which had windows in its upper room open toward Jerusalem, and to get down on his knees three times a day to pray to his God and praise him, just as he had done previously. The conspirators came and found Daniel praying and seeking mercy before his God. Then they approached the king and said concerning the interdict, "O king! Did you not sign an interdict, that anyone who prays to anyone, divine or human, within thirty days except to you, O king, shall be thrown into a den of lions?" The king answered, "The thing stands fast, according to the law of the Medes and Persians, which cannot be revoked." Then they responded to the king, "Daniel, one of the exiles from Judah, pays no attention to you, O king, or to the interdict you have signed, but he is saying his prayers three times a day."

When the king heard the charge, he was very much distressed. He was determined to save Daniel, and until the sun went down he made every effort to rescue him. Then the conspirators came to the king and said to him, "Know, O king, that it is a law of the Medes and Persians that no interdict or ordinance that the king establishes can be changed."

Then the king gave the command, and Daniel was brought and thrown into the den of lions. The king said to Daniel, "May your God, whom you faithfully serve, deliver you!" A stone was brought and laid on the mouth of the den, and the king sealed it with his own signet and with the signet of his lords, so that nothing might be changed concerning Daniel. Then the king went to his palace and spent the night fasting; no food was brought to him, and sleep fled from him.

Then, at break of day, the king got up and hurried to the den of lions. When he came near the den where Daniel was, he cried out anxiously to Daniel, "O Daniel, servant of the living God, has your God whom you faithfully serve been able to deliver you from the lions?" Daniel then said to the king, "O king, live forever! My God sent his angel and shut the lions' mouths so that they would not hurt me, because I was found blameless before him; and also before you, O king, I have done no wrong." Then the king was exceedingly glad and commanded that Daniel be taken up out of the den. So Daniel was taken up out of the den, and no kind of harm was found on him, because he had trusted in his God. The king gave a command, and those who had accused Daniel were brought and thrown into the den of lions—they, their children, and their wives. Before they reached the bottom of the den the lions overpowered them and broke all their bones in pieces.

AMOS: "LET JUSTICE ROLL DOWN"

The visionary power of Martin Luther King Jr. was profoundly biblical. Many of the most memorable images and phrases in his speeches came directly from the biblical pool of prophetic imagination. These words from the prophet Amos are the source of one of King's most well known calls for justice in a world of injustice. As you read the larger passage from which King drew the line about justice rolling down "like waters," ask what about its context might have drawn him to it. How does this ancient text reach across more than two and a half millennia, from ancient Israel to modern-day Washington, D.C.?

AMOS 5:21-24

I hate, I despise your festivals,
    and I take no delight in your
    solemn assemblies.
Even though you offer me your
    burnt offerings and grain
    offerings,
    I will not accept them;
and the offerings of well-being of
    your fatted animals
    I will not look upon.
Take away from me the noise of
    your songs;
    I will not listen to the melody
    of your harps.
But let justice roll down like
    waters,
    and righteousness like an ever-
flowing stream.

We can never be satisfied as long as our children are stripped of their selfhood and robbed of their dignity by signs stating "For whites only." We cannot be satisfied as long as a Negro in Mississippi cannot vote and a Negro in New York believes he has nothing for which to vote. No, no, we are not satisfied, and we will not be satisfied until "justice rolls down like waters, and righteousness like a mighty stream."

—Martin Luther King Jr., "I Have a Dream," speech at the March on Washington for Jobs and Freedom, August 28, 1963

JONAH AND THE WHALE

Jonah's is the story of a reluctant prophet fleeing his calling. The biblical story doesn't dwell on what it was like spending three days inside a fish, but that's what has often captured our imaginations. Sometimes the ordeal is remembered light-heartedly, as in the 1980s MTV hit music video "Belly of the Whale" by the Burning Sensations. More often, however, to find yourself in the belly of the whale means to stop running away from responsibility, to face yourself and your true calling. Sometimes, as when Pinocchio finds his father Geppetto inside Monstro, it is in the belly of the whale that you find the one you've been looking for and realize he or she has been looking for you too.

But there's much more to the story than the big fish. Jonah's character is particularly fascinating as his reluctance turns to indignation. In the end, he remains silent. Had he been given the last word, what might he have said?

Troubled Water

JONAH 1:1-17

Now the word of the LORD came to Jonah son of Amittai, saying, "Go at once to Nineveh, that great city, and cry out against it; for their wickedness has come up before me." But Jonah set out to flee to Tarshish from the presence of the LORD. He went down to Joppa and found a ship going to Tarshish; so he paid his fare and went on board, to go with them to Tarshish, away from the presence of the LORD.

But the LORD hurled a great wind upon the sea, and such a mighty storm came upon the sea that the ship threatened to break up. Then the mariners were afraid, and each cried to his god. They threw the cargo that was in the ship into the sea, to lighten it for them. Jonah, meanwhile, had gone down into the hold of the ship and had lain down, and was fast asleep. The captain came and said to him, "What are you doing sound asleep? Get up, call on your god! Perhaps the god will spare us a thought so that we do not perish."

The sailors said to one another, "Come, let us cast lots, so that we may know on whose account this calamity has come upon us." So they cast lots, and the lot fell on Jonah. Then they said to him, "Tell us why this calamity has come upon us. What is your occupation? Where do you come from? What is your country? And of what people are you?" "I am a Hebrew," he replied. "I worship the LORD, the God of heaven, who made the sea and the dry land." Then the men were even more afraid, and said to him, "What is this that you have done!" For the men knew that he was fleeing from the presence of the LORD, because he had told them so.

Then they said to him, "What shall we do to you, that the sea may quiet down for us?" For the sea was growing more and more tempestuous. He said to them, "Pick me up and throw me into the sea; then the sea will

———

In a memorable episode from the hit television show *Northern Exposure* ("Big Fish"), Joel Fleischman is fishing on a small Alaskan lake one evening, wondering whether he should accept his gentile girlfriend Maggie O'Connell's offer to host a Passover seder for him, when he catches his childhood rabbi and hauls him into the boat. Moments later, they find themselves in the belly of a big fish.

quiet down for you; for I know it is because of me that this great storm has come upon you." Nevertheless the men rowed hard to bring the ship back to land, but they could not, for the sea grew more and more stormy against them. Then they cried out to the LORD, "Please, O LORD, we pray, do not let us perish on account of this man's life. Do not make us guilty of innocent blood; for you, O LORD, have done as it pleased you." So they picked Jonah up and threw him into the sea; and the sea ceased from its raging. Then the men feared the LORD even more, and they offered a sacrifice to the LORD and made vows.

But the LORD provided a large fish to swallow up Jonah; and Jonah was in the belly of the fish three days and three nights.

A Second Time

JONAH 3:1–4:11

The word of the LORD came to Jonah a second time, saying, "Get up, go to Nineveh, that great city, and proclaim to it the message that I tell you." So Jonah set out and went to Nineveh, according to the word of the LORD. Now Nineveh was an exceedingly large city, a three days' walk across. Jonah began to go into the city, going a day's walk. And he cried out, "Forty days more, and Nineveh shall be overthrown!" And the people of Nineveh believed God; they proclaimed a fast, and everyone, great and small, put on sackcloth.

When the news reached the king of Nineveh, he rose from his throne, removed his robe, covered himself with sackcloth, and sat in ashes. Then he had a proclamation made in Nineveh: "By the decree of the king and his nobles: No human being or animal, no herd or flock, shall taste anything. They shall not feed, nor shall they drink water. Human beings and animals shall be covered with sackcloth, and they shall cry mightily to God. All shall turn from their evil ways and from the violence that is in their hands. Who knows? God may relent and change his mind; he may turn from his fierce anger, so that we do not perish."

When God saw what they did, how they turned from their evil ways, God changed his mind about the calamity that he had said he would bring upon them; and he did not do it.

But this was very displeasing to Jonah, and he became angry. He prayed to the LORD and said, "O LORD! Is not this what I said while I was still in my own country? That is why I fled to Tarshish at the beginning; for I knew that you are a gracious God and merciful, slow to anger, and abounding in steadfast love, and ready to relent from punishing. And now, O LORD, please take my life from me, for it is better for me to die than to live." And the LORD said, "Is it right for you to be angry?" Then Jonah went out of the

"I think Jonah is the key to all of this," Joel"s rabbi explains. "Why was Jonah swallowed by the whale in the first place? The Lord said, 'Go to Nineveh. Cry out against their wickedness.' Instead, Jonah cuts the boat and goes to Tarshish. The Lord raises a ruckus, Jonah gets the heave-ho. What's the meaning behind all of this?"

"Next time go to Nineveh," Joel replies.

"Responsibility. Jonah was trying to avoid his responsibility."

"So you think I should have Passover with O'Connell?"

"She may be your Nineveh, Joel. This is what you're running away from. It may not be my field, but maybe by denying her Passover, you're denying her intimacy."

city and sat down east of the city, and made a booth for himself there. He sat under it in the shade, waiting to see what would become of the city.

The LORD God appointed a bush, and made it come up over Jonah, to give shade over his head, to save him from his discomfort; so Jonah was very happy about the bush. But when dawn came up the next day, God appointed a worm that attacked the bush, so that it withered. When the sun rose, God prepared a sultry east wind, and the sun beat down on the head of Jonah so that he was faint and asked that he might die. He said, "It is better for me to die than to live."

But God said to Jonah, "Is it right for you to be angry about the bush?" And he said, "Yes, angry enough to die." Then the LORD said, "You are concerned about the bush, for which you did not labor and which you did not grow; it came into being in a night and perished in a night. And should I not be concerned about Nineveh, that great city, in which there are more than a hundred and twenty thousand persons who do not know their right hand from their left, and also many animals?"

PART 2

The New Testament

Introduction

No matter how religious or irreligious we are, we live in a Christ-haunted world. Images of and references to Jesus pervade popular culture, from WWJD bracelets to sacred-heart tattoos, from "Jesus loves you" billboards to Rapture-ready bestsellers, from Mel Gibson's dead serious *The Passion of the Christ* to Lee Demarbre's kung-fu action comedy *Jesus Christ, Vampire Hunter.* Even our calendar is structured and punctuated by holidays that link to his story. The school year is divided by Christmastime, which commemorates his birth (albeit integrated, more recently, with Kwanza and Hanukkah), for example, and most spring breaks are linked to Holy Week and Easter, which commemorate his trial, crucifixion, and resurrection. Jesus is a most familiar presence.

And yet, at the same time, he remains a most mysterious figure. At the heart of all these familiar cultural images and references to Jesus is an uneasy sense of mystery. As accustomed as we are to his being part of our world, he never quite fits in. His is an uncomfortable presence. I'm reminded of one of my favorite bumper stickers: "Jesus is coming again. Look busy."

Speaking of second comings, what about all the popular books and movies that imagine him, or a figure like him, returning to our world in the flesh? Does that ever go well? Recall Dostoyevsky's chilling story of the Grand Inquisitor in his novel *The Brothers Karamazov,* in which Jesus returns only to be sentenced to death, again, by a high priest who's figured out that people don't want what he has to offer. Or John Sayles's film *The Brother from Another Planet,* in which a mute, dark-skinned alien with Christlike powers of empathy and healing crash-lands on Ellis Island and winds up homeless in Harlem. Second comings rarely get what you'd call a warm welcome. Jesus didn't fit in then, and he still doesn't.

That's what I mean when I say that we live in a Christ-haunted world. A haunting presence is not the same as a full presence. It's a feeling that someone is simultaneously here and not here, everywhere and nowhere. It's a presence you feel, but can't quite pin down. It's a familiar mystery. Jesus's question to his disciples, "But who do *you* say that I am?" still echoes in our world, no matter how post-Christian that world sometimes seems to be.

As you go back to the source, that is, the New Testament, you may find that its stories about Jesus do more to underscore the question than to answer it. Start with the fact that it includes four different gospels, that is, four versions of the Jesus story. Our word "gospel" comes from the Old English *godspel*, "good story" or "good news," which is an apt translation of the Greek name for these stories, *euangelion* (*eu*, "happy," plus *angelion*, "message" or "news"). Each of the four gospels offers its own interpretation of the story of Jesus and what makes it such a good story, such good news. And they don't altogether agree.

Then come the other writings of the New Testament—the story of the early Jesus movement in Acts, the letters of the apostle Paul and other early leaders, and the book of Revelation. Each of these adds its voice, offering still more perspectives and raising additional questions. The New Testament is a richly diverse, fascinating collection of stories, letters, and visions. What holds them together is not unanimity, but the mysterious and illusive figure around which they all revolve.

Expect to be surprised. The Jesus we meet in these stories is at least as haunting and hard to pin down as he is in today's popular culture. A highly unpredictable dinner guest, a relentlessly demanding leader, and a frequently perplexing teacher, he could be passionately indignant one minute and compassionately loving the next, as likely to cast out as to welcome in, as likely to knock over your table as to sit down and eat. Never a dull moment. It is this deeply compelling and disturbing figure that drives these stories and keeps us reading.

Now, a few brief words of advice, things to keep in mind as you dive in.

First, remember that, although you're reading what we now think of as Christian Scripture, it was Jewish from the get-go. Early Christianity began as a Jewish movement among many other Jewish movements within the Roman Empire of the first century. Jesus and all his disciples lived and died as devout Jews. The same is true of the movement's most influential early leader, the apostle Paul. So when you read about Jesus arguing with members of other Jewish sects like the Pharisees or Sadducees, think of it more like an argument between American Baptists and Southern Baptists than one between proponents of two different religions. They were all Jewish.

Second, the New Testament was literally centuries in the making. The earliest writings, Paul's letters, were written in the 50s and 60s CE, a couple decades after Jesus. The gospels were written later still, during the last three decades of the first century. Other writings date to the early part of the second century. And none of these writings started out as part of the New Testament. They were independent texts. Copies of them circulated among early Christian communities on their own. Gradually, they gained authority as interpretations of Jewish scriptural tradition in light of Jesus. Eventually, by the second half of the fourth century—yes, more than three centuries after Jesus—an official canon, or authoritative list, of the twenty-seven documents now in our New Testament had taken form. Around the same time, and probably not coincidentally, the medium of the bound book had developed to the point that it could hold them all in a single volume. So, like the Hebrew Bible, the New Testament didn't drop down from the sky ready-formed.

Third and finally, make room for difference. Don't expect all that you read to agree. How did the birth of Jesus take place? Who was there? When did he host the Last Supper? How did Judas die? Who witnessed the empty tomb? To these and other questions, different texts yield different answers and perspectives, which is why the organization of the selections that follow keeps each of the gospels separate. The New Testament canon did not choose just one authoritative version. Nor did it go with a harmonization of the four (such gospel harmonies had been made by the late second century). It embraced a diversity of voices. So should we.

Above all, and again I say, trust your own good instincts. Any question or thought that emerges from the details of the text is legitimate, no matter how unorthodox it might seem. At times you'll probably feel drawn in. That's great. Go with it. At other times you may feel frustrated. That's perfectly okay too. Go with that feeling. Wrestle with the text. What is it that you're reacting to? Meaning is in the relationship between you and what you're reading. Sometimes that relationship is simpatico, sometimes not. So let it happen, and let meaning emerge in the process.

The Gospel of Matthew

NATIVITY

Such a fragile, tentative opening: a teenager is pregnant, and her fiancé has been told in a dream to believe something pretty unbelievable about how she got that way. But he does. And she gives birth. And so the iffy, vulnerable new life of the anointed one begins.

A new beginning, to be sure. But the Gospel of Matthew takes pains to show continuity with Jewish tradition. It's no accident, for instance, that Joseph reminds us of the biblical patriarch Joseph from Genesis, who also got divine revelations in dreams and had to go down to Egypt. Note too how this gospel frequently describes events and actions as "fulfillments" of Scripture—not in the sense of a "prediction" that has "come true," but in the sense that the meaning of the Jewish Scriptures is being "filled out" in new and surprising ways.

Do you notice anything missing here? Where's the annunciation to Mary by the angel Gabriel? What about Mary's visit to Elizabeth? The birth of John the Baptist? No room in the inn? Away in a manger? Shepherds watching flocks by night? None of that is part of this story. That's all in the Gospel of Luke. In fact, the story of Jesus's birth that most of us know from "The Little Drummer Boy" and Christmas pageants is an amalgam of Matthew and Luke, bringing together characters and events from both gospels into one story. How does your experience of the story change when you read it on its own terms?

MATTHEW 1:18-25

Now the birth of Jesus the Messiah took place in this way. When his mother Mary had been engaged to Joseph, but before they lived together, she was found to be with child from the Holy Spirit. Her husband Joseph, being a righteous man and unwilling to expose her to public disgrace, planned to dismiss her quietly. But just when he had resolved to do this, an angel of the Lord appeared to him in a dream and said, "Joseph, son of David, do not be afraid to take Mary as your wife, for the child conceived in her is from the Holy Spirit. She will bear a son, and you are to name him Jesus, for he will save his people from their sins." All this took place to fulfill what had been spoken by the Lord through the prophet:

"Look, the virgin shall conceive and bear a son,
    and they shall name him Emmanuel,"

which means, "God is with us." When Joseph awoke from sleep, he did as the angel of the Lord commanded him; he took her as his wife, but had no marital relations with her until she had borne a son; and he named him Jesus.

THE WISE AND THE GREAT

Here, at the heart of the nativity story, toward the very beginning of the first gospel, we find our first interfaith gathering: the "wise men" (Latin *magi,* Greek *magoi*) who came to visit the baby Jesus were probably Persian priests of Zoroastrianism. Indeed, they found Jesus by means of their own kind of divination, astrology. Nor did they convert. They came as Zoroastrians, and they left as Zoroastrians.

As you read, pay attention to the dynamics of the relationship between these Persian visitors and Herod the Great, ruler of Judea, whose murderous grasping after power is contrasted with their wise discernment about how the stars are aligning. Today, sadly, Herod's slaughter of innocent children, driven by political insecurity, is far more believable than the image of prominent leaders from one religion coming to pay homage to the future leader of another.

Note that we are never told how many wise men there were. The tradition that there were three comes from the fact that they brought three gifts.

MATTHEW 2:1-16

In the time of King Herod, after Jesus was born in Bethlehem of Judea, wise men from the East came to Jerusalem, asking, "Where is the child who has been born king of the Jews? For we observed his star at its rising, and have come to pay him homage." When King Herod heard this, he was frightened, and all Jerusalem with him; and calling together all the chief priests and scribes of the people, he inquired of them where the Messiah was to be born. They told him, "In Bethlehem of Judea; for so it has been written by the prophet:

'And you, Bethlehem, in the land of Judah,
 are by no means least among the rulers of Judah;
for from you shall come a ruler
 who is to shepherd my people Israel.'"

Then Herod secretly called for the wise men and learned from them the exact time when the star had appeared. Then he sent them to Bethlehem, saying, "Go and search diligently for the child; and when you have found him, bring me word so that I may also go and pay him homage." When they had heard the king, they set out; and there, ahead of them, went the star that they had seen at its rising, until it stopped over the place where the child was. When they saw that the star had stopped, they were overwhelmed with joy. On entering the house, they saw the child with Mary his mother; and they knelt down and paid him homage. Then, opening their treasure chests, they offered him gifts of gold, frankincense, and myrrh. And having been warned in a dream not to return to Herod, they left for their own country by another road.

Now after they had left, an angel of the Lord appeared to Joseph in a dream and said, "Get up, take the child and his mother, and flee to Egypt, and remain there until I tell you; for Herod is about to search for the child, to destroy him." Then Joseph got up, took the child and his mother by night, and went to Egypt, and remained there until the death of Herod. This was to fulfill what had been spoken by the Lord through the prophet, "Out of Egypt I have called my son."

When Herod saw that he had been tricked by the wise men, he was infuriated, and he sent and killed all the children in and around Bethlehem who were two years old or under, according to the time that he had learned from the wise men.

> **Your naked infants spitted upon pikes,**
> **Whiles the mad mothers with their howls confused**
> **Do break the clouds, as did the wives of Jewry**
> **At Herod's bloody-hunting slaughtermen.**
> —King Henry, threatening Harfleur, in William Shakespeare's *Henry V*

JOHN THE BAPTIST

The half-naked, sweaty-faced, straggly-haired prophet in Martin Scorsese's *The Last Temptation of Christ,* berating the small crowd that had come out to the Jordan to see him, is an apt depiction of John the Baptist. Like his biblical predecessor Elijah, he's edgy, to say the least. He lives on the edge of the wilderness, and he says edgy, provocative things—the kinds of things that can cost you your head, then as now.

So what made him so popular that even Sadducees and Pharisees, rival movements in the diverse world of first-century Judaism, would come out to hear him preach and to be baptized by him? And how does his radical preaching presage Jesus's own?

MATTHEW 3:1-17

In those days John the Baptist appeared in the wilderness of Judea, proclaiming, "Repent, for the kingdom of heaven has come near." This is the one of whom the prophet Isaiah spoke when he said,

"The voice of one crying out in the wilderness:
'Prepare the way of the Lord,
    make his paths straight.'"

Now John wore clothing of camel's hair with a leather belt around his waist, and his food was locusts and wild honey. Then the people of Jerusalem and all Judea were going out to him, and all the region along the Jordan, and they were baptized by him in the river Jordan, confessing their sins.

But when he saw many Pharisees and Sadducees coming for baptism, he said to them, "You brood of vipers! Who warned you to flee from the wrath to come? Bear fruit worthy of repentance. Do not presume to say to yourselves, 'We have Abraham as our ancestor'; for I tell you, God is able from these stones to raise up children to Abraham. Even now the ax is lying at the root of the trees; every tree therefore that does not bear good fruit is cut down and thrown into the fire.

"I baptize you with water for repentance, but one who is more powerful than I is coming after me; I am not worthy to carry his sandals. He will baptize you with the Holy Spirit and fire. His winnowing fork is in his hand, and he will clear his threshing floor and will gather his wheat into the granary; but the chaff he will burn with unquenchable fire."

Then Jesus came from Galilee to John at the Jordan, to be baptized by him. John would have prevented him, saying, "I need to be baptized by you, and do you come to me?" But Jesus answered him, "Let it be so now; for it is proper for us in this way to fulfill all righteousness." Then he consented. And when Jesus had been baptized, just as he came up from the water, suddenly the heavens were opened to him and he saw the Spirit of God descending like a dove and alighting on him. And a voice from heaven said, "This is my Son, the Beloved, with whom I am well pleased."

DIALOGUE WITH THE DEVIL

Immediately after his baptism, Jesus is driven into the wilderness for a time of trial. Chosenness leads not to happiness or an immediate rise to power, but to a wilderness experience. In the Jesus story, as in countless stories since, from Henry David Thoreau's *Walden* to Jon Krakauer's *Into the Wild,* the wilderness is a primordial place of purification and preparation. One returns from it to begin a new chapter, even a new life.

Jesus ends up in a biblical debate with the devil. But this character is not so much the cosmically evil anti-God we know from

Mel Gibson's *Passion.* He's more like "the Accuser" in the book
of Job, playing his part in the divine plan by testing Jesus. Note
too how long he was in the wilderness. Does the number forty
ring a bell? Remember the Israelites wandering in the wilderness
for forty years?

MATTHEW 4:1–11

Then Jesus was led up by the Spirit into the wilderness to be tempted by
the devil. He fasted forty days and forty nights, and afterwards he was
famished. The tempter came and said to him, "If you are the Son of God,
command these stones to become loaves of bread." But he answered, "It
is written,

'One does not live by bread alone,
   but by every word that comes from the mouth of God.'"

Then the devil took him to the holy city and placed him on the pin-
nacle of the temple, saying to him, "If you are the Son of God, throw
yourself down; for it is written,

'He will command his angels concerning you,'
   and 'On their hands they will bear you up,
so that you will not dash your foot against a stone.'"

Jesus said to him, "Again it is written, 'Do not put the Lord your God to
the test.'"
   Again, the devil took him to a very high mountain and showed him
all the kingdoms of the world and their splendor; and he said to him, "All
these I will give you, if you will fall down and worship me." Jesus said to
him, "Away with you, Satan! for it is written,

'Worship the Lord your God,
   and serve only him.'"

Then the devil left him, and suddenly angels came and waited on him.

RABBI JESUS

Our everyday speech is peppered, or rather salted, with phrases and images from Jesus's teachings: blessed peacemakers, being "persecuted for righteousness' sake," "the light of the world," not storing your treasures "where moth and rust consume," not trying to "serve two masters," letting the day's trouble be enough for the day, the mustard seed, the eye of the needle, "rendering unto Caesar," and, of course, being "the salt of the earth." Yet when we read these teachings in context, they often seem more riddling than practical.

The Gospel of Matthew grounds Jesus's authority in his brilliance as a rabbi, an interpreter of the Jewish Scriptures. As you read this selection of Jesus's teachings from throughout the gospel, reflect on the general feelings and images they evoke when taken together, rather than on finding the point. Indeed, you may decide there is no single point. What would that say about this unusual newcomer, Rabbi Jesus?

The Sermon on the Mount

MATTHEW 5:1-20; 6:5-15, 19, 24-34

When Jesus saw the crowds, he went up the mountain; and after he sat down, his disciples came to him. Then he began to speak, and taught them, saying:

"Blessed are the poor in spirit, for theirs is the kingdom of heaven.

"Blessed are those who mourn, for they will be comforted.

"Blessed are the meek, for they will inherit the earth.

"Blessed are those who hunger and thirst for righteousness, for they will be filled.

"Blessed are the merciful, for they will receive mercy.

"Blessed are the pure in heart, for they will see God.

"Blessed are the peacemakers, for they will be called children of God.

"Blessed are those who are persecuted for righteousness' sake, for theirs is the kingdom of heaven.

Compare the Beatitudes ("blessings") of Jesus in Matthew's Sermon on the Mount with Luke's version in the Sermon on the Plain (Luke 6:20–26):

"Blessed are you who are poor,
　for yours is the kingdom of God.
"Blessed are you who are hungry now,
　for you will be filled.
"Blessed are you who weep now,
　for you will laugh.

"Blessed are you when people revile you and persecute you and utter all kinds of evil against you falsely on my account. Rejoice and be glad, for your reward is great in heaven, for in the same way they persecuted the prophets who were before you.

"You are the salt of the earth; but if salt has lost its taste, how can its saltiness be restored? It is no longer good for anything, but is thrown out and trampled under foot.

"You are the light of the world. A city built on a hill cannot be hid. No one after lighting a lamp puts it under the bushel basket, but on the lampstand, and it gives light to all in the house. In the same way, let your light shine before others, so that they may see your good works and give glory to your Father in heaven.

"Do not think that I have come to abolish the law or the prophets; I have come not to abolish but to fulfill. For truly I tell you, until heaven and earth pass away, not one letter, not one stroke of a letter, will pass from the law until all is accomplished. Therefore, whoever breaks one of the least of these commandments, and teaches others to do the same, will be called least in the kingdom of heaven; but whoever does them and teaches them will be called great in the kingdom of heaven. For I tell you, unless your righteousness exceeds that of the scribes and Pharisees, you will never enter the kingdom of heaven.

. . . "And whenever you pray, do not be like the hypocrites; for they love to stand and pray in the synagogues and at the street corners, so that they may be seen by others. Truly I tell you, they have received their reward. But whenever you pray, go into your room and shut the door and pray to your Father who is in secret; and your Father who sees in secret will reward you.

"When you are praying, do not heap up empty phrases as the Gentiles do; for they think that they will be heard because of their many words.

Do not be like them, for your Father knows what you need before you ask him.

"Pray then in this way:

Our Father in heaven,
hallowed be your name.
Your kingdom come.
Your will be done,
on earth as it is in heaven.
Give us this day our daily bread.
And forgive us our debts,
as we also have forgiven our debtors.
And do not bring us to the time of trial,
but rescue us from the evil one.

For if you forgive others their trespasses, your heavenly Father will also forgive you; but if you do not forgive others, neither will your Father forgive your trespasses.

. . . "Do not store up for yourselves treasures on earth, where moth and rust consume and where thieves break in and steal; but store up for yourselves treasures in heaven, where neither moth nor rust consumes and where thieves do not break in and steal. For where your treasure is, there your heart will be also.

. . . "No one can serve two masters; for a slave will either hate the one and love the other, or be devoted to the one and despise the other. You cannot serve God and wealth.

"Therefore I tell you, do not worry about your life, what you will eat or what you will drink, or about your body, what you will wear. Is not life more than food, and the body more than clothing? Look at the birds

"Blessed are you when people hate you, and when they exclude you, revile you, and defame you on account of the Son of Man. Rejoice in that day and leap for joy, for surely your reward is great in heaven; for that is what their ancestors did to the prophets.

"But woe to you who are rich, for you have received your consolation.
"Woe to you who are full now, for you will be hungry.
"Woe to you who are laughing now, for you will mourn and weep.

"Woe to you when all speak well of you, for that is what their ancestors did to the false prophets."

of the air; they neither sow nor reap nor gather into barns, and yet your heavenly Father feeds them. Are you not of more value than they? And can any of you by worrying add a single hour to your span of life? And why do you worry about clothing? Consider the lilies of the field, how they grow; they neither toil nor spin, yet I tell you, even Solomon in all his glory was not clothed like one of these. But if God so clothes the grass of the field, which is alive today and tomorrow is thrown into the oven, will he not much more clothe you—you of little faith? Therefore do not worry, saying, 'What will we eat?' or 'What will we drink?' or 'What will we wear?' For it is the Gentiles who strive for all these things; and indeed your heavenly Father knows that you need all these things. But strive first for the kingdom of God and his righteousness, and all these things will be given to you as well.

"So do not worry about tomorrow, for tomorrow will bring worries of its own. Today's trouble is enough for today."

Not Peace but a Sword

MATTHEW 10:34–38

"Do not think that I have come to bring peace to the earth; I have not come to bring peace, but a sword.

For I have come to set a man against his father,
and a daughter against her mother,
and a daughter-in-law against her mother-in-law;
and one's foes will be members of one's own household.

Whoever loves father or mother more than me is not worthy of me; and whoever loves son or daughter more than me is not worthy of me; and whoever does not take up the cross and follow me is not worthy of me. Those who find their life will lose it, and those who lose their life for my sake will find it."

HOW TO READ A PARABLE

Jesus's signature teaching tool was the parable. Think of a parable as a story-shaped metaphor in which an unexpected association is made between an unfamiliar idea and a story drawn from everyday experience. We are used to metaphors that equate two things that seem unrelated. "God is a rock," for example. But the metaphorical mode of the parable looks more like this: "God is a rock on which a storm-tossed ship crashed and splintered to pieces in the night. The people on the ship survived by clinging to its sharp edges. The next morning, when the sun rose in a clear blue sky, they all gave thanks for their lives."

The central theme in Jesus's parables is the "kingdom of God" or, in Matthew, the "kingdom of heaven." How remarkable, then, that he never clearly defines or explains what he means by this phrase! Instead he points to it poetically by means of parables that appeal to the metaphorical imagination. Sometimes, as in chapter 13 of Matthew, he offers several parables in a row, piling metaphor on metaphor. It's a mustard seed, it's yeast, it's a treasure in a field, it's a merchant. Each unfolds in its own surprising story. Each offers a fresh way of envisioning this illusive "kingdom." As readers, we are left with a series of unexpected associations, creating tensions between the unfamiliar and the familiar. Jesus's parables are more like Zen koans than theological propositions.

Resist the temptation to try to reduce each parable to a single, straightforward meaning. Ask yourself, what are the two parts of the metaphor? What is surprising about the association? What is unexpected? How does this metaphor interact with others Jesus offers, here and elsewhere? Don't be discouraged if you don't find a clear picture emerging. Don't worry if you don't feel like you "get it." Take comfort in the fact that the disciples didn't seem to get it either.

Speaking in Parables

MATTHEW 13:1-9, 24-35, 44-46

That same day Jesus went out of the house and sat beside the sea. Such great crowds gathered around him that he got into a boat and sat there, while the whole crowd stood on the beach. And he told them many things in parables, saying: "Listen! A sower went out to sow. And as he sowed, some seeds fell on the path, and the birds came and ate them up. Other seeds fell on rocky ground, where they did not have much soil, and they sprang up quickly, since they had no depth of soil. But when the sun rose, they were scorched; and since they had no root, they withered away. Other seeds fell among thorns, and the thorns grew up and choked them. Other seeds fell on good soil and brought forth grain, some a hundred-fold, some sixty, some thirty. Let anyone with ears listen!"

. . . He put before them another parable: "The kingdom of heaven may be compared to someone who sowed good seed in his field; but while everybody was asleep, an enemy came and sowed weeds among the wheat, and then went away. So when the plants came up and bore grain, then the weeds appeared as well. And the slaves of the householder came and said to him, 'Master, did you not sow good seed in your field? Where, then, did these weeds come from?' He answered, 'An enemy has done this.' The slaves said to him, 'Then do you want us to go and gather them?' But he replied, 'No; for in gathering the weeds you would uproot the wheat along with them. Let both of them grow together until the harvest; and at harvest time I will tell the reapers, Collect the weeds first and bind them in bundles to be burned, but gather the wheat into my barn.'"

He put before them another parable: "The kingdom of heaven is like a mustard seed that someone took and sowed in his field; it is the smallest of all the seeds, but when it has grown it is the greatest of shrubs and becomes a tree, so that the birds of the air come and make nests in its branches."

He told them another parable: "The kingdom of heaven is like yeast that a woman took and mixed in with three measures of flour until all of it was leavened."

Jesus told the crowds all these things in parables; without a parable he told them nothing. This was to fulfill what had been spoken through the prophet:

"I will open my mouth to speak in parables;
   I will proclaim what has been hidden from the foundation of the
   world."

. . . "The kingdom of heaven is like treasure hidden in a field, which someone found and hid; then in his joy he goes and sells all that he has and buys that field.

"Again, the kingdom of heaven is like a merchant in search of fine pearls; on finding one pearl of great value, he went and sold all that he had and bought it."

Little Children

MATTHEW 19:13-15

Then little children were being brought to him in order that he might lay his hands on them and pray. The disciples spoke sternly to those who brought them; but Jesus said, "Let the little children come to me, and do not stop them; for it is to such as these that the kingdom of heaven belongs." And he laid his hands on them and went on his way.

The Eye of the Needle

MATTHEW 19:16-26

Then someone came to him and said, "Teacher, what good deed must I do to have eternal life?" And he said to him, "Why do you ask me about what is good? There is only one who is good. If you wish to enter into life, keep the commandments." He said to him, "Which ones?" And Jesus said, "You shall not murder; You shall not commit adultery; You shall not steal; You shall not bear false witness; Honor your father and mother; also, You shall love your neighbor as yourself." The young man said to him, "I have kept all these; what do I still lack?" Jesus said to him, "If you wish to be perfect, go, sell your possessions, and give the money to the poor, and you will have treasure in heaven; then come, follow me." When the young man heard this word, he went away grieving, for he had many possessions.

Then Jesus said to his disciples, "Truly I tell you, it will be hard for a rich person to enter the kingdom of heaven. Again I tell you, it is easier for a camel to go through the eye of a needle than for someone who is rich to enter the kingdom of God." When the disciples heard this, they were greatly astounded and said, "Then who can be saved?" But Jesus looked at them and said, "For mortals it is impossible, but for God all things are possible."

Render unto Caesar

MATTHEW 22:15-22

> Christ answered the Herodians according to their condition. "Show me the tribute-money," said he. . . . "Render therefore to Caesar that which is Caesar's, and to God those things which are God's"—leaving them no wiser than before as to which was which; for they did not wish to know.
>
> —Henry David Thoreau,
> *Civil Disobedience*

Then the Pharisees went and plotted to entrap him in what he said. So they sent their disciples to him, along with the Herodians, saying, "Teacher, we know that you are sincere, and teach the way of God in accordance with truth, and show deference to no one; for you do not regard people with partiality. Tell us, then, what you think. Is it lawful to pay taxes to the emperor, or not?" But Jesus, aware of their malice, said, "Why are you putting me to the test, you hypocrites? Show me the coin used for the tax." And they brought him a denarius. Then he said to them, "Whose head is this, and whose title?" They answered, "The emperor's." Then he said to them, "Give therefore to the emperor the things that are the emperor's, and to God the things that are God's." When they heard this, they were amazed; and they left him and went away.

"The Least of These"

MATTHEW 25:31-46

"When the Son of Man comes in his glory, and all the angels with him, then he will sit on the throne of his glory. All the nations will be gathered before him, and he will separate people one from another as a shepherd separates the sheep from the goats, and he will put the sheep at his right hand and the goats at the left. Then the king will say to those at his right hand, 'Come, you that are blessed by my Father, inherit the kingdom prepared for you from the foundation of the world; for I was hungry and you gave me food, I was thirsty and you gave me something to drink, I was a stranger and you welcomed me, I was naked and you gave me clothing, I was sick and you took care of me, I was in prison and you visited me.' Then the righteous will answer him, 'Lord, when was it that we saw you hungry and gave you food, or thirsty and gave you

Inspired by this story, the Matthew 25 Network is an American ecumenical dialogue and political action organization whose basic standard for judging a government or society is how it treats "the least of these."

something to drink? And when was it that we saw you a stranger and welcomed you, or naked and gave you clothing? And when was it that we saw you sick or in prison and visited you?' And the king will answer them, 'Truly I tell you, just as you did it to one of the least of these who are members of my family, you did it to me.' Then he will say to those at his left hand, 'You that are accursed, depart from me into the eternal fire prepared for the devil and his angels; for I was hungry and you gave me no food, I was thirsty and you gave me nothing to drink, I was a stranger and you did not welcome me, naked and you did not give me clothing, sick and in prison and you did not visit me.' Then they also will answer, 'Lord, when was it that we saw you hungry or thirsty or a stranger or naked or sick or in prison, and did not take care of you?' Then he will answer them, 'Truly I tell you, just as you did not do it to one of the least of these, you did not do it to me.' And these will go away into eternal punishment, but the righteous into eternal life."

A HEAD ON A PLATTER

When we last saw John the Baptist, he was delivering his radical critique of the powers that be to a diverse crowd of Jews, including Jesus, at the Jordan River. Apparently, he did not hold back when it came to the ruling family.

Although the gospel text never mentions the name of Herodias's dancing daughter, the Jewish historian Josephus informs us that it was Salome. The modern image of her as a dangerous young seductress is thanks especially to Oscar Wilde's play *Salome,* which imbues her with a sense of "evil chastity," as Wilde himself put it. Numerous appearances on the silver screen since then have reinforced that image, beginning with the 1908 silent movie based on Wilde's play and directed by J. Stuart Blackton. And so once again we find the Bible being recruited to reinforce a negative image of female sexual power that takes down a godly strong man. Remember Delilah? Jezebel? Is there another, more sympathetic way to read Salome in this story?

MATTHEW 14:1-12

At that time Herod the ruler heard reports about Jesus; and he said to his servants, "This is John the Baptist; he has been raised from the dead, and for this reason these powers are at work in him." For Herod had arrested John, bound him, and put him in prison on account of Herodias, his brother Philip's wife, because John had been telling him, "It is not lawful for you to have her." Though Herod wanted to put him to death, he feared the crowd, because they regarded him as a prophet. But when Herod's birthday came, the daughter of Herodias danced before the company, and she pleased Herod so much that he promised on oath to grant her whatever she might ask. Prompted by her mother, she said, "Give me the head of John the Baptist here on a platter." The king was grieved, yet out of regard for his oaths and for the guests, he commanded it to be given; he sent and had John beheaded in the prison. The head was brought on a platter and given to the girl, who brought it to her mother. His disciples came and took the body and buried it; then they went and told Jesus.

EVERYDAY MIRACLES

As we saw in Jesus's parables, the extraordinary is often discovered in the ordinary. Here, similarly, a mundane, everyday problem—a hungry crowd and a short supply of bread and fish—becomes the occasion for a miracle. And then, in the very next story, we have another miracle, likewise occasioned by a very

typical situation: fishermen having a tough time making head-
way on a choppy lake.

Notice how little Jesus himself makes of his miraculous acts.
Indeed, as his actions continue to attract attention, his desire to
be alone seems to increase, like that of a rising star trying to get
away from fans and the paparazzi.

Loaves and Fishes

MATTHEW 14:13-21

Now when Jesus heard this, he withdrew from there in a boat to a deserted place by himself. But when the crowds heard it, they followed him
on foot from the towns. When he went ashore, he saw a great crowd; and
he had compassion for them and cured their sick. When it was evening,
the disciples came to him and said, "This is a deserted place, and the
hour is now late; send the crowds away so that they may go into the vil-
lages and buy food for themselves." Jesus said to them, "They need not go
away; you give them something to eat." They replied, "We have nothing
here but five loaves and two fish." And he said, "Bring them here to me."
Then he ordered the crowds to sit down on the grass. Taking the five
loaves and the two fish, he looked up to heaven, and blessed and broke
the loaves, and gave them to the disciples, and the disciples gave them to
the crowds. And all ate and were filled; and they took up what was left
over of the broken pieces, twelve baskets full. And those who ate were
about five thousand men, besides women and children.

Walking on Water

MATTHEW 14:22-33

Immediately he made the disciples get into the boat and go on ahead to
the other side, while he dismissed the crowds. And after he had dismissed
the crowds, he went up the mountain by himself to pray. When evening
came, he was there alone, but by this time the boat, battered by the
waves, was far from the land, for the wind was against them. And early
in the morning he came walking toward them on the sea. But when the
disciples saw him walking on the sea, they were terrified, saying, "It is a

ghost!" And they cried out in fear. But immediately Jesus spoke to them and said, "Take heart, it is I; do not be afraid."

Peter answered him, "Lord, if it is you, command me to come to you on the water." He said, "Come." So Peter got out of the boat, started walking on the water, and came toward Jesus. But when he noticed the strong wind, he became frightened, and beginning to sink, he cried out, "Lord, save me!" Jesus immediately reached out his hand and caught him, saying to him, "You of little faith, why did you doubt?" When they got into the boat, the wind ceased. And those in the boat worshiped him, saying, "Truly you are the Son of God."

"GET BEHIND ME, SATAN!"

"Who do other people say I am?" "Who do you say I am?" These two questions are so simple, yet so profound, running straight to the core of identity and meaning. Would you ask them of your nearest companions? Do you know the answers? Did Jesus? Did he need Peter to give him the answer he hoped to hear?

But this story is as much about Jesus's volatile relationship with Peter, his right-hand man, as it is about his identity. Praised as the foundation rock of the church one second and rebuked as Satan the next—where does this leave Peter?

Pop culture has been less interested in these existential questions than with the theme of temptation, taking Jesus's rebuke, "Get behind me, Satan!" beyond questions of identity and power and into the realm of—what else?—love and lust.

MATTHEW 16:13-23

Now when Jesus came into the district of Caesarea Philippi, he asked his disciples, "Who do people say that the Son of Man is?" And they said, "Some say John the Baptist, but others Elijah, and still others Jeremiah or one of the prophets." He said to them, "But who do you say that I am?" Simon Peter answered, "You are the Messiah, the Son of the living God." And Jesus answered him, "Blessed are you, Simon son of Jonah! For flesh and blood has not revealed this to you, but my Father in heaven. And I tell you, you are Peter, and on this rock I will build my church, and the gates of Hades will not prevail against it. I will give you the keys of the kingdom of heaven, and whatever you bind on earth will be bound in heaven, and whatever you loose on earth will be loosed in heaven." Then he sternly ordered the disciples not to tell anyone that he was the Messiah.

From that time on, Jesus began to show his disciples that he must go to Jerusalem and undergo great suffering at the hands of the elders and chief priests and scribes, and be killed, and on the third day be raised. And Peter took him aside and began to rebuke him, saying, "God forbid it, Lord! This must never happen to you." But he turned and said to Peter, "Get behind me, Satan! You are a stumbling block to me; for you are setting your mind not on divine things but on human things."

Someone I'm mad about
Is waiting in the night for me,
Someone that I mustn't see—
Satan, get thee behind me.
He promised to wait,
But I won't appear
And he may come here—
Satan, he's at my gate,
Get thee behind me—
Stay where you are,
It's too late.

—Irving Berlin, "Get Thee
Behind Me, Satan"

CHANGING TABLES

Immediately after Jesus's triumphal entry into Jerusalem, he goes straight to the Temple, overturns the money changers' tables, and drives the dealers out. Just as his public recognition seems to be peaking, he stirs up trouble. Such an action, especially during Passover season, would certainly have drawn the attention of Roman officials, who were quick to put down potential uprisings and keep the Pax Romana, the "peace of Rome," by whatever means necessary.

In movies, the climactic moment in this story is Jesus's raid on the Temple. But notice how the actual story culminates not in driving out the money changers and dealers, but in welcoming the blind, the lame, and the children (Pier Paolo Pasolini's exceptional *Gospel According to Saint Matthew* is one of the only Jesus movies to get it right). Why is it that we tend to remember the casting out more than the welcoming in? Which is more radical?

MATTHEW 21:1-17

When they had come near Jerusalem and had reached Bethphage, at the Mount of Olives, Jesus sent two disciples, saying to them, "Go into the village ahead of you, and immediately you will find a donkey tied, and a colt with her; untie them and bring them to me. If anyone says anything to you, just say this, 'The Lord needs them.' And he will send them immediately." This took place to fulfill what had been spoken through the prophet, saying,

> "Tell the daughter of Zion,
>   Look, your king is coming to you,
> humble, and mounted on a donkey,
>   and on a colt, the foal of a donkey."

The disciples went and did as Jesus had directed them; they brought the donkey and the colt, and put their cloaks on them, and he sat on them. A very large crowd spread their cloaks on the road, and others cut branches from the trees and spread them on the road. The crowds that went ahead of him and that followed were shouting,

> "Hosanna to the Son of David!
>   Blessed is the one who comes in the name of the Lord!
> Hosanna in the highest heaven!"

When he entered Jerusalem, the whole city was in turmoil, asking, "Who is this?" The crowds were saying, "This is the prophet Jesus from Nazareth in Galilee."

Then Jesus entered the temple and drove out all who were selling and buying in the temple, and he overturned the tables of the money changers and the seats of those who sold doves. He said to them, "It is written,

> 'My house shall be called a house of prayer';
>   but you are making it a den of robbers."

The blind and the lame came to him in the temple, and he cured them. But when the chief priests and the scribes saw the amazing things that he did, and heard the children crying out in the temple, "Hosanna to the Son of David," they became angry and said to him, "Do you hear what these are saying?" Jesus said to them, "Yes; have you never read,

'Out of the mouths of infants and nursing babies
   you have prepared praise for yourself'?"

He left them, went out of the city to Bethany, and spent the night there.

BETRAYED EXPECTATIONS

The end of Jesus's story in Matthew is full of betrayed expectations. The messianic expectation of his followers that he would quickly ascend to power in Jerusalem turns into one more case of Roman capital punishment (the Romans crucified insurrectionists and rabble-rousers all the time). Judas, prominent among Jesus's disciples, sells him out. The crowds, who earlier heralded his triumphal entry into the city, now jeer and call for his blood. Peter, the rock on which he says he will build his church, denies him three times, almost despite himself. Even God seems to have forsaken him.

Some may identify with Jesus. But many of us are drawn to the all too human betrayers, compelled by the inner conflicts that are revealed in their betrayals: Peter, who has seemed so perfectly, zealously devoted until now, and especially Judas, whose regret drives him to suicide. Indeed, it is the pathos of Judas—his jealousy, his anger, and his love—more than the character of Jesus that so draws us to Tim Rice and Andrew Lloyd Webber's 1971 rock opera *Jesus Christ Superstar.*

Look for the subtle signs of internal conflict and uncertainty that motivate the characters and drive the story as it builds, moving from one betrayal to the next. Also, which of Jesus's companions never fail, right to the very end?

The Last Supper

MATTHEW 26:17–30

On the first day of Unleavened Bread the disciples came to Jesus, saying, "Where do you want us to make the preparations for you to eat the Passover?" He said, "Go into the city to a certain man, and say to him, 'The Teacher says, My time is near; I will keep the Passover at your house with my disciples.'" So the disciples did as Jesus had directed them, and they prepared the Passover meal.

The gospel narratives of the Last Supper are the earliest known accounts of a Passover seder.

When it was evening, he took his place with the twelve; and while they were eating, he said, "Truly I tell you, one of you will betray me." And they became greatly distressed and began to say to him one after another, "Surely not I, Lord?" He answered, "The one who has dipped his hand into the bowl with me will betray me. The Son of Man goes as it is written of him, but woe to that one by whom the Son of Man is betrayed! It would have been better for that one not to have been born." Judas, who betrayed him, said, "Surely not I, Rabbi?" He replied, "You have said so."

While they were eating, Jesus took a loaf of bread, and after blessing it he broke it, gave it to the disciples, and said, "Take, eat; this is my body." Then he took a cup, and after giving thanks he gave it to them, saying, "Drink from it, all of you; for this is my blood of the covenant, which is poured out for many for the forgiveness of sins. I tell you, I will never again drink of this fruit of the vine until that day when I drink it new with you in my Father's kingdom."

When they had sung the hymn, they went out to the Mount of Olives.

Denial, Betrayal, Arrest

MATTHEW 26:31–27:2

Then Jesus said to them, "You will all become deserters because of me this night; for it is written,

'I will strike the shepherd,
  and the sheep of the flock will be scattered.'

But after I am raised up, I will go ahead of you to Galilee." Peter said to him, "Though all become deserters because of you, I will never desert you." Jesus said to him, "Truly I tell you, this very night, before the cock crows, you will deny me three times." Peter said to him, "Even though I must die with you, I will not deny you." And so said all the disciples.

Then Jesus went with them to a place called Gethsemane; and he said to his disciples, "Sit here while I go over there and pray." He took with him Peter and the two sons of Zebedee, and began to be grieved and agitated. Then he said to them, "I am deeply grieved, even to death; remain here, and stay awake with me." And going a little farther, he threw himself on the ground and prayed, "My Father, if it is possible, let this cup pass from me; yet not what I want but what you want." Then he came to the disciples and found them sleeping; and he said to Peter, "So, could you not stay awake with me one hour? Stay awake and pray that you may not come into the time of trial; the spirit indeed is willing, but the flesh is weak." Again he went away for the second time and prayed, "My Father, if this cannot pass unless I drink it, your will be done." Again he came and found them sleeping, for their eyes were heavy. So leaving them again, he went away and prayed for the third time, saying the same words. Then he came to the disciples and said to

The character of Judas in the rock opera *Jesus Christ Superstar* is among the most moving interpretations of this biblical figure. From the opening scene, in which he strives to "strip away the myth from the man," he's a deeply conflicted disciple, torn by feelings of love, jealousy, and righteous indignation. Never greed. "These sordid kind of things are coming hard to me," he tells the high priest, who later commends him, "You'll be remembered forever for this." Indeed. Realizing the role he has been made to play, he agonizes, "When he's cold and dead, will he let me be? Does he love me too? Does he care for me?"

them, "Are you still sleeping and taking your rest? See, the hour is at hand, and the Son of Man is betrayed into the hands of sinners. Get up, let us be going. See, my betrayer is at hand."

While he was still speaking, Judas, one of the twelve, arrived; with him was a large crowd with swords and clubs, from the chief priests and the elders of the people. Now the betrayer had given them a sign, saying, "The one I will kiss is the man; arrest him." At once he came up to Jesus and said, "Greetings, Rabbi!" and kissed him. Jesus said to him, "Friend, do what you are here to do." Then they came and laid hands on Jesus and arrested him. Suddenly, one of those with Jesus put his hand on his sword, drew it, and struck the slave of the high priest, cutting off his ear. Then Jesus said to him, "Put your sword back into its place; for all who take the sword will perish by the sword. Do you think that I cannot appeal to my Father, and he will at once send me more than twelve legions of angels? But how then would the scriptures be fulfilled, which say it must happen in this way?" At that hour Jesus said to the crowds, "Have you come out with swords and clubs to arrest me as though I were a bandit? Day after day I sat in the temple teaching, and you did not arrest me. But all this has taken place, so that the scriptures of the prophets may be fulfilled." Then all the disciples deserted him and fled.

Those who had arrested Jesus took him to Caiaphas the high priest, in whose house the scribes and the elders had gathered. But Peter was following him at a distance, as far as the courtyard of the high priest; and going inside, he sat with the guards in order to see how this would end. Now the chief priests and the whole council were looking for false testimony against Jesus so that they might put him to death, but they found none, though many false witnesses came forward. At last two came forward and said, "This fellow said, 'I am able to destroy the temple of God and to build it in three days.'" The high priest stood up and said, "Have you no answer? What is it that they testify against you?" But Jesus was silent. Then the high priest said to him, "I put you under oath before the living God, tell us if you are the Messiah, the Son of God." Jesus said to him, "You have said so. But I tell you,

From now on you will see the Son of Man
　　seated at the right hand of Power
　　and coming on the clouds of heaven."

Then the high priest tore his clothes and said, "He has blasphemed! Why do we still need witnesses? You have now heard his blasphemy. What is your verdict?" They answered, "He deserves death." Then they spat in his face and struck him; and some slapped him, saying, "Prophesy to us, you Messiah! Who is it that struck you?"

Now Peter was sitting outside in the courtyard. A servant-girl came to him and said, "You also were with Jesus the Galilean." But he denied it before all of them, saying, "I do not know what you are talking about." When he went out to the porch, another servant-girl saw him, and she said to the bystanders, "This man was with Jesus of Nazareth." Again he denied it with an oath, "I do not know the man." After a little while the bystanders came up and said to Peter, "Certainly you are also one of them, for your accent betrays you." Then he began to curse, and he swore an oath, "I do not know the man!" At that moment the cock crowed. Then Peter remembered what Jesus had said: "Before the cock crows, you will deny me three times." And he went out and wept bitterly.

When morning came, all the chief priests and the elders of the people conferred together against Jesus in order to bring about his death. They bound him, led him away, and handed him over to Pilate the governor.

Poor Old Judas

MATTHEW 27:3-10

When Judas, his betrayer, saw that Jesus was condemned, he repented and brought back the thirty pieces of silver to the chief priests and the elders. He said, "I have sinned by betraying innocent blood." But they said, "What is that to us? See to it yourself." Throwing down the pieces of silver in the temple, he departed; and he went and hanged himself. But the chief priests, taking the pieces of silver, said, "It is not lawful to put them into the treasury, since

Compare Matthew's story of Judas's death to the one in the book of Acts (1:18–19):

Now this man [Judas] acquired a field with the reward of his wickedness; and falling headlong, he burst open in the middle and all his bowels gushed out. This became known to all the

residents of Jerusalem, so that the field was called in their language Hakeldama, that is, Field of Blood.

Why is Matthew's version so much better known than this one, where the "bad guy" gets his ultimate reward?

they are blood money." After conferring together, they used them to buy the potter's field as a place to bury foreigners. For this reason that field has been called the Field of Blood to this day. Then was fulfilled what had been spoken through the prophet Jeremiah, "And they took the thirty pieces of silver, the price of the one on whom a price had been set, on whom some of the people of Israel had set a price, and they gave them for the potter's field, as the Lord commanded me."

Before Pilate

MATTHEW 27:11-26

Now Jesus stood before the governor; and the governor asked him, "Are you the King of the Jews?" Jesus said, "You say so." But when he was accused by the chief priests and elders, he did not answer. Then Pilate said to him, "Do you not hear how many accusations they make against you?" But he gave him no answer, not even to a single charge, so that the governor was greatly amazed.

Now at the festival the governor was accustomed to release a prisoner for the crowd, anyone whom they wanted. At that time they had a notorious prisoner, called Jesus Barabbas. So after they had gathered, Pilate said to them, "Whom do you want me to release for you, Jesus Barabbas or Jesus who is called the Messiah?" For he realized that it was out of jealousy that they had handed him over. While he was sitting on the judgment seat, his wife sent word to him, "Have nothing to do with that innocent man, for today I have suffered a great deal because of a dream about him." Now the chief priests and the elders persuaded the crowds to ask for Barabbas and to have Jesus killed. The governor again said to them, "Which of the two do you want me to release for you?" And they said, "Barabbas." Pilate said to them, "Then what should I do with Jesus who is called the Messiah?" All of them said, "Let him be crucified!" Then he asked, "Why, what evil has he done?" But they shouted all the more, "Let him be crucified!"

So when Pilate saw that he could do nothing, but rather that a riot was beginning, he took some water and washed his hands before the crowd, saying, "I am innocent of this man's blood; see to it yourselves." Then the people as a whole answered, "His blood be on us and on our children!" So he released Barabbas for them; and after flogging Jesus, he handed him over to be crucified.

The Crucifixion

MATTHEW 27:27-61

Then the soldiers of the governor took Jesus into the governor's head-quarters, and they gathered the whole cohort around him. They stripped him and put a scarlet robe on him, and after twisting some thorns into a crown, they put it on his head. They put a reed in his right hand and knelt before him and mocked him, saying, "Hail, King of the Jews!" They spat on him, and took the reed and struck him on the head. After mocking him, they stripped him of the robe and put his own clothes on him. Then they led him away to crucify him.

As they went out, they came upon a man from Cyrene named Simon; they compelled this man to carry his cross. And when they came to a place called Golgotha (which means Place of a Skull), they offered him wine to drink, mixed with gall; but when he tasted it, he would not drink it. And when they had crucified him, they divided his clothes among themselves by casting lots; then they sat down there and kept watch over him. Over his head they put the charge against him, which read, "This is Jesus, the King of the Jews."

Then two bandits were crucified with him, one on his right and one on his left. Those who passed by derided him, shaking their heads and saying, "You who would destroy the temple and build it in three days, save yourself! If you are the Son of God, come down from the cross." In the same way the chief priests also, along with the scribes and elders, were mocking him, saying, "He saved others; he cannot save himself. He is the King of Israel; let him come down from the cross now, and we will believe in him. He trusts in God; let God deliver him now, if he wants to; for he said, 'I am God's Son.'" The bandits who were crucified with him also taunted him in the same way.

From noon on, darkness came over the whole land until three in the afternoon. And about three o'clock Jesus cried with a loud voice, "Eli, Eli, lema sabachthani?" that is, "My God, my God, why have you forsaken me?" When some of the bystanders heard it, they said, "This man is calling for Elijah." At once one of them ran and got a sponge, filled it with sour wine, put it on a stick, and gave it to him to drink. But the others said, "Wait, let us see whether Elijah will come to save him." Then Jesus cried again with a loud voice and breathed his last. At that moment the curtain of the temple was torn in two, from top to bottom. The earth shook, and the rocks were split. The tombs also were opened, and many bodies of the saints who had fallen asleep were raised. After his resurrection they came out of the tombs and entered the holy city and appeared to many. Now when the centurion and those with him, who were keeping watch over Jesus, saw the earthquake and what took place, they were terrified and said, "Truly this man was God's Son!"

Each of the four gospels names different women as the first witnesses to the empty tomb. In Mark, they are Mary Magdalene, Mary the mother of James, and Salome (presumably not the one who danced before Herod). In Luke, they are Mary Magdalene, Joanna (otherwise unknown), Mary the mother of James, and "the other women with them." And in John, it is Mary Magdalene only. The fact that Mary Magdalene is mentioned in all four may indicate that she was an especially prominent member of the early Jesus movement. Note too that none of the gospels mention any men.

Many women were also there, looking on from a distance; they had followed Jesus from Galilee and had provided for him. Among them were Mary Magdalene, and Mary the mother of James and Joseph, and the mother of the sons of Zebedee.

When it was evening, there came a rich man from Arimathea, named Joseph, who was also a disciple of Jesus. He went to Pilate and asked for the body of Jesus; then Pilate ordered it to be given to him. So Joseph took the body and wrapped it in a clean linen cloth and laid it in his own new tomb, which he had hewn in the rock. He then rolled a great stone to the door of the tomb and went away. Mary Magdalene and the other Mary were there, sitting opposite the tomb.

Death Betrayed

MATTHEW 28:1–10

After the sabbath, as the first day of the week was dawning, Mary Magdalene and the other Mary went to see the tomb. And suddenly there was a great earthquake; for an angel of the Lord, descending from heaven, came and rolled back the stone and sat on it. His appearance was like lightning, and his clothing white as snow. For fear of him the guards shook and became like dead men. But the angel said to the women, "Do not be afraid; I know that you are looking for Jesus who was crucified. He is not here; for he has been raised, as he said. Come, see the place where he lay. Then go quickly and tell his disciples, 'He has been raised from the dead, and indeed he is going ahead of you to Galilee; there you will see him.' This is my message for you." So they left the tomb quickly with fear and great joy, and ran to tell his disciples. Suddenly Jesus met them and said, "Greetings!" And they came to him, took hold of his feet, and worshiped him. Then Jesus said to them, "Do not be afraid; go and tell my brothers to go to Galilee; there they will see me."

WHY FOUR DIFFERENT GOSPELS?

There are four different gospels in the New Testament, and each offers a unique perspective and interpretation of the story of Jesus Christ. Matthew emphasizes Jesus's identity as a rabbi and interpreter of Torah and thus includes many instructions concerning how to conduct one's life in a godly way. John's Jesus, by contrast, says very little about what his followers must do and much more about who he is and how to know him. Mark's Jesus often tells those who recognize him as the Messiah to keep quiet and tell no one. Luke's emphasizes social justice, envisioning the coming kingdom of God as especially good news for the poor and the oppressed.

Often, the gospels disagree on important details of the Jesus story. For example, each one includes different women as the first witnesses of the empty tomb; Matthew and Luke-Acts give contradictory accounts of Judas's death; and whereas Jesus's last meal with his disciples is a Passover seder in Matthew, Mark, and Luke, it takes place the day before in the Gospel of John. The New Testament is comfortable with contradiction. It embraces different voices, different accounts, and different interpretations even when they can't be harmonized.

Now here's a New Testament puzzle. Although every gospel is different, three of them—Matthew, Mark, and Luke—have a lot in common. They share much of the same content, sometimes word for word. Yet each is also significantly different from the others. The puzzle is how to explain their relationship. Because the Gospel of Mark is the shortest of the three, and because Matthew and Luke include most of Mark's contents (sometimes correcting it along the way), most conclude that Mark must have been the earliest gospel (about 70 CE) and that Matthew and Luke both used it as a source. Another twist is that Matthew and Luke also share a good deal of other material that is not part of Mark. Most of that material is sayings of Jesus. Scholars therefore hypothesize that these two gospels got that material from a source they had in common that was a collection of Jesus's sayings. This hypothetical text is known as Q, for *Quelle* (German for "source"). There are other possible solutions to the puzzle. Can you come up with one?

The Gospel of Mark

MESSIANIC SECRET

In the Gospel of Mark, Jesus hits the ground running. No nativity. No Mary, no Joseph, no angel. No childhood stories. Within a few verses, he is in the thick of it, healing and exorcising people left and right.

In these opening stories, count how many times "immediately" and "at once" are repeated. How do these and other details give a sense of momentum and unstoppable power to the beginning of this story of Jesus? At the same time, notice how Jesus keeps admonishing people not to tell anyone about him, and how the more he urges people to keep this "messianic secret," the more the word spreads.

MARK 1:21–28, 40–45

They went to Capernaum; and when the sabbath came, he entered the synagogue and taught. They were astounded at his teaching, for he taught them as one having authority, and not as the scribes. Just then there was in their synagogue a man with an unclean spirit, and he cried out, "What have you to do with us, Jesus of Nazareth? Have you come to destroy us? I know who you are, the Holy One of God." But Jesus rebuked him, saying, "Be silent, and come out of him!" And the unclean spirit, convulsing him and crying with a loud voice, came out of him. They were all amazed, and they kept on asking one another, "What is this? A new teaching—with authority! He commands even the unclean spirits, and they obey him." At once his fame began to spread throughout the surrounding region of Galilee.

. . . A leper came to him begging him, and kneeling he said to him, "If you choose, you can make me clean." Moved with pity, Jesus stretched out his hand and touched him, and said to him, "I do choose. Be made clean!" Immediately the leprosy left him, and he was made clean. After sternly warning him he sent him away at once, saying to him, "See that you say nothing to anyone; but go, show yourself to the priest, and offer for your cleansing what Moses commanded, as a testimony to them." But he went out and began to proclaim it freely, and to spread the word, so that Jesus could no longer go into a town openly, but stayed out in the country; and people came to him from every quarter.

TOUCHING THE HEM

Again we find Jesus among the crowds, carried along by the momentum. Jairus, a prominent member of the synagogue, hurries him along to save his dying daughter. But another "daughter," a stranger along the way, interrupts. And for a moment, everything comes to a standstill.

That she draws healing power from his garment but not his body suggests both intimacy and distance—touching, but not quite touching. The mix of desire and faith presented in this biblical moment of connection was powerfully conveyed in Sam Cooke's famous recording of "Touch the Hem of His Garment," which retells this story from the woman's perspective. Performed with his original gospel group, the Soul Stirrers, this song conveyed a sense of longing that anticipated the soulful secular love songs he would soon be famous for.

MARK 5:21-43

When Jesus had crossed again in the boat to the other side, a great crowd gathered around him; and he was by the sea. Then one of the leaders of the synagogue named Jairus came and, when he saw him, fell at his feet and begged him repeatedly, "My little daughter is at the point of death. Come and lay your hands on her, so that she may be made well, and live." So he went with him.

And a large crowd followed him and pressed in on him. Now there was a woman who had been suffering from hemorrhages for twelve years.

She had endured much under many physicians, and had spent all that she had; and she was no better, but rather grew worse. She had heard about Jesus, and came up behind him in the crowd and touched his cloak, for she said, "If I but touch his clothes, I will be made well." Immediately her hemorrhage stopped; and she felt in her body that she was healed of her disease. Immediately aware that power had gone forth from him, Jesus turned about in the crowd and said, "Who touched my clothes?" And his disciples said to him, "You see the crowd pressing in on you; how can you say, 'Who touched me?'" He looked all around to see who had done it. But the woman, knowing what had happened to her, came in fear and trembling, fell down before him, and told him the whole truth. He said to her, "Daughter, your faith has made you well; go in peace, and be healed of your disease."

While he was still speaking, some people came from the leader's house to say, "Your daughter is dead. Why trouble the teacher any further?" But overhearing what they said, Jesus said to the leader of the synagogue, "Do not fear, only believe." He allowed no one to follow him except Peter, James, and John, the brother of James. When they came to the house of the leader of the synagogue, he saw a commotion, people weeping and wailing loudly. When he had entered, he said to them, "Why do you make a commotion and weep? The child is not dead but sleeping." And they laughed at him. Then he put them all outside, and took the child's father and mother and those who were with him, and went in where the child was. He took her by the hand and said to her, "Talitha cum," which means, "Little girl, get up!" And immediately the girl got up and began to walk about (she was twelve years of age). At this they were overcome with amazement. He strictly ordered them that no one should know this, and told them to give her something to eat.

IN CONCLUSION

The Gospel of Mark ends as abruptly as it begins. If you feel as though something's missing, you're not alone. Although this is most likely the original ending, other early versions of the gospel include additions that try to wrap things up more securely. In them, the risen Jesus returns and speaks once more with his disciples, commissioning them to go into the world and spread the good news. In the longest versions, Jesus says that believers "will pick up snakes in their hands, and if they drink any deadly thing, it will not hurt them." This is the biblical basis for the practices of churches that drink poison and handle snakes as part of their worship services.

Still, the original ending leaves us with terror, amazement, fear, and silence. Why? What is the effect of concluding so inconclusively?

MARK 16:1-8

When the sabbath was over, Mary Magdalene, and Mary the mother of James, and Salome bought spices, so that they might go and anoint him. And very early on the first day of the week, when the sun had risen, they went to the tomb. They had been saying to one another, "Who will roll away the stone for us from the entrance to the tomb?" When they looked up, they saw that the stone, which was very large, had already been rolled back. As they entered the tomb, they saw a young man, dressed in a white robe, sitting on the right side; and they were alarmed. But he said to them, "Do not be alarmed; you are looking for Jesus of Nazareth, who was crucified. He has been raised; he is not here. Look, there is the place they laid him. But go, tell his disciples and Peter that he is going ahead of you to Galilee; there you will see him, just as he told you." So they went out and fled from the tomb, for terror and amazement had seized them; and they said nothing to anyone, for they were afraid.

The Gospel of Luke

MOTHERS AND SONS

Here in Luke we have a very self-conscious new beginning: the writer knows what others have done and boldly intends to do it differently.

Remember how Matthew's nativity narrative focuses at least as much on the men in the story as on Mary and baby Jesus? There it was Joseph, not Mary, who got the news from the angel; then the wise men got it using their astrological methods; then Herod got it from the wise men; and so on. In Matthew's version, men seemed to move the story along. Not so in Luke. Here, the central actors are two women, Mary the mother of Jesus and her relative Elizabeth, the mother of John (the Baptist). They're the ones in the know. Their husbands are left mostly in the dark.

Our pop-culture version of the nativity, familiar from holiday television specials and Christmas pageants, typically blends Matthew and Luke. Matthew's wise men join Luke's shepherds in Luke's stable. Luke's stories about Elizabeth, Zechariah, and the birth of their son John usually get cut.

Now read Luke's narrative on its own, as the story of two spiritually tuned-in women and their two auspicious births. How does this beginning frame the rest of the story?

LUKE 1:1–2:20

Since many have undertaken to set down an orderly account of the events that have been fulfilled among us, just as they were handed on to us by those who from the beginning were eyewitnesses and servants of the word, I too decided, after investigating everything carefully from the very first, to write an orderly account for you, most excellent Theophilus, so that you may know the truth concerning the things about which you have been instructed.

In the days of King Herod of Judea, there was a priest named Zechariah, who belonged to the priestly order of Abijah. His wife was a descendant of Aaron, and her name was Elizabeth. Both of them were righteous before God, living blamelessly according to all the commandments and regulations of the Lord. But they had no children, because Elizabeth was barren, and both were getting on in years.

Once when he was serving as priest before God and his section was on duty, he was chosen by lot, according to the custom of the priesthood, to enter the sanctuary of the Lord and offer incense. Now at the time of the incense offering, the whole assembly of the people was praying outside. Then there appeared to him an angel of the Lord, standing at the right side of the altar of incense. When Zechariah saw him, he was terrified; and fear overwhelmed him. But the angel said to him, "Do not be afraid, Zechariah, for your prayer has been heard. Your wife Elizabeth will bear you a son, and you will name him John. You will have joy and gladness, and many will rejoice at his birth, for he will be great in the sight of the Lord. He must never drink wine or strong drink; even before his birth he will be filled with the Holy Spirit. He will turn many of the people of Israel to the Lord their God. With the spirit and power of Elijah he will go before him, to turn the hearts of parents to their children, and the disobedient to the wisdom of the righteous, to make ready a people prepared for the Lord." Zechariah said to the angel, "How will I know that this is so? For I am an old man, and my wife is getting on in years." The angel replied, "I am Gabriel. I stand in the presence of God, and I have been sent to speak to you and to bring you this good news. But now, because you did not believe my words, which will be fulfilled in their time, you will become mute, unable to speak, until the day these things occur."

Meanwhile the people were waiting for Zechariah, and wondered at his delay in the sanctuary. When he did come out, he could not speak to them, and they realized that he had seen a vision in the sanctuary. He kept motioning to them and remained unable to speak. When his time of service was ended, he went to his home.

After those days his wife Elizabeth conceived, and for five months she remained in seclusion. She said, "This is what the Lord has done for me when he looked favorably on me and took away the disgrace I have endured among my people."

In the sixth month the angel Gabriel was sent by God to a town in Galilee called Nazareth, to a virgin engaged to a man whose name was Joseph, of the house of David. The virgin's name was Mary. And he came to her and said, "Greetings, favored one! The Lord is with you." But she was much perplexed by his words and pondered what sort of greeting this might be. The angel said to her, "Do not be afraid, Mary, for you have found favor with God. And now, you will conceive in your womb and bear a son, and you will name him Jesus. He will be great, and will be called the Son of the Most High, and the Lord God will give to him the throne of his ancestor David. He will reign over

> "Every angel is terrifying," wrote poet Rainer Maria Rilke. Which is why one of the first things they have to say is "do not be afraid." But note: Mary is perplexed, not afraid. In her celebrated poem "Annunciation," Denise Levertov declared her the "bravest of all humans." The poem concludes:
>
> Consent,
>   courage unparalleled,
> opened her utterly.

the house of Jacob forever, and of his kingdom there will be no end." Mary said to the angel, "How can this be, since I am a virgin?" The angel said to her, "The Holy Spirit will come upon you, and the power of the Most High will overshadow you; therefore the child to be born will be holy; he will be called Son of God. And now, your relative Elizabeth in her old age has also conceived a son; and this is the sixth month for her who was said to be barren. For nothing will be impossible with God." Then Mary said, "Here am I, the servant of the Lord; let it be with me according to your word." Then the angel departed from her.

In those days Mary set out and went with haste to a Judean town in the hill country, where she entered the house of Zechariah and greeted Elizabeth. When Elizabeth heard Mary's greeting, the child leaped in her womb. And Elizabeth was filled with the Holy Spirit and exclaimed with a loud cry, "Blessed are you among women, and blessed is the fruit of your womb. And why has this happened to me, that the mother of my Lord comes to me? For as soon as I heard the sound of your greeting, the child in my womb leaped for joy. And blessed is she who believed that there would be a fulfillment of what was spoken to her by the Lord."

And Mary said,

"My soul magnifies the Lord,
    and my spirit rejoices in God my Savior,
for he has looked with favor on the lowliness of his servant.
    Surely, from now on all generations will call me blessed;
for the Mighty One has done great things for me,
    and holy is his name.
His mercy is for those who fear him
    from generation to generation.
He has shown strength with his arm;
    he has scattered the proud in the thoughts of their hearts.
He has brought down the powerful from their thrones,
    and lifted up the lowly;
he has filled the hungry with good things,
    and sent the rich away empty.
He has helped his servant Israel,
    in remembrance of his mercy,
according to the promise he made to our ancestors,
    to Abraham and to his descendants forever."

And Mary remained with her about three months and then returned to her home.

Now the time came for Elizabeth to give birth, and she bore a son. Her neighbors and relatives heard that the Lord had shown his great mercy to her, and they rejoiced with her.

On the eighth day they came to circumcise the child, and they were going to name him Zechariah after his father. But his mother said, "No; he is to be called John." They said to her, "None of your relatives has this name." Then they began motioning to his father to find out what name he wanted to give him. He asked for a writing tablet and wrote, "His name is John." And all of them were amazed. Immediately his mouth was opened and his tongue freed, and he began to speak, praising God. Fear came over all their neighbors, and all these things were talked about throughout the entire hill country of Judea. All who heard them pondered them and said, "What then will this child become?" For, indeed, the hand of the Lord was with him.

Then his father Zechariah was filled with the Holy Spirit and spoke this prophecy:

"Blessed be the Lord God of Israel,
　for he has looked favorably on his people and redeemed them.
He has raised up a mighty savior for us
　in the house of his servant David,
as he spoke through the mouth of his holy prophets from of old,
　that we would be saved from our enemies and from the hand of all
　who hate us.
Thus he has shown the mercy promised to our ancestors,
　and has remembered his holy covenant,
the oath that he swore to our ancestor Abraham,
　to grant us that we, being rescued from the hands of our enemies,
might serve him without fear, in holiness and righteousness
　before him all our days.
And you, child, will be called the prophet of the Most High;
　for you will go before the Lord to prepare his ways,
to give knowledge of salvation to his people
　by the forgiveness of their sins.
By the tender mercy of our God,
　the dawn from on high will break upon us,
to give light to those who sit in darkness and in the shadow of death,
　to guide our feet into the way of peace."

The child grew and became strong in spirit, and he was in the wilderness until the day he appeared publicly to Israel.

In those days a decree went out from Emperor Augustus that all the world should be registered. This was the first registration and was taken while Quirinius was governor of Syria. All went to their own towns to be registered. Joseph also went from the town of Nazareth in Galilee to Judea, to the city of David called Bethlehem, because he was descended from the house and family of David. He went to be registered with Mary, to whom he was engaged and who was expecting a child. While they were there, the time came for her to deliver her child. And she gave birth to her firstborn son and wrapped him in bands of cloth, and laid him in a manger, because there was no place for them in the inn.

In that region there were shepherds living in the fields, keeping watch over their flock by night. Then an angel of the Lord stood before them, and the glory of the Lord shone around them, and they were terrified. But the angel said to them, "Do not be afraid; for see—I am bringing you good news of great joy for all the people: to you is born this day in the city of David a Savior, who is the Messiah, the Lord. This will be a sign for you: you will find a child wrapped in bands of cloth and lying in a manger." And suddenly there was with the angel a multitude of the heavenly host, praising God and saying,

"Glory to God in the highest heaven,
    and on earth peace among those whom he favors!"

When the angels had left them and gone into heaven, the shepherds said to one another, "Let us go now to Bethlehem and see this thing that has taken place, which the Lord has made known to us." So they went with haste and found Mary and Joseph, and the child lying in the manger. When they saw this, they made known what had been told them about this child; and all who heard it were amazed at what the shepherds told them. But Mary treasured all these words and pondered them in her heart. The shepherds returned, glorifying and praising God for all they had heard and seen, as it had been told them.

THE BOY JESUS

Children's books about Jesus include lots of pictures of him working with Dad in the woodshop, interacting with Mom and other adoring relatives, and so on. These childhood portraits speak to our desire to fill the gap between his birth stories and his adult life. Yet no such images of him can be found in the Bible. In fact, the story of Jesus in the Temple is the only New Testament story of Jesus as a boy, the only bridge between birth and adulthood. What does it reveal about him? Why did this story and no others make the cut?

LUKE 2:41–51

Now every year his parents went to Jerusalem for the festival of the Passover. And when he was twelve years old, they went up as usual for the festival. When the festival was ended and they started to return, the boy Jesus stayed behind in Jerusalem, but his parents did not know it. Assuming that he was in the group of travelers, they went a day's journey. Then they started to look for him among their relatives and friends. When they did not find him, they returned to Jerusalem to search for him. After three days they found him in the temple, sitting among the teachers, listening to them and asking them questions. And all who heard him were amazed at his understanding and his answers. When his parents saw him they were astonished; and his mother said to him, "Child, why have you treated us like this? Look, your father and I have been searching for you in great anxiety." He said to them, "Why were you searching for me? Did you not know that I must be in my Father's house?" But they did not understand what he said to them. Then he went down with them and came to Nazareth, and was obedient to them. His mother treasured all these things in her heart.

HOMECOMING

A homecoming is always, in some sense, a return to one's former self. "Isn't that so-and-so's kid? Who does he think he is?" No matter how well you do for yourself out on your own, the folks back home are still going to remember you as you were. And then try to kill you? Okay. Not your typical homecoming.

What provokes such rage from the hometown congregation? It's not the content of his reading from Isaiah, as revolutionary as that is. It's what he says next. Is he trying to provoke them? Is their rejection of him a self-fulfilling prophecy? Who is this riddling, provocative person at the center of the story?

LUKE 4:16-30

When he came to Nazareth, where he had been brought up, he went to the synagogue on the sabbath day, as was his custom. He stood up to read, and the scroll of the prophet Isaiah was given to him. He unrolled the scroll and found the place where it was written:

"The Spirit of the Lord is upon me,
  because he has anointed me
  to bring good news to the poor.
He has sent me to proclaim release to the captives
  and recovery of sight to the blind,
  to let the oppressed go free,
to proclaim the year of the Lord's favor."

And he rolled up the scroll, gave it back to the attendant, and sat down. The eyes of all in the synagogue were fixed on him. Then he began to say to them, "Today this scripture has been fulfilled in your hearing." All spoke well of him and were amazed at the gracious words that came from his mouth. They said, "Is not this Joseph's son?" He said to them, "Doubtless you will quote to me this proverb, 'Doctor, cure yourself!' And you will say, 'Do here also in your hometown the things that we have heard you did at Capernaum.'" And he said, "Truly I tell you, no prophet is accepted in the prophet's hometown. But the truth is, there were many widows in Israel in the time of Elijah, when the heaven was shut up three years and six months, and there was a severe famine over all the land; yet Elijah was sent to none of them except to a widow at Zarephath in Sidon. There were also many lepers in Israel in the time of the prophet Elisha, and none of them was cleansed except Naaman the Syrian." When they heard this, all in the synagogue were filled with rage. They got up, drove him out of the town, and led him to the brow of the hill on which their town was built, so that they might hurl him off the cliff. But he passed through the midst of them and went on his way.

THE GOOD SAMARITAN

Ever wonder about those "Good Sam Club" bumper stickers on motor homes? The club began as an informal network of RV campers who were committed to helping out other travelers in need. Good Sam is a cute nickname for the hero of this story, the "good Samaritan" who helped a traveler in distress when other, more righteous people walked on by (the Samaritans were descended from Northern tribes and were looked down upon by other Jewish groups of the time).

Notice how this story is set within another story: Jesus is in a discussion with a student of Jewish law, and the good Samaritan story is his answer to the student's follow-up question, "Who is my neighbor?" How does the story answer that question, then and now?

LUKE 10:25-37

Just then a lawyer stood up to test Jesus. "Teacher," he said, "what must I do to inherit eternal life?" He said to him, "What is written in the law? What do you read there?" He answered, "You shall love the Lord your God with all your heart, and with all your soul, and with all your strength, and with all your mind; and your neighbor as yourself." And he said to him, "You have given the right answer; do this, and you will live."

But wanting to justify himself, he asked Jesus, "And who is my neighbor?" Jesus replied, "A man was going down from Jerusalem to Jericho, and fell into the hands of robbers, who stripped him, beat him, and went away, leaving him half dead. Now by chance a priest was going down that road; and when he saw him, he passed by on the other side. So likewise a Levite, when he came to the place and saw him, passed by on the other side. But a Samaritan while traveling came near him; and when he saw him, he was moved with pity. He went to him and bandaged his wounds, having poured oil and wine on them. Then he put him on his own animal, brought him to an inn, and took care of him. The next day he took out two denarii, gave them to the innkeeper, and said, 'Take care of him; and when I come back, I will repay you whatever more you spend.' Which of these three, do you think, was a neighbor to the man who fell into the hands of the robbers?" He said, "The one who showed him mercy." Jesus said to him, "Go and do likewise."

MARTHA AND MARY

"The 'Mary' and the 'Martha' in my life have an eternal war." So wrote Lady Bird Johnson in her *White House Diary,* reflecting on her role as First Lady (1963–69). Martha has become shorthand for a woman who worries more about the details of hospitality and, in the process, loses out on more meaningful social engagement with the guests. Still, doesn't Martha have a point? Somebody has to be responsible for the details. And sharing them might help.

LUKE 10:38-42

Now as they went on their way, he entered a certain village, where a woman named Martha welcomed him into her home. She had a sister named Mary, who sat at the Lord's feet and listened to what he was saying. But Martha was distracted by her many tasks; so she came to him and asked, "Lord, do you not care that my sister has left me to do all the work by myself? Tell her then to help me." But the Lord answered her, "Martha, Martha, you are worried and distracted by many things; there is need of only one thing. Mary has chosen the better part, which will not be taken away from her."

THE PRODIGAL SON

The parable of the prodigal ("wasteful," "reckless") son is woven into the narrative fabric of popular culture. So familiar and influential is this story that no novelist, filmmaker, or songwriter could tell a new story about a runaway or a child gone bad without at least alluding to it.

Part of what makes it such a powerful story is its openness to multiple perspectives. Different readers identify with different characters. How about you? Perhaps you can relate most to the prodigal. Or maybe your sympathies lie with the older, more responsible sibling. You get Dad's point. Still, could letting the younger son off the hook be part of a codependent pattern at the root of the problem? Here again, then, parables inevitably open themselves to more than one interpretation.

LUKE 15:11–32

Then Jesus said, "There was a man who had two sons. The younger of them said to his father, 'Father, give me the share of the property that will belong to me.' So he divided his property between them. A few days later the younger son gathered all he had and traveled to a distant country, and there he squandered his property in dissolute living. When he had spent everything, a severe famine took place throughout that country, and he began to be in need. So he went and hired himself out to one of the citizens of that country, who sent him to his fields to feed the pigs. He would gladly have filled himself with the pods that the pigs were eating; and no one gave him anything. But when he came to himself he said, 'How many of my father's hired hands have bread enough and to spare, but here I am dying of hunger! I will get up and go to my father, and I will say to him, "Father, I have sinned against heaven and before you; I am no longer worthy to be called your son; treat me like one of your hired hands."' So he set off and went to his father. But while he was still far off, his father saw him and was filled with compassion; he ran and put his arms around him and kissed him. Then the son said to him, 'Father, I have sinned against heaven and before you; I am no longer worthy to be called your son.' But the father said to his slaves, 'Quickly, bring out a robe—the best one—and put it on him; put a ring on his finger and sandals on his feet. And get the fatted calf and kill it, and let us eat and celebrate; for this son of mine was dead and is alive again; he was lost and is found!' And they began to celebrate.

"Now his elder son was in the field; and when he came and approached the house, he heard music and dancing. He called one of the slaves and asked what was going on. He replied, 'Your brother has come, and your father has killed the fatted calf, because he has got him back safe and sound.' Then he became angry and refused to go in. His father came out and began to plead with him. But he answered his father, 'Listen! For all these years I have been working like a slave for you, and I have never disobeyed your command; yet you have never given me even a young goat so that I might celebrate with my friends. But when this son of yours came back, who has devoured your property with prostitutes, you killed the fatted calf for him!' Then the father said to him, 'Son, you are always with me, and all that is mine is yours. But we had to celebrate and rejoice, because this brother of yours was dead and has come to life; he was lost and has been found.'"

The Gospel of John

"IN THE BEGINNING WAS THE WORD"

We all want to be in the know, to "get it." The Gospel of John often speaks to that desire. Here Jesus is less of a doer and more of a talker. His actions are few, but he talks a lot about who he is. His emphasis is not on what one needs to do, but what one needs to believe in order to have insider knowledge.

That Jesus is a talker is one possible reason for calling him "the Word" in this famous prologue. But the Greek word here, *logos,* has many meanings. In Greek and Jewish philosophy, it referred to words, speaking, logic, reason, meaning. It was also associated with the female personification of Wisdom (remember her in Proverbs, present at the beginning of creation?). All these nuances and more may be found here. One single meaning is not what it's about.

So we face an immediate irony in these opening words, and the opening Word. We are being drawn into the story as insiders, in the know; but are we? Are we allowed all the way in? For many of us, this sense of being inside and outside, in the light and in the dark, at the same time haunts us right through to the end, and beyond.

JOHN 1:1–18

In the beginning was the Word, and the Word was with God, and the Word was God. He was in the beginning with God. All things came into being through him, and without him not one thing came into being. What has come into being in him was life, and the life was the light of all people. The light shines in the darkness, and the darkness did not overcome it.

There was a man sent from God, whose name was John. He came as a witness to testify to the light, so that all might believe through him. He himself was not the light, but he came to testify to the light. The true light, which enlightens everyone, was coming into the world.

He was in the world, and the world came into being through him; yet the world did not know him. He came to what was his own, and his own people did not accept him. But to all who received him, who believed in his name, he gave power to become children of God, who were born, not of blood or of the will of the flesh or of the will of man, but of God.

And the Word became flesh and lived among us, and we have seen his glory, the glory as of a father's only son, full of grace and truth. (John testified to him and cried out, "This was he of whom I said, 'He who comes after me ranks ahead of me because he was before me.'") From his fullness we have all received, grace upon grace. The law indeed was given through Moses; grace and truth came through Jesus Christ. No one has ever seen God. It is God the only Son, who is close to the Father's heart, who has made him known.

WATER INTO WINE

Jesus was the life of the party, turning water into wine. Not just any wine, mind you, but the finest of the evening. Many a pious teetotaler has secretly wished that this story had not made it into the Bible. Along with the apostle Paul's comment that a little wine is good for digestion, Jesus's miracle of fermentation has required them to argue, weakly, that wine back then was so low in alcohol that it was really more like grape juice (which temperance activist Thomas Welch invented as a nonalcoholic alternative to wine for Communion!). Leaving behind such gymnastic interpretive moves, what does it say about John's Jesus that his first miracle (and one of only a handful in this gospel) is to keep the wine flowing at a wedding party?

JOHN 2:1-11

On the third day there was a wedding in Cana of Galilee, and the mother of Jesus was there. Jesus and his disciples had also been invited to the wedding. When the wine gave out, the mother of Jesus said to him, "They have no wine." And Jesus said to her, "Woman, what concern is that to you and to me? My hour has not yet come." His mother said to the servants, "Do whatever he tells you." Now standing there were six stone water jars for the Jewish rites of purification, each holding twenty or thirty gallons. Jesus said to them, "Fill the jars with water." And they filled them up to the brim. He said to them, "Now draw some out, and take it to the chief steward." So they took it. When the steward tasted the water that had become wine, and did not know where it came from (though the servants who had drawn the water knew), the steward called the bridegroom and said to him, "Everyone serves the good wine first, and then the inferior wine after the guests have become drunk. But you have kept the good wine until now." Jesus did this, the first of his signs, in Cana of Galilee, and revealed his glory; and his disciples believed in him.

'Tis melancholy, and a fearful sign
  Of human frailty, folly, also crime,
That love and marriage rarely can combine,
  Although they both are born in the same clime;
Marriage from love, like vinegar from wine—
  A sad, sour, sober beverage—by time
Is sharpen'd from its high celestial flavour
Down to a very homely household savour.

—Lord Byron, *Don Juan*

BORN AGAIN

Sometimes, we want to know without being known. Perhaps we're searching for something, or someone, in a book or on the Internet. We want to remain anonymous, at least for the time being. So too Nicodemus, who seeks out Jesus by night. He wants to know, but not in the light of day. He's not ready to commit, to "go public." Which is ironic, since his story has become one of the most well known in the Bible!

In fact, Jesus's final statement to him is perhaps the most famous of all New Testament verses: John 3:16, "For God so loved the world . . ." For many evangelicals today, it is biblical bedrock, the core of the gospel message. And thanks to "Rainbow Man" Rollen Stewart, who began holding up a big "John 3:16" sign in the end zone during nationally televised football games, it has become familiar to many, many others. Rollen actually got life in prison for kidnapping in 1992, but others have taken up his mantle.

JOHN 3:1–16

Here, Nicodemus is put off. Jesus scolds him for not getting it, not having the inside knowledge. Yet he continued to follow, albeit at some distance. Several chapters later we find him defending Jesus against the Temple priests, saying that he should be given a fair hearing (7:50–51). And at the end he is among Jesus's disciples, providing myrrh and aloes for his crucified body (19:39).

Now there was a Pharisee named Nicodemus, a leader of the Jews. He came to Jesus by night and said to him, "Rabbi, we know that you are a teacher who has come from God; for no one can do these signs that you do apart from the presence of God." Jesus answered him, "Very truly, I tell you, no one can see the kingdom of God without being born from above." Nicodemus said to him, "How can anyone be born after having grown old? Can one enter a second time into the mother's womb and be born?" Jesus answered, "Very truly, I tell you, no one can enter the kingdom of God without being born of water and Spirit. What is born of the flesh is flesh, and what is born of the Spirit is spirit. Do not be astonished that I said to you, 'You must be born from above.' The wind blows where it chooses, and you hear the sound of it, but you do not know where it comes from or where it goes. So it is with everyone who is born of the Spirit." Nicodemus said to him, "How can these things be?" Jesus answered him, "Are you a teacher of Israel, and yet you do not understand these things?

"Very truly, I tell you, we speak of what we know and testify to what we have seen; yet you do not receive our testimony. If I have told you about earthly things and you do not believe, how can you believe if I tell you about heavenly things? No one has ascended into heaven except the one who descended from heaven, the Son of Man. And just as Moses lifted up the serpent in the wilderness, so must the Son of Man be lifted up, that whoever believes in him may have eternal life.

"For God so loved the world that he gave his only Son, so that everyone who believes in him may not perish but may have eternal life.

THE FIRST STONE

Here Jesus interprets the law with a mirror. Look at your own selves, he essentially says to his fellow Torah scholars. And so he removes the stinger from a patriarchal law.

Again we find mystery at the center of this story. It says that he was writing on the ground with his finger, but it doesn't say what he wrote. Why not? What do you imagine it was?

JOHN 8:2–11

Early in the morning he came again to the temple. All the people came to him and he sat down and began to teach them. The scribes and the Pharisees brought a woman who had been caught in adultery; and making her stand before all of them, they said to him, "Teacher, this woman was caught in the very act of committing adultery. Now in the law Moses commanded us to stone such women. Now what do you say?" They said this to test him, so that they might have some charge to bring against him. Jesus bent down and wrote with his finger on the ground. When they kept on questioning him, he straightened up and said to them, "Let anyone among you who is without sin be the first to throw a stone at her." And once again he bent down and wrote on the ground. When they heard it, they went away, one by one, beginning with the elders; and Jesus was left alone with the woman standing before him. Jesus straightened up and said to her, "Woman, where are they? Has no one condemned you?" She said, "No one, sir." And Jesus said, "Neither do I condemn you. Go your way, and from now on do not sin again."

LAZARUS

"Come out!" The story of Jesus calling forth his dead friend
Lazarus from the tomb is as much about liberation and release as it is about the miracle of resurrection. It is in that spirit
that Eugene O'Neill's play *Lazarus Laughed* tells the story of
Lazarus's postresurrection life, which is filled with a fearless,
death-defying "laughter of God."

Especially striking here is the eruption of emotion from Jesus
when he sees his friends racked with grief. In fact, this is the
only place in the Bible where Jesus cries. As it happens, verse
35, "Jesus began to weep" ("Jesus wept" in the King James Version), is also the shortest verse in the Bible.

JOHN 11:17-44

When Jesus arrived, he found that Lazarus had already been in the tomb
four days. Now Bethany was near Jerusalem, some two miles away, and
many of the Jews had come to Martha and Mary to console them about
their brother. When Martha heard that Jesus was coming, she went and
met him, while Mary stayed at home. Martha said to Jesus, "Lord, if you
had been here, my brother would not have died. But even now I know
that God will give you whatever you ask of him." Jesus said to her, "Your
brother will rise again." Martha said to him, "I know that he will rise
again in the resurrection on the last day." Jesus said to her, "I am the
resurrection and the life. Those who believe in me, even though they die,
will live, and everyone who lives and believes in me will never die. Do
you believe this?" She said to him, "Yes, Lord, I believe that you are the
Messiah, the Son of God, the one coming into the world."

When she had said this, she went back and called her sister Mary, and
told her privately, "The Teacher is here and is calling for you." And when
she heard it, she got up quickly and went to him. Now Jesus had not yet
come to the village, but was still at the place where Martha had met him.
The Jews who were with her in the house, consoling her, saw Mary get
up quickly and go out. They followed her because they thought that she
was going to the tomb to weep there. When Mary came where Jesus was
and saw him, she knelt at his feet and said to him, "Lord, if you had been
here, my brother would not have died." When Jesus saw her weeping, and

the Jews who came with her also weeping, he was greatly disturbed in spirit and deeply moved. He said, "Where have you laid him?" They said to him, "Lord, come and see." Jesus began to weep. So the Jews said, "See how he loved him!" But some of them said, "Could not he who opened the eyes of the blind man have kept this man from dying?"

Then Jesus, again greatly disturbed, came to the tomb. It was a cave, and a stone was lying against it. Jesus said, "Take away the stone." Martha, the sister of the dead man, said to him, "Lord, already there is a stench because he has been dead four days." Jesus said to her, "Did I not tell you that if you believed, you would see the glory of God?" So they took away the stone. And Jesus looked upward and said, "Father, I thank you for having heard me. I knew that you always hear me, but I have said this for the sake of the crowd standing here, so that they may believe that you sent me." When he had said this, he cried with a loud voice, "Lazarus, come out!" The dead man came out, his hands and feet bound with strips of cloth, and his face wrapped in a cloth. Jesus said to them, "Unbind him, and let him go."

TOUCH ME NOT

Mary Magdalene has gotten a bad rap. In this story and others, she is a prominent follower of Jesus. In fact, she is the only person mentioned in all four gospels as a witness to the empty tomb. Attempting to play down her prominence, preachers since Pope Gregory the Great have falsely identified her with the unnamed woman caught in adultery that Jesus saves from stoning (John 8:2–11). Adding insult to injury, they have also asserted that she was not only an adulterer, but a prostitute. Indeed, since the seventeenth century, "Magdalene" has been another name for a reformed prostitute. Blockbusters from *The Last Temptation of Christ* to *The Passion of the Christ* have reinforced this false image. Forget all of that when you're reading this story.

JOHN 20:1–18

Early on the first day of the week, while it was still dark, Mary Magdalene came to the tomb and saw that the stone had been removed from the tomb. So she ran and went to Simon Peter and the other disciple, the one whom Jesus loved, and said to them, "They have taken the Lord out of the tomb, and we do not know where they have laid him." Then Peter and the other disciple set out and went toward the tomb. The two were running together, but the other disciple outran Peter and reached the tomb first. He bent down to look in and saw the linen wrappings lying there, but he did not go in. Then Simon Peter came, following him, and went into the tomb. He saw the linen wrappings lying there, and the cloth that had been on Jesus' head, not lying with the linen wrappings but rolled up in a place by itself. Then the other disciple, who reached the tomb first, also went in, and he saw and believed; for as yet they did not understand the scripture, that he must rise from the dead. Then the disciples returned to their homes.

Noli me tangere, "Touch me not," is the Latin Vulgate version of the phrase here translated "Do not hold on to me." It has found many postbiblical lives, from the name of a flower, *Impatiens noli-tangere,* to the motto of a number of U.S. military divisions.

But Mary stood weeping outside the tomb. As she wept, she bent over to look into the tomb; and she saw two angels in white, sitting where the body of Jesus had been lying, one at the head and the other at the feet. They said to her, "Woman, why are you weeping?" She said to them, "They have taken away my Lord, and I do not know where they have laid him." When she had said this, she turned around and saw Jesus standing there, but she did not know that it was Jesus. Jesus said to her, "Woman, why are you weeping? Whom are you looking for?" Supposing him to be the gardener, she said to him, "Sir, if you have carried him away, tell me where you have laid him, and I will take him away." Jesus said to her, "Mary!" She turned and said to him in Hebrew, "Rabbouni!" (which means Teacher). Jesus said to her, "Do not hold on to me, because I have not yet ascended to the Father. But go to my brothers and say to them, 'I am ascending to my Father and your Father, to my God and your God.'" Mary Magdalene went and announced to the disciples, "I have seen the Lord"; and she told them that he had said these things to her.

DOUBTING THOMAS

"Doubting Thomas," who needed to touch Jesus's wounds for himself in order to believe that he had risen from the dead, was Mark Twain's favorite disciple. He was the first scientist, making a careful examination of the empirical data before accepting the resurrection as a fact. "It seems to me," Twain wrote, "that we owe that hard-headed—or sound-headed—witness something more than a slur."

JOHN 20:19–29

When it was evening on that day, the first day of the week, and the doors of the house where the disciples had met were locked for fear of the Jews, Jesus came and stood among them and said, "Peace be with you." After he said this, he showed them his hands and his side. Then the disciples rejoiced when they saw the Lord. Jesus said to them again, "Peace be with you. As the Father has sent me, so I send you." When he had said this, he breathed on them and said to them, "Receive the Holy Spirit. If you forgive the sins of any, they are forgiven them; if you retain the sins of any, they are retained."

But Thomas (who was called the Twin), one of the twelve, was not with them when Jesus came. So the other disciples told him, "We have seen the Lord." But he said to them, "Unless I see the mark of the nails in his hands, and put my finger in the mark of the nails and my hand in his side, I will not believe."

A week later his disciples were again in the house, and Thomas was with them. Although the doors were shut, Jesus came and stood among them and said, "Peace be with you." Then he said to Thomas, "Put your finger here and see my hands. Reach out your hand and put it in my side. Do not doubt but believe." Thomas answered him, "My Lord and my God!" Jesus said to him, "Have you believed because you have seen me? Blessed are those who have not seen and yet have come to believe."

Acts of the Apostles

PENTECOST

A century ago, the charismatic movement known as Pentecostalism was born among a racially and economically mixed group of women and men in a house on Azusa Street in Los Angeles. Assailed by reporters and mainline ministers as possessed or drunken lunatics, they saw their own story, in light of this biblical story, as a rebirth of the church, richly blessed with gifts of the spirit. The birth of the church in the biblical story also looked to outsiders like some kind of drunken orgy.

Note how the story from Acts (the second part to Luke) emphasizes the continuity of the new church with Judaism. Those present were observing the Jewish holiday of Pentecost, which is the Greek name for Shavuot, the Festival of Weeks, commemorating the giving of the Ten Commandments. Is there a parallel here between the giving of the Holy Spirit, guiding this new community, and the giving of the law, guiding the newly liberated Israelites through the wilderness? Taking it in another direction, might this be a reversal of Babel?

ACTS 2:1-13

When the day of Pentecost had come, they were all together in one place. And suddenly from heaven there came a sound like the rush of a violent wind, and it filled the entire house where they were sitting. Divided tongues, as of fire, appeared among them, and a tongue rested on each of them. All of them were filled with the Holy Spirit and began to speak in other languages, as the Spirit gave them ability.

Now there were devout Jews from every nation under heaven living in Jerusalem. And at this sound the crowd gathered and was bewildered, because each one heard them speaking in the native language of each. Amazed and astonished, they asked, "Are not all these who are speaking Galileans? And how is it that we hear, each of us, in our own native language? Parthians, Medes, Elamites, and residents of Mesopotamia, Judea and Cappadocia, Pontus and Asia, Phrygia and Pamphylia, Egypt and the parts of Libya belonging to Cyrene, and visitors from Rome, both Jews and proselytes, Cretans and Arabs—in our own languages we hear them speaking about God's deeds of power." All were amazed and perplexed, saying to one another, "What does this mean?" But others sneered and said, "They are filled with new wine."

ALL THINGS IN COMMON

Jesus was not the three-car-garage type. He saw riches as a major obstacle to salvation—harder than putting a camel through the eye of a needle. It looks as though the newly formed community of his followers was just as radical. How is this not an ancient form of communism? In any case, this story has been a bit of a problem for those preachers who glorify material wealth.

ACTS 2:43-47; 4:32-37

Awe came upon everyone, because many wonders and signs were being done by the apostles. All who believed were together and had all things in common; they would sell their possessions and goods and distribute the proceeds to all, as any had need. Day by day, as they spent much time together in the temple, they broke bread at home and ate their food with glad and generous hearts, praising God and having the goodwill of all the people. And day by day the Lord added to their number those who were being saved.

. . . Now the whole group of those who believed were of one heart and soul, and no one claimed private ownership of any possessions, but everything they owned was held in common. With great power the apostles gave their testimony to the resurrection of the Lord Jesus, and great grace was upon them all. There was not a needy person among them, for as many as owned lands or houses sold them and brought the proceeds of what was sold. They laid it at the apostles' feet, and it was distributed to each as any had need. There was a Levite, a native of Cyprus, Joseph, to whom the apostles gave the name Barnabas (which means "son of encouragement"). He sold a field that belonged to him, then brought the money, and laid it at the apostles' feet.

ON THE ROAD TO DAMASCUS

Sometimes the call to conversion can hit you like a truck, knocking you off course and setting you on a new one. So it goes for Saul. One moment he's bound and determined to squelch the new Jesus movement, and the next he's on his way to becoming its greatest advocate.

Everything is changed. And yet, in another sense, nothing has changed. The former self is still there. As the narrator of Ralph Ellison's *Invisible Man* recalls his wise grandfather saying, "You start Saul, and end up Paul. . . . When you're a young'un, you Saul, but let life whup your head a bit and you starts trying to be Paul—though you still Sauls around on the side." Conversion is never really complete, as Paul occasionally confesses in his own letters.

ACTS 9:1–25

Meanwhile Saul, still breathing threats and murder against the disciples of the Lord, went to the high priest and asked him for letters to the synagogues at Damascus, so that if he found any who belonged to the Way, men or women, he might bring them bound to Jerusalem. Now as he was going along and approaching Damascus, suddenly a light from heaven flashed around him. He fell to the ground and heard a voice saying to him, "Saul, Saul, why do you persecute me?" He asked, "Who are you, Lord?" The reply came, "I am Jesus, whom you are persecuting. But get up and enter the city, and you will be told what you are to do." The men who were traveling with him stood speechless because they heard the voice but saw no one. Saul got up from the ground, and though his eyes were open, he could see nothing; so they led him by the hand and brought him into Damascus. For three days he was without sight, and neither ate nor drank.

Now there was a disciple in Damascus named Ananias. The Lord said to him in a vision, "Ananias." He answered, "Here I am, Lord." The Lord said to him, "Get up and go to the street called Straight, and at the house of Judas look for a man of Tarsus named Saul. At this moment he is praying, and he has seen in a vision a man named Ananias come in and lay his hands on him so that he might regain his sight." But Ananias answered, "Lord, I have heard from many about this man, how much evil he has done to your saints in Jerusalem; and here he has authority from the chief priests to bind all who invoke your name." But the Lord said to him, "Go, for he is an instrument whom I have chosen to bring my name before Gentiles and kings and before the people of Israel; I myself will show him how much he must suffer for the sake of my name." So Ananias went and entered the house. He laid his hands on Saul and said, "Brother Saul, the Lord Jesus, who appeared to you on your way here, has sent me so that you may regain your sight and be filled with the Holy Spirit." And immediately something like scales fell from his eyes, and his sight was restored. Then he got up and was baptized, and after taking some food, he regained his strength.

For several days he was with the disciples in Damascus, and immediately he began to proclaim Jesus in the synagogues, saying, "He is the Son of God." All who heard him were amazed and said, "Is not this the man who made havoc in Jerusalem among those who invoked this name? And has he not come here for the purpose of bringing them bound before the chief priests?" Saul became increasingly more powerful and confounded the Jews who lived in Damascus by proving that Jesus was the Messiah.

After some time had passed, the Jews plotted to kill him, but their plot became known to Saul. They were watching the gates day and night so that they might kill him; but his disciples took him by night and let him down through an opening in the wall, lowering him in a basket.

The Letters of Paul

It would be tough to overestimate the influence of Paul on American culture, let alone religion. Indeed, Christianity bears Paul's imprint almost as much as Jesus's. Yet Paul didn't write theological treatises; he wrote letters to real people dealing with real issues that came from their own unique situations. It was those very practical, personal, pastoral interactions that inspired the many phrases and images that continue to find their way into contemporary culture.

Letters aren't stories, but there are stories behind them. As you read, remember that you are eavesdropping on one side of a two-way conversation in progress. What's the story? What was the other side saying?

ONE BODY, MANY PARTS

1 CORINTHIANS 12:12-26

For just as the body is one and has many members, and all the members of the body, though many, are one body, so it is with Christ. For in the one Spirit we were all baptized into one body—Jews or Greeks, slaves or free—and we were all made to drink of one Spirit.

Indeed, the body does not consist of one member but of many. If the foot would say, "Because I am not a hand, I do not belong to the body," that would not make it any less a part of the body. And if the ear would say, "Because I am not an eye, I do not belong to the body," that would not make it any less a part of the body. If the whole body were an eye, where would the hearing be? If the whole body were hearing, where would the sense of smell be? But as it is, God arranged the members in the body, each one of them, as he chose. If all were a single member, where would the body be? As it is, there are many members, yet one body. The eye cannot say to the hand, "I have no need of you," nor again the head to the feet, "I have no need of you." On the contrary, the members of the body that seem to be weaker are indispensable, and those members of the body that we think less honorable we clothe with greater honor, and our less respectable members are treated with greater respect; whereas our more respectable members do not need this. But God has so arranged the body, giving the greater honor to the inferior member, that there may be no dissension within the body, but the members may have the same care for one another. If one member suffers, all suffer together with it; if one member is honored, all rejoice together with it.

"THE GREATEST OF THESE IS LOVE"

1 CORINTHIANS 13:1-13

In his 2009 inaugural address, President Barack Obama called for his country to move beyond political partisanship with reference to this passage when he said, "We remain a young nation, but in the words of Scripture, the time has come to set aside childish things." In the final stanzas of her inaugural poem, "Praise Song for the Day," Elizabeth Alexander also alludes to this passage, this time speaking explicitly of love. "What if the mightiest word is love?" she wonders, and then elaborates

If I speak in the tongues of mortals and of angels, but do not have love, I am a noisy gong or a clanging cymbal. And if I have prophetic powers, and understand all mysteries and all knowledge, and if I have all faith, so as to remove mountains, but do not have love, I am nothing. If I give away all my possessions, and if I hand over my body so that I may boast, but do not have love, I gain nothing.

Love is patient; love is kind; love is not envious or boastful or arrogant or rude. It does not insist on its own way; it is not irritable or resentful; it does not rejoice in wrongdoing, but rejoices in the truth. It bears all things, believes all things, hopes all things, endures all things.

Love never ends. But as for prophecies, they will come to an end; as for tongues, they will cease; as for knowledge, it will come to an end. For we know only in part, and we prophesy only in part; but when the complete comes, the partial will come to an end. When I was a child, I spoke like a child, I thought like a child, I reasoned like a child; when I became an adult, I put an end to childish ways. For now we see in a mirror, dimly, but then we will see face to face. Now I know only in part; then I will know fully, even as I have been fully known. And now faith, hope, and love abide, these three; and the greatest of these is love.

on what she means in a way very reminiscent of Paul's own poetics of love: beyond love of spouse, family, or even nation, this love is expansive, fearless, hopeful: "love that casts a widening pool of light ... with no need to pre-empt grievance." With this mighty possibility in mind, she concludes,

On the brink, on the brim,
  on the cusp,
praise song for walking
  forward in that light.

"A THORN IN THE FLESH"

2 CORINTHIANS 12:1–10

It is necessary to boast; nothing is to be gained by it, but I will go on to visions and revelations of the Lord. I know a person in Christ who fourteen years ago was caught up to the third heaven—whether in the body or out of the body I do not know; God knows. And I know that such a person—whether in the body or out of the body I do not know; God knows—was caught up into Paradise and heard things that are not to be told, that no mortal is permitted to repeat. On behalf of such a one I will boast, but on my own behalf I will not boast, except of my weaknesses. But if I wish to boast, I will not be a fool, for I will be speaking the truth. But I refrain from it, so that no one may think better of me than what is seen in me or heard from me, even considering the exceptional character of the revelations. Therefore, to keep me from being too elated, a thorn was given me in the flesh, a messenger of Satan to torment me, to keep me

SIGNATURE PAUL?

Of the twenty-one letters in the New Testament, thirteen are attributed to the apostle Paul. Paul never met Jesus, nor did he know the gospels (they were written well over a decade after he died, and he never mentions any of their stories). Yet his influence on early Christianity as it spread throughout the Roman Empire was huge. What, if anything, would Christianity be without him? It's impossible to know.

Paul was very popular among the early Christians. His name carried a lot of weight. It's no surprise, then, that others wrote letters using his name as a pseudonym. Could it be that some of those pseudonymous letters made it into the New Testament? Absolutely. Based on careful analysis of vocabulary, writing style, and other evidence, many scholars consider some of the Pauline letters to be "deutero-Pauline," that is, written in his name by later authors who identified with his legacy. The most likely candidates are the "Pastoral Letters," 1–2 Timothy and Titus, which presume a level of ecclesiastical structure and hierarchy that probably didn't exist in Paul's time. This would help explain some discrepancies between these and other Pauline letters. At the end of his letter to the Romans, for example, Paul happily acknowledges several women who are authoritative leaders in the emerging Jesus movement, including Junia, whom he calls "prominent among the apostles" (16:7); and in Galatians, he proclaims that there is "no longer male and female; for all of you are one in Christ Jesus" (3:28). Yet in the first letter to Timothy, we read, "I permit no woman to teach or to have authority over a man; she is to keep silent" (2:12).

from being too elated. Three times I appealed to the Lord about this, that it would leave me, but he said to me, "My grace is sufficient for you, for power is made perfect in weakness." So, I will boast all the more gladly of my weaknesses, so that the power of Christ may dwell in me. Therefore I am content with weaknesses, insults, hardships, persecutions, and calamities for the sake of Christ; for whenever I am weak, then I am strong.

"NO LONGER JEW OR GREEK"

GALATIANS 3:28

There is no longer Jew or Greek, there is no longer slave or free, there is no longer male and female; for all of you are one in Christ Jesus.

JewGreek is greekjew. Extremes meet.

—James Joyce, *Ulysses*

Revelation

SACRED HORROR

Horror master Clive Barker once said that you can find two books in almost every American home, a Bible and a Stephen King novel. If there's a Bible in King's home, or in Barker's, it probably falls open to Revelation. This biblical book of horrors has been a veritable monster-making manual for modern writers and directors. The initial vision of the risen Christ is a good example. As you read, try to imagine what's being described. Does it come together in a single, unified picture? Or is this description beyond depiction?

REVELATION 1:9-19

I, John, your brother who share with you in Jesus the persecution and the kingdom and the patient endurance, was on the island called Patmos because of the word of God and the testimony of Jesus. I was in the spirit on the Lord's day, and I heard behind me a loud voice like a trumpet saying, "Write in a book what you see and send it to the seven churches, to Ephesus, to Smyrna, to Pergamum, to Thyatira, to Sardis, to Philadelphia, and to Laodicea."

Then I turned to see whose voice it was that spoke to me, and on turning I saw seven golden lampstands, and in the midst of the lampstands I saw one like the Son of Man, clothed with a long robe and with a golden sash across his chest. His head and his hair were white as white wool, white as snow; his eyes were like a flame of fire, his feet were like burnished bronze, refined as in a furnace, and his voice was like the sound of many waters. In his right hand he held seven stars, and from his mouth

LEAVING "LEFT BEHIND" BEHIND

The book of Revelation, also known as the Apocalypse of John, is the only work of apocalyptic literature in the New Testament. There were other apocalyptic scriptures in circulation in the early centuries of Christianity, but Revelation was the only one that made the cut. And even its inclusion was controversial well into the fourth century.

An apocalypse, from the Greek *apokalupto,* "uncover" or "reveal," is a text that claims to mediate a divine revelation. It might be about the future or the past. Most often, it's about an alternative way of seeing the present and the very near future. So it is in Revelation, where the Roman Empire is reimagined as a new Babylon, a monstrously diabolical oppressor of the people of God. In its climactic vision of the Second Coming, it envisions a time soon to come in which that oppressive regime will be overcome and a New Jerusalem will be established.

Most of us are familiar with the ways televangelists and bestselling Christian writers use the book of Revelation

came a sharp, two-edged sword, and his face was like the sun shining with full force.

When I saw him, I fell at his feet as though dead. But he placed his right hand on me, saying, "Do not be afraid; I am the first and the last, and the living one. I was dead, and see, I am alive forever and ever; and I have the keys of Death and of Hades. Now write what you have seen, what is, and what is to take place after this.

SEVEN SEALS AND FOUR HORSEMEN

The opening of the seven seals by the Lamb (an image of the risen Christ) is as fascinating as it is confusing. It's a revelation of something that remains hidden, shrouded in symbolism that we can't quite decipher.

to predict an imminent Judgment Day, the Rapture, and so on. They read it as an encoded script for the unfolding of the "end times." Locusts are seen as fighter planes, Babylon as the Soviet Union or Iraq or the World Bank, the mark of the beast as a credit-card number or digital chip, and Armageddon as the impending Third World War. Most of us avoid these overzealous decryptions of the book of Revelation like the plague. And, because they claim such absolute authority over the meaning of the book itself, we steer clear of it too. That's unfortunate, because Revelation is a remarkable work of literature in its own right.

So, leave the Left-Behinders behind long enough to read the text on its own terms. As you do, try to resist the temptation to decode it, linking its various images, characters, and events to our contemporary world. Instead, consider the richly poetic, suggestive qualities of its visions, which have inspired so many very different meanings and reimaginings over the centuries.

The four horsemen, released with the first four seals, have had many postbiblical resurrections, including quartets of football backfielders, groups of professional tag-team wrestlers, and the four members of Metallica performing their hit song "The Four Horsemen." Perhaps the most popular apocalyptic horseman is the mysterious, death-dealing preacher of few words in Clint Eastwood's *Pale Rider* (1985).

As you read, notice how the successive opening of each seal builds drama and suspense into the process of revelation, culminating with the seventh seal.

REVELATION 6:1-17; 8:1-5

Then I saw the Lamb open one of the seven seals, and I heard one of the four living creatures call out, as with a voice of thunder, "Come!"

I looked, and there was a white horse! Its rider had a bow; a crown was given to him, and he came out conquering and to conquer.

When he opened the second seal, I heard the second living creature call out, "Come!" And out came another horse, bright red; its rider was permitted to take peace from the earth, so that people would slaughter one another; and he was given a great sword.

When he opened the third seal, I heard the third living creature call out, "Come!" I looked, and there was a black horse! Its rider held a pair of scales in his hand, and I heard what seemed to be a voice in the midst of the four living creatures saying, "A quart of wheat for a day's pay, and three quarts of barley for a day's pay, but do not damage the olive oil and the wine!"

When he opened the fourth seal, I heard the voice of the fourth living creature call out, "Come!" I looked and there was a pale green horse! Its rider's name was Death, and Hades followed with him; they were given authority over a fourth of the earth, to kill with sword, famine, and pestilence, and by the wild animals of the earth.

This opening of *New York Herald-Tribune* writer Grantland Rice's report on the University of Notre Dame's win over Army on October 18, 1924, is the most famous newspaper lead in the history of sports journalism:

> Outlined against a blue-gray October sky, the Four Horsemen rode again. In dramatic lore they are known as Famine, Pestilence, Destruction and Death. These are only aliases. Their real names are

When he opened the fifth seal, I saw under the altar the souls of those who had been slaughtered for the word of God and for the testimony they had given; they cried out with a loud voice, "Sovereign Lord, holy and true, how long will it be before you judge and avenge our blood on the inhabitants of the earth?" They were each given a white robe and told to rest a little longer, until the number would be complete both of their fellow servants and of their brothers and sisters, who were soon to be killed as they themselves had been killed.

When he opened the sixth seal, I looked, and there came a great earthquake; the sun became black as sackcloth, the full moon became like blood, and the stars of the sky fell to the earth as the fig tree drops its winter fruit when shaken by a gale. The sky vanished like a scroll rolling itself up, and every mountain and island was removed from its place. Then the kings of the earth and the magnates and the generals and the rich and the powerful, and everyone, slave and free, hid in the caves and among the rocks of the mountains, calling to the mountains and rocks, "Fall on us and hide us from the face of the one seated on the throne and from the wrath of the Lamb; for the great day of their wrath has come, and who is able to stand?"

Stuhldreher, Miller, Crowley and Layden. They formed the crest of the South Bend cyclone before which another fighting Army football team was swept over the precipice at the Polo Grounds yesterday afternoon as 55,000 spectators peered down on the bewildering panorama spread on the green plain below.

. . . When the Lamb opened the seventh seal, there was silence in heaven for about half an hour. And I saw the seven angels who stand before God, and seven trumpets were given to them. Another angel with a golden censer came and stood at the altar; he was given a great quantity of incense to offer with the prayers of all the saints on the golden altar that is before the throne. And the smoke of the incense, with the prayers of the saints, rose before God from the hand of the angel. Then the angel took the censer and filled it with fire from the altar and threw it on the earth; and there were peals of thunder, rumblings, flashes of lightning, and an earthquake.

THE RED DRAGON

A warrior saves a damsel in distress from a dragon. Sound familiar? This story has given shape to countless postbiblical stories of dragon slayers—from Beowulf and St. George to Harry Potter, who saves Ginny from the Basilisk in *Harry Potter and the Chamber of Secrets*. But the dragon has also inspired more than one diabolical antihero. The iconic cannibal Hannibal Lecter, in Thomas Harris's *Silence of the Lambs* and *Red Dragon* (famously

played by Anthony Hopkins in the movie versions), for example, was obsessed with William Blake's biblically inspired paintings of the Red Dragon and the Woman Clothed with the Sun. What would draw Blake and Lecter, and perhaps even us, to this rebellious monster and his fallen angels?

REVELATION 12:1–9, 13–18

A great portent appeared in heaven: a woman clothed with the sun, with the moon under her feet, and on her head a crown of twelve stars. She was pregnant and was crying out in birth pangs, in the agony of giving birth. Then another portent appeared in heaven: a great red dragon, with seven heads and ten horns, and seven diadems on his heads. His tail swept down a third of the stars of heaven and threw them to the earth. Then the dragon stood before the woman who was about to bear a child, so that he might devour her child as soon as it was born. And she gave birth to a son, a male child, who is to rule all the nations with a rod of iron. But her child was snatched away and taken to God and to his throne; and the woman fled into the wilderness, where she has a place prepared by God, so that there she can be nourished for one thousand two hundred sixty days.

And war broke out in heaven; Michael and his angels fought against the dragon. The dragon and his angels fought back, but they were defeated, and there was no longer any place for them in heaven. The great dragon was thrown down, that ancient serpent, who is called the Devil and Satan, the deceiver of the whole world—he was thrown down to the earth, and his angels were thrown down with him.

. . . So when the dragon saw that he had been thrown down to the earth, he pursued the woman who had given birth to the male child. But the woman was given the two wings of the great eagle, so that she could fly from the serpent into the wilderness, to her place where she is nourished for a time, and times, and half a time. Then from his mouth the serpent poured water like a river after the woman, to sweep her away with the flood. But the earth came to the help of the woman; it opened its mouth and swallowed the river that the dragon had poured from his mouth. Then the dragon was angry with the woman, and went off to make war on the rest of her children, those who keep the commandments of God and hold the testimony of Jesus.

Then the dragon took his stand on the sand of the seashore.

SYMBOLISM IN REVELATION

Although much of the symbolism in Revelation is lost to us, some of it can be deciphered, at least partially. Here are some common meanings of familiar symbols from the book. The numbers derive from Jewish numerology and Greek mathematics.

Numbers

Three: the spiritual world, divinity

Four: creation, humanity

Seven: perfection and completion (three and a half is imperfection, incompletion)

Ten: totality

Twelve: Israel, the people of God (as in the twelve tribes)

Colors

White: overpowering victory

Red: war, bloodshed

Black: famine

Pale green: rot, death

Animals

Beasts, monsters, dragons: Satanic, evil, anti-God

Horns: power

Multiple heads: oligarchy

Lamb: sacrificial animal

Lion: royalty

Eagles, oxen: nobility, superiority

THE MARK OF THE BEAST

The blasphemous, many-headed beast, given authority to rule over humankind, seems to leap off the page and into our imaginations. How could such a monstrous figure attract such a huge following? From there, it's a short step to demonizing any world leader, religious or otherwise, who seems to enjoy a lot more popular appeal than we think he or she should. Then again, maybe we too have been seduced. How can we be sure that we are not already bearing the "mark of the beast"? What is it about this fantasy that invites us into what-if scenarios, pressing the question about which side we would be on?

REVELATION 13:1–18

And I saw a beast rising out of the sea, having ten horns and seven heads; and on its horns were ten diadems, and on its heads were blasphemous names. And the beast that I saw was like a leopard, its feet were like a bear's, and its mouth was like a lion's mouth. And the dragon gave it his power and his throne and great authority. One of its heads seemed to have received a death-blow, but its mortal wound had been healed. In amazement the whole earth followed the beast. They worshiped the dragon, for he had given his authority to the beast, and they worshiped the beast, saying, "Who is like the beast, and who can fight against it?"

The beast was given a mouth uttering haughty and blasphemous words, and it was allowed to exercise authority for forty-two months. It opened its mouth to utter blasphemies against God, blaspheming his name and his dwelling, that is, those who dwell in heaven. Also it was allowed to make war on the saints and to conquer them. It was given authority over every tribe and people and language and nation, and all the inhabitants of the earth will worship it, everyone whose name has not been written from the foundation of the world in the book of life of the Lamb that was slaughtered.

Let anyone who has an ear listen:

If you are to be taken captive,
　　into captivity you go;
if you kill with the sword,
　　with the sword you must be killed.

Here is a call for the endurance and faith of the saints.

Then I saw another beast that rose out of the earth; it had two horns like a lamb and it spoke like a dragon. It exercises all the authority of the first beast on its behalf, and it makes the earth and its inhabitants worship the first beast, whose mortal wound had been healed. It performs great signs, even making fire come down from heaven to earth in the sight of all; and by the signs that it is allowed to perform on behalf of the beast, it deceives the inhabitants of earth, telling them to make an image for the beast that had been wounded by the sword and yet lived; and it was allowed to give breath to the image of the beast so that the image of the beast could even speak and cause those who would not worship the image of the beast to be killed. Also it causes all, both small and great, both rich and poor, both free and slave, to be marked on the right hand or the forehead, so that no one can buy or sell who does not have the mark, that is, the name of the beast or the number of its name. This calls for wisdom: let anyone with understanding calculate the number of the beast, for it is the number of a person. Its number is six hundred sixty-six.

> The darkness drops again;
>   but now I know
> That twenty centuries of
>   stony sleep
> Were vexed to nightmare by
>   a rocking cradle,
> And what rough beast, its
>   hour come round at last,
> Slouches toward Bethlehem
>   to be born?
> —William Butler Yeats,
>   "Second Coming"

THE GRAPES OF WRATH

"Mine eyes have seen the glory of the coming of the Lord; He is trampling out the vintage where the grapes of wrath are stored." So begins the abolitionist anthem "Battle Hymn of the Republic," written in 1861 by Julia Ward Howe. The biblical passage that inspired her underscores how bloody its vision of deliverance from oppression is. In his novel *The Grapes of Wrath,* John Steinbeck transforms Howe's image into the wine press of the Dust Bowl, a context of suffering from which some redemption may ultimately come. Like so many biblical images, this one has proven to be highly adaptable to new pressing situations.

Then I looked, and there was a white cloud, and seated on the cloud was one like the Son of Man, with a golden crown on his head, and a sharp sickle in his hand! Another angel came out of the temple, calling with a loud voice to the one who sat on the cloud, "Use your sickle and reap, for the hour to reap has come, because the harvest of the earth is fully ripe." So the one who sat on the cloud swung his sickle over the earth, and the earth was reaped.

Then another angel came out of the temple in heaven, and he too had a sharp sickle. Then another angel came out from the altar, the angel who has authority over fire, and he called with a loud voice to him who had the sharp sickle, "Use your sharp sickle and gather the clusters of the vine of the earth, for its grapes are ripe." So the angel swung his sickle over the earth and gathered the vintage of the earth, and he threw it into the great wine press of the wrath of God. And the wine press was trodden outside the city, and blood flowed from the wine press, as high as a horse's bridle, for a distance of about two hundred miles.

END TIMES

A bumper sticker reads, "In case of Rapture this vehicle will be unmanned." The driver, apparently, expects to be swept up into heaven before things get ugly. Most of us, however, are not so sure how it's all going to pan out, or if it ever will. Still, it is a fascinating exercise of our imaginations to read how John of Patmos conceives the culmination of his grand vision. One thing is clear here: the end is not absolute. That is beyond even John's imagination. This ending is also a new beginning. It's the edge of the world as we know it.

Then I saw an angel standing in the sun, and with a loud voice he called to all the birds that fly in midheaven, "Come, gather for the great supper of God, to eat the flesh of kings, the flesh of captains, the flesh of the mighty, the flesh of horses and their riders—flesh of all, both free and slave, both small and great." Then I saw the beast and the kings of the earth with their armies gathered to make war against the rider on the horse and against his army. And the beast was captured, and with it the false prophet who had performed in its presence the signs by which he deceived those who had received the mark of the beast and those who worshiped its image. These two were thrown alive into the lake of fire that burns with sulfur. And the rest were killed by the sword of the rider on the horse, the sword that came from his mouth; and all the birds were gorged with their flesh.

As with many other images in Revelation, Gog and Magog are taken from the prophet Ezekiel (chapters 38–39). There, as here, they seem to be the names of the leaders of enemy armies gathering against God's people.

Then I saw an angel coming down from heaven, holding in his hand the key to the bottomless pit and a great chain. He seized the dragon, that ancient serpent, who is the Devil and Satan, and bound him for a thousand years, and threw him into the pit, and locked and sealed it over him, so that he would deceive the nations no more, until the thousand years were ended. After that he must be let out for a little while.

Then I saw thrones, and those seated on them were given authority to judge. I also saw the souls of those who had been beheaded for their testimony to Jesus and for the word of God. They had not worshiped the beast or its image and had not received its mark on their foreheads or their hands. They came to life and reigned with Christ a thousand years. (The rest of the dead did not come to life until the thousand years were ended.) This is the first resurrection. Blessed and holy are those who share in the first resurrection. Over these the second death has no power, but they will be priests of God and of Christ, and they will reign with him a thousand years.

When the thousand years are ended, Satan will be released from his prison and will come out to deceive the nations at the four corners of the earth, Gog and Magog, in order to gather them for battle; they are as numerous as the sands of the sea. They marched up over the breadth of the earth and surrounded the camp of the saints and the beloved city. And fire came down from heaven and consumed them. And the devil who had deceived them was thrown into the lake of fire and sulfur, where the beast and the false prophet were, and they will be tormented day and night forever and ever.

Then I saw a great white throne and the one who sat on it; the earth and the heaven fled from his presence, and no place was found for them. And I saw the dead, great and small, standing before the throne, and books were opened. Also another book was opened, the book of life. And the dead were judged according to their works, as recorded in the books. And the sea gave up the dead that were in it, Death and Hades gave up the dead that were in them, and all were judged according to what they had done. Then Death and Hades were thrown into the lake of fire. This is the second death, the lake of fire; and anyone whose name was not found written in the book of life was thrown into the lake of fire.

PART 3

Extras

Familiar Biblical Phrases and Images

ALL THINGS TO ALL PEOPLE (1 Corinthians 9:22):

To the weak I became weak, so that I might win the weak. I have become all things to all people, that I might by all means save some.

ALL THINGS WORK TOGETHER FOR GOOD (Romans 8:28):

We know that all things work together for good for those who love God, who are called according to his purpose.

AM I MY BROTHER'S KEEPER? (Genesis 4:9):

Then the LORD said to Cain, "Where is your brother Abel?" He said, "I do not know; am I my brother's keeper?"

ANCIENT OF DAYS (Daniel 7:9):

As I watched,
thrones were set in place,
    and an Ancient One [KJV: "ancient of days"] took his throne,
his clothing was white as snow,
    and the hair of his head like pure wool;
his throne was fiery flames,
    and its wheels were burning fire.

APPLE OF MY EYE (Deuteronomy 32:10; also Zechariah 2:8):

He sustained him in a desert land,
    in a howling wilderness waste;
he shielded him, cared for him,
    guarded him as the apple of his eye.

AS OLD AS METHUSELAH (Genesis 5:27):

Thus all the days of Methuselah were nine hundred sixty-nine years; and he died.

ASSURANCE OF THINGS HOPED FOR (Hebrews 11:1):

Now faith is the assurance of things hoped for, the conviction of things not seen.

AT WITS' END (Psalm 107:27):

They reeled and staggered like drunkards,
  and were at their wits' end.

BEGINNING OF SORROWS (Matthew 24:7–8):

For nation will rise against nation, and kingdom against kingdom, and there will be famines and earthquakes in various places: all this is but the beginning of the birth pangs [KJV: "beginning of sorrows"].

BLIND LEADING THE BLIND (Matthew 15:14):

Let them alone; they are blind guides of the blind. And if one blind person guides another, both will fall into a pit.

BY THE RIVERS OF BABYLON (Psalm 137:1):

By the rivers of Babylon—
there we sat down and there we wept
  when we remembered Zion.

CAN A LEOPARD CHANGE ITS SPOTS? (Jeremiah 13:23):

Can Ethiopians change their skin
  or leopards their spots?

CAST THE FIRST STONE (John 8:7):

Let anyone among you who is without sin be the first to throw a stone at her.

COAT OF MANY COLORS (Genesis 37:3):

Now Israel loved Joseph more than any other of his children, because he was the son of his old age; and he had made him a long robe with sleeves [KJV: "coat of many colors"].

COVER A MULTITUDE OF SINS (James 5:20; also 1 Peter 4:8):

You should know that whoever brings back a sinner from wandering will save the sinner's soul from death and will cover a multitude of sins.

CUP RUNNETH OVER (Psalm 23:5):
You prepare a table before me
   in the presence of my enemies;
you anoint my head with oil;
   my cup overflows [KJV: "runneth over"].

DEN OF ROBBERS (Jeremiah 7:11; also Matthew 21:13; Mark 11:17; Luke 19:46):
   Has this house, which is called by my name, become a den of robbers in your sight? You know, I too am watching, says the LORD.

DON'T HIDE YOUR LIGHT UNDER A BUSHEL BASKET (Matthew 5:15):
   No one after lighting a lamp puts it under the bushel basket, but on the lampstand, and it gives light to all in the house.

DON'T LET THE SUN GO DOWN ON YOUR ANGER (Ephesians 4:26):
   Be angry but do not sin; do not let the sun go down on your anger.

DON'T LOOK BACK (Genesis 19:17):
   When they had brought them outside, they said, "Flee for your life; do not look back or stop anywhere in the Plain; flee to the hills, or else you will be consumed."

DOUBTING THOMAS (John 20:24–25):
   But Thomas (who was called the Twin), one of the twelve, was not with them when Jesus came. So the other disciples told him, "We have seen the Lord." But he said to them, "Unless I see the mark of the nails in his hands, and put my finger in the mark of the nails and my hand in his side, I will not believe."

DROP IN A BUCKET (Isaiah 40:15):
Even the nations are like a drop from a bucket,
   and are accounted as dust on the scales;
   see, he takes up the isles like fine dust.

EARS TINGLE (1 Samuel 3:11):
   Then the LORD said to Samuel, "See, I am about to do something in Israel that will make both ears of anyone who hears of it tingle."

EAST OF EDEN (Genesis 4:16):

Then Cain went away from the presence of the Lord, and settled in the land of Nod, east of Eden.

EAT AND DRINK FOR TOMORROW WE DIE (Isaiah 22:12–13; also 1 Corinthians 15:32):

In that day the Lord God of hosts
   called to weeping and mourning,
   to baldness and putting on sackcloth;
but instead there was joy and festivity,
   killing oxen and slaughtering sheep,
   eating meat and drinking wine.
"Let us eat and drink,
   for tomorrow we die."

EAT, DRINK, BE MERRY (Luke 12:19):

And I will say to my soul, "Soul, you have ample goods laid up for many years; relax, eat, drink, be merry."

ENTERTAINING ANGELS UNAWARE (Hebrews 13:2):

Do not neglect to show hospitality to strangers, for by doing that some have entertained angels without knowing it.

EVERY WIND OF DOCTRINE (Ephesians 4:14):

We must no longer be children, tossed to and fro and blown about by every wind of doctrine, by people's trickery, by their craftiness in deceitful scheming.

EYE FOR AN EYE (Exodus 21:23–24; also Leviticus 24:19–20; Deuteronomy 19:21; Matthew 5:38):

If any harm follows, then you shall give life for life, eye for eye, tooth for tooth, hand for hand, foot for foot . . .

FALL FROM GRACE (Galatians 5:4):

You who want to be justified by the law have cut yourselves off from Christ; you have fallen away from grace.

FAT OF THE LAND (Genesis 45:18):

Take your father and your households and come to me, so that I may give you the best of the land of Egypt, and you may enjoy the fat of the land.

FEAR NO EVIL (Psalm 23:4):

Even though I walk through the darkest valley,

I fear no evil.

FIGHT THE GOOD FIGHT (1 Timothy 6:12):

Fight the good fight of the faith; take hold of the eternal life, to which you were called and for which you made the good confession in the presence of many witnesses.

FLY IN THE OINTMENT (Ecclesiastes 10:1):

Dead flies make the perfumer's ointment give off a foul odor;

so a little folly outweighs wisdom and honor.

FOR EVERYTHING THERE IS A SEASON (Ecclesiastes 3:1):

For everything there is a season, and a time for every matter under heaven.

FORBIDDEN FRUIT (Genesis 3:2–3):

The woman said to the serpent, "We may eat of the fruit of the trees in the garden; but God said, 'You shall not eat of the fruit of the tree that is in the middle of the garden, nor shall you touch it, or you shall die.'"

GET BEHIND ME, SATAN (Mark 8:33; also Matthew 16:23):

But turning and looking at his disciples, he rebuked Peter and said, "Get behind me, Satan! For you are setting your mind not on divine things but on human things."

GIVE UP THE GHOST (Acts 12:23):

And immediately, because he had not given the glory to God, an angel of the Lord struck him down, and he was eaten by worms and died [KJV: "gave up the ghost"].

GO FROM STRENGTH TO STRENGTH (Psalm 84:7):

They go from strength to strength;

the God of gods will be seen in Zion.

HARD-HEARTED (Exodus 7:3):

But I will harden Pharaoh's heart, and I will multiply my signs and wonders in the land of Egypt.

HOW THE MIGHTY HAVE FALLEN (2 Samuel 1:19):
Your glory, O Israel, lies slain upon your high places!
How the mighty have fallen!

LET MY PEOPLE GO (Exodus 5:1):

Afterward Moses and Aaron went to Pharaoh and said, "Thus says the LORD, the God of Israel, 'Let my people go, so that they may celebrate a festival to me in the wilderness.'"

LET THERE BE LIGHT (Genesis 1:3):

Then God said, "Let there be light"; and there was light.

LIGHT OF THE WORLD (Matthew 5:14):

You are the light of the world. A city built on a hill cannot be hid.

LIKE A LAMB TO THE SLAUGHTER (Isaiah 53:7; also Jeremiah 11:19):
He was oppressed, and he was afflicted,
    yet he did not open his mouth;
like a lamb that is led to the slaughter,
    and like a sheep that before its shearers is silent,
    so he did not open his mouth.

LIVE AND MOVE AND HAVE OUR BEING (Acts 17:28):

For "In him we live and move and have our being"; as even some of your own poets have said,
"For we too are his offspring."

LOVE OF MONEY (1 Timothy 6:10):

For the love of money is a root of all kinds of evil, and in their eagerness to be rich some have wandered away from the faith and pierced themselves with many pains.

MAN AFTER HIS OWN HEART (1 Samuel 13:13–14; also Acts 13:22):

Samuel said to Saul, "You have done foolishly; you have not kept the commandment of the LORD your God, which he commanded you. The LORD would have established your kingdom over Israel forever, but now your kingdom will not continue; the LORD has sought out a man after his own heart; and the LORD has appointed him to be ruler over his people, because you have not kept what the LORD commanded you."

MANY ARE CALLED BUT FEW ARE CHOSEN (Matthew 22:13–14):
Then the king said to the attendants, "Bind him hand and foot, and throw him into the outer darkness, where there will be weeping and gnashing of teeth." For many are called, but few are chosen.

NO REST FOR THE WICKED (Isaiah 57:20–21):
But the wicked are like the tossing sea
    that cannot keep still;
    its waters toss up mire and mud.
There is no peace, says my God, for the wicked.

OLD AS THE HILLS (Job 15:7):
Are you the firstborn of the human race?
    Were you brought forth before the hills?

OUT OF THE MOUTHS OF BABES (Psalm 8:2; also Matthew 21:16):
Out of the mouths of babes and infants
you have founded a bulwark because of your foes,
    to silence the enemy and the avenger.

PERSECUTED FOR RIGHTEOUSNESS' SAKE (Matthew 5:10):
Blessed are those who are persecuted for righteousness' sake, for theirs is the kingdom of heaven.

PHYSICIAN, HEAL THYSELF (Luke 4:23):
Doubtless you will quote to me this proverb, "Doctor, cure yourself!"

PLOWSHARES INTO SWORDS (Joel 3:10):
Beat your plowshares into swords,
and your pruning hooks into spears;
    let the weakling say, "I am a warrior."

POWERS THAT BE (Romans 13:1):
Let every person be subject to the governing authorities; for there is no authority except from God, and those authorities that exist [KJV: "powers that be"] have been instituted by God.

REAP THE WHIRLWIND (Hosea 8:7):
For they sow the wind,
    and they shall reap the whirlwind.

REAP WHAT YOU SOW (Galatians 6:7; also Job 4:8; Matthew 25:24; Luke 19:21):

Do not be deceived; God is not mocked, for you reap whatever you sow.

RISE AND SHINE (Isaiah 60:1):
Arise, shine; for your light has come,
  and the glory of the LORD has risen upon you.

ROOT OF THE MATTER (Job 19:28–29):
If you say, "How we will persecute him!"
  and, "The root of the matter is found in him";
be afraid of the sword,
  for wrath brings the punishment of the sword,
  so that you may know there is a judgment.

SALT OF THE EARTH (Matthew 5:13):

You are the salt of the earth; but if salt has lost its taste, how can its saltiness be restored? It is no longer good for anything, but is thrown out and trampled under foot.

SEE THROUGH A GLASS DARKLY (1 Corinthians 13:12):

For now we see in a mirror, dimly [KJV: "through a glass, darkly"], but then we will see face to face. Now I know only in part; then I will know fully, even as I have been fully known.

SIGHS TOO DEEP FOR WORDS (Romans 8:26):

Likewise the Spirit helps us in our weakness; for we do not know how to pray as we ought, but that very Spirit intercedes with sighs too deep for words.

SIGNS OF THE TIMES (Matthew 16:2–3):

When it is evening, you say, "It will be fair weather, for the sky is red." And in the morning, "It will be stormy today, for the sky is red and threatening." You know how to interpret the appearance of the sky, but you cannot interpret the signs of the times.

SKIN OF MY TEETH (Job 19:20):
My bones cling to my skin and to my flesh,
  and I have escaped by the skin of my teeth.

SOUR GRAPES (Ezekiel 18:2; also Jeremiah 31:29–30):

What do you mean by repeating this proverb concerning the land of Israel, "The parents have eaten sour grapes, and the children's teeth are set on edge"?

SPIRIT IS WILLING BUT THE FLESH IS WEAK (Matthew 26:41):

Stay awake and pray that you may not come into the time of trial; the spirit indeed is willing, but the flesh is weak.

SWORDS INTO PLOWSHARES (Isaiah 2:4; also Micah 4:3):

He shall judge between the nations,
   and shall arbitrate for many peoples;
they shall beat their swords into plowshares,
   and their spears into pruning hooks;
nation shall not lift up sword against nation,
   neither shall they learn war any more.

THORN IN THE FLESH (2 Corinthians 12:7):

Therefore, to keep me from being too elated, a thorn was given me in the flesh, a messenger of Satan to torment me, to keep me from being too elated.

WARS AND RUMORS OF WARS (Matthew 24:6):

And you will hear of wars and rumors of wars; see that you are not alarmed; for this must take place, but the end is not yet.

WHAT GOD HAS JOINED TOGETHER (Matthew 19:6):

So they are no longer two, but one flesh. Therefore what God has joined together, let no one separate.

WHERE NEITHER MOTH NOR RUST CONSUMES (Matthew 6:20):

Store up for yourselves treasures in heaven, where neither moth nor rust consumes and where thieves do not break in and steal.

WHERE TWO OR THREE ARE GATHERED (Matthew 18:20):

For where two or three are gathered in my name, I am there among them.

WOE IS ME (Job 10:15):

If I am wicked, woe to me!
   If I am righteous, I cannot lift up my head,

for I am filled with disgrace
  and look upon my affliction.

WRITING ON THE WALL (Daniel 5:4–6):

They drank the wine and praised the gods of gold and silver, bronze, iron, wood, and stone. Immediately the fingers of a human hand appeared and began writing on the plaster of the wall of the royal palace, next to the lampstand. The king was watching the hand as it wrote. Then the king's face turned pale, and his thoughts terrified him. His limbs gave way, and his knees knocked together.

VALLEY OF THE SHADOW OF DEATH (Psalm 23:4):

Even though I walk through the darkest valley,
[KJV: "Yea, though I walk through the valley of the shadow of death,"]
  I fear no evil.

Glossary of Biblical Key Words

AARON, Moses's older brother, co-leader of the Exodus, and first leader of the priesthood.

ABEL, one of the two first sons of Eve and Adam; he is killed by his brother Cain.

ABRAHAM, the first patriarch of Israel; God changed his name from Abram ("father on high") to Abraham ("father of many").

ABSALOM, David's beloved son and rival. When Absalom's sister Tamar is raped by his half brother Amnon, he has Amnon killed and then flees, becoming an enemy of the Davidic kingdom. At one point he takes Jerusalem, but his armies are eventually defeated and he is killed.

ACTS OF THE APOSTLES (New Testament), part two of the Gospel of Luke, recounting the beginnings of the Jesus movement as it grows and spreads throughout the Roman Empire. The central figures are Peter, the leader of the church in Jerusalem, and Paul (formerly Saul), an opponent of the movement who converts and becomes its greatest proponent. Acts ends with Paul's arrest in Jerusalem and transfer to Rome, where he is eventually executed.

AD (*Anno Domini,* Latin, "year of our Lord"), the older, Christian designation for the era now more commonly called CE, "Common Era."

ADAM AND EVE, the first human couple. In Hebrew *'adam* is the generic term for "human" (either sex) as well as the proper name for the first man, Adam. It is related to *'adamah,* "earth." God creates *ha'adam,* "the human" (with the definite article *ha*), from *ha'adamah,* "the humus." Once divided into male and female, the male part is given the proper name Adam. Adam then names the female part Eve, that is, *havvah,* related to the verb "live," because she is the mother of all living.

ADONAI ("my lord," from Hebrew *'adon,* "lord" or "master"), a term used both for human masters ("my lord") and for God, usually in combination with the divine name YHWH (i.e., *'adonai yhwh,* translated "Lord God" in small capitals). *See also* tetragrammaton.

ADONIJAH, David's son who failed to succeed him as king; Solomon has him executed.

AHAB, ruler of the Northern Kingdom (Israel), husband of Jezebel, and opponent of the prophets Elijah and Elisha.

AHASUERUS, the insecure and showy king of Persia in the story of Esther, also known as Xerxes I (486–465 BCE), the grandson of Cyrus the Great.

AMALEKITES, according to biblical legend, the descendants of Jacob's brother Esau. They were frequent foes of the Israelites in Canaan from the time of Moses to the time of David.

AMMONITES, enemies of the Israelites during their conquest of Canaan. They were located in the plateau area just east of the Jordan River. Biblical legend demeans them as descendants of Lot resulting from his incestuous relationship with his younger daughter. *See also* Moabites.

AMORITES, one of the populations living in Canaan before the Israelite conquest; also the ancient people from the north who founded Mari and Babylon.

AMOS (Hebrew Bible), one of the twelve Minor Prophets. Amos prophesied against the Northern Kingdom during the eighth century BCE. His impassioned judgments against the injustices of powerful religious and political leaders made him unpopular in his day.

ANGEL (from Greek *angelos,* "messenger"; Hebrew *mal'ak*), a messenger of God. As revelations of divine otherness, angels tend to terrify—most often the first thing they say is, "Fear not."

ANNA, a prophetess in the Jerusalem Temple who, along with Simeon, recognizes the baby Jesus as Israel's promised Messiah in Luke.

ANNUNCIATION, the story in Luke of the angel Gabriel's announcement to Mary that she will bear the Messiah.

ANTICHRIST, a term used in 2 and 3 John to describe opponents of the gospel. Later uses of the term in reference to someone who will come before Christ's return and falsely claim to be God derive from other texts, especially 2 Thessalonians 2 and Revelation 13.

ANTIOCHUS, Antiochus IV Epiphanes, the ruler of the Seleucid Empire remembered for his "abomination of desolation" against the Jerusalem Temple in 167 BCE (mentioned in Daniel and 1 Maccabees). His actions led to the Maccabean revolt, which led to the rededication of the Temple, celebrated during Hanukkah.

APOCALYPSE (from Greek *apokalupto,* "uncover" or "unhide," the equivalent of Latin *revelare,* "unveil"), a text that claims to mediate a divine revelation.

APOCALYPSE OF JOHN (New Testament). *See* Revelation.

APOCRYPHA, the name of the deuterocanonical works that were part of the Greek Septuagint version of the Hebrew Bible and are included in the Roman Catholic and Orthodox canons of Scripture. The term "apocryphal" also sometimes refers to other noncanonical writings that are roughly contemporary with canonical ones (e.g., the *Gospel of Thomas*).

APOSTLE, someone who is sent, as a messenger. Jesus's disciples are called apostles because Jesus, after his resurrection, sends them forth to spread the good news to the ends of the earth. Paul is called an apostle after he is called to do the same.

ARAMAIC, the lingua franca of Jewish people in Palestine and Mesopotamia during the time of Jesus. It is closely related to Hebrew and uses the same alphabet and script. Parts of Daniel and Ezra in the Hebrew Bible are written in Aramaic.

ARK, the boat that Noah, his family, and the animals lived in during the flood.

ARK OF THE COVENANT, an ornate box containing the Ten Commandments, Aaron's staff, and a portion of manna. Its construction is described in Exodus (25:10–22). The Philistines capture it from King Saul; David is the hero for bringing it back.

ARMAGEDDON, a Greek transliteration of the Hebrew *har-megiddon,* "mountain of Megiddo." Megiddo was a plain in the Jezreel Valley of northern Palestine where the Israelites fought several battles. In Revelation, Armageddon is the site of the final battle between the forces of God and the forces of evil.

ASCENSION, Jesus's departure into the heavens after his resurrection, described in Acts 1.

ASSYRIA, the ancient Mesopotamian superpower that competed with Egypt for dominance over Palestine from the eleventh to the seventh century BCE. The Assyrians conquered the Northern Kingdom, Israel, in 722 BCE and laid siege to Jerusalem, the capital of Judah, the Southern Kingdom, in 701 BCE.

AUGUSTUS, Julius Caesar's adopted heir and Roman emperor (27 BCE–14 CE) at the time of Jesus's birth.

BAAL, a Canaanite word meaning "lord" and the name of a popular deity associated with fertility. Baal and the God of Israel are often depicted as rivals in biblical stories (e.g., in Elijah's challenge to the prophets of Baal in 1 Kings 18).

BABEL. *See* Tower of Babel.

BABYLON, an ancient city on the Euphrates that was the capital of both the Old Babylonian and the Neo-Babylonian empires, Mesopotamian superpowers that competed for dominance in the region of Palestine.

BABYLONIAN EXILE, the forced deportation of Judeans to Babylon after the Neo-Babylonians sacked Jerusalem and destroyed its Temple in 587 BCE. This is *the* formative event in the Hebrew Bible, a crisis that forced many Jews to look back on their history in search of a theological explanation for how God could allow them to be removed from the Promised Land.

BALAAM, a prophet hired by the king of Moab to curse the Israelites. On his way there, his donkey sees an angel blocking the way and refuses to move. When Balaam beats the donkey, the donkey talks back. Then Balaam too sees the angel and repents (Numbers 22–24).

BAPTISM, in Christian tradition, the central rite of passage signifying a new state of being. The immersion in water signifies a new birth and adoption by God. The story of John the Baptist baptizing Jesus along with others in the Jordan River suggests that the practice derived from an earlier Jewish rite of initiation or reinitiation.

BARABBAS, the Jewish criminal whom Pontius Pilate releases instead of Jesus.

BARUCH, the disciple and scribe of the prophet Jeremiah. His stories about Jeremiah are included in the prophetic book.

BATHSHEBA, the mother of Solomon. She was married to one of David's loyal soldiers, Uriah. When David got her pregnant, he had Uriah killed in battle and then took her as a wife.

BCE, "Before the Common Era," a less Christocentric designation for the era formerly referred to as BC, "Before Christ."

BEATITUDES, "Blessings," the series of blessings given by Jesus in his Sermon on the Mount (Matthew 5) and in his Sermon on the Plain (Luke 6).

BEHEMOTH, the monstrous land creature described in Job 40 along with the sea monster Leviathan.

BELSHAZZAR, in the book of Daniel, the son of Nebuchadnezzar and the last king of Babylon. In fact, he was the son of Nabonidus and was a prince, but never king. He was in charge of protecting Babylon when Nabonidus surrendered to Cyrus of Persia in 539 BCE.

BETHLEHEM, the small village near Jerusalem where David and Jesus were born.

BILHAH, Jacob's concubine and mother of Dan and Naphtali.

BOAZ, the prominent citizen of Bethlehem who marries Ruth and becomes the great-grandfather of David.

BURNING BUSH, the form from which God called Moses to lead the Hebrews out of slavery. The fire burned, but the bush was not consumed.

CAIAPHAS, the high priest of the Jerusalem Temple during the reign of the Roman emperor Tiberius; he oversaw the Sanhedrin's trial of Jesus.

CAIN, the oldest son of Eve and Adam. After he killed his brother Abel, God exiled him from his homeland to wander the earth. God also gave him a mark so no one would dare kill him.

CALEB, a spy sent, along with Joshua, into Canaan to report back on the Israelites' chances for successful conquest. Because of his faith, he is the only one of his generation who does not die in the wilderness, but is allowed to enter the Promised Land.

CALVARY, the Latin equivalent of "Golgotha," the "place of the skull," where Jesus was crucified.

CANAAN, the biblical name for the land of Palestine, the region west of the Jordan River, from Egypt in the south to Syria in the north; also known as the Promised Land, because God promises it to Abraham's offspring (Genesis 12:7).

CANON, an official, authoritative list. The canon of the New Testament, for example, includes twenty-seven texts, no more, no less.

CE, "Common Era," a less Christocentric designation for the era formerly referred to as AD, *Anno Domini,* "Year of our Lord."

CEPHAS. *See* Peter.

CHERUBIM, winged creatures with animal bodies and human faces that serve as guardians of the divine. Familiar in Israelite as well as Babylonian mythologies, they were used to decorate the tabernacle and the Jerusalem Temple.

CHRIST (from Greek *christos,* the equivalent of Hebrew *messiah,* "anointed"), designation for Jesus; "Jesus Christ" means Jesus the Messiah.

CHRISTOLOGY, a particular theological understanding of the meaning of the gospel of Jesus Christ. Different New Testament gospels and letters develop different Christologies, that is, interpretations of what it means to call Jesus of Nazareth the Christ.

CHRONICLES, 1 AND 2 (Hebrew Bible), two books retelling Israelite and Judean history from creation to Cyrus's defeat of Babylon. Written more than a century after the restoration of Jerusalem, they draw heavily from other biblical texts, especially the books of Samuel and Kings, often quoting from them directly. In their revisionist history, they are more flattering of King David and more critical of the Northern Kingdom.

COAT OF MANY COLORS, the King James Version description of the coat given to Joseph by his father, Jacob. Modern versions more correctly translate "long robe with long sleeves."

CODEX, the Greek name for a bound book. The earliest codices were small notebooks used for keeping records or notes. It was not until the third century that the codex began to replace the scroll as the dominant medium for literature in the Greco-Roman world. Christians appear to have been early adopters of the codex. *See also* scroll.

COLOSSIANS (New Testament), Paul's letter to the community at Colossae in Asia Minor. It argues against "false teachers" who were apparently promoting various ascetic practices and regulations as a means of attaining mystical union with God. The authorship of this Pauline letter is a matter of scholarly debate.

CONSTANTINE, the emperor of Rome (306–337 CE), who converted to Christianity. In 313 CE, he issued the Edict of Milan, which enforced tolerance of the Christian religion. In 325 CE, he presided over the Council of Nicea. He inaugurated a new era in which Christianity came to be identified with imperial power.

CORINTHIANS, 1 AND 2 (New Testament), two letters from Paul to the community at Corinth, where he had lived for a year and a half. The first focuses on issues within the community and refers to other letters between Paul and the Corinthians that are lost to us today. In 2 Corinthians, which may have been compiled from more than one original letter, Paul defends himself and his teachings against challenges from others who are competing for authority. In it he famously "boasts" in his "weakness."

COVENANT, an agreement or contract between two individuals or groups. Some covenants are more like promises, as when God covenants with Noah and Abraham to make their descendants a great nation. Others are conditional, as when God commands certain behaviors from the Israelites, vowing to bless their obedience and curse their disobedience (e.g., in Deuteronomy).

CRUCIFIXION, a common Roman (not Jewish) method of execution in which the criminal is nailed to a cross (Latin *cruci-fixus,* "fixed to a cross") and left until dead. This is how Jesus was executed.

CYRUS, the king of Persia who conquered the Babylonians in 539 BCE and allowed the Jews to return to Jerusalem and rebuild the Temple. Isaiah calls him God's messiah.

DANIEL (Hebrew Bible), a collection of stories about Jews in the Diaspora struggling to remain faithful in the face of pressures to assimilate. The latter chapters (7–12) offer a series of prophetic visions concerning divine judgment on the four empires that ruled the region after the fall of Judah (Babylon, Medea, Persia, and the Greeks). These symbol-rich visions influenced later apocalyptic writings, most notably the New Testament book of Revelation.

DAVID, the successor to Saul and second king of the United Monarchy. With the possible exception of Moses, he is the most prominent and complex biblical character in the Hebrew Bible. His stories are found in 1–2 Samuel, 1 Kings, and 1–2 Chronicles, and later tradition attributed several of the Psalms to him.

DAY OF ATONEMENT, Yom Kippur ("day of covering"), an annual Jewish rite associated with the fall New Year festival of Rosh Hashanah. People confess and are forgiven for any wrongdoings. The biblical directions for the rite are given in Leviticus 16.

DEAD SEA SCROLLS, a vast collection of Jewish writings, many of them biblical, that were found in caves near Qumran along the northwest bank of the Dead Sea. They date between the second century BCE and the first century CE and include the oldest copies of Hebrew Scriptures ever discovered. Among them are many different versions of the same biblical texts.

DECALOGUE, another name for the Ten Commandments, given in Exodus 20 and Deuteronomy 5.

DELILAH, the woman who is bribed by the Philistines to discover the secret of Samson's strength, which turns out to be his long hair (Judges 16).

DEUTERONOMISTIC HISTORY, a term coined by Martin Noth for the narrative that runs from Deuteronomy through 2 Kings. Although this material comes from several different sources, it appears to have been edited together in light of Deuteronomy. Defeat and exile by foreign superpowers (2 Kings 17 and 25) were interpreted as the result of the failure to maintain pure religious devotion, allowing God's law to be compromised by relations with non-Israelite peoples and religions.

DEUTERONOMY (Hebrew Bible), the fifth book of the Bible and final book of the Torah. Presented as Moses's farewell address to the Israelites, who are about to enter the Promised Land without him, it recalls their story of deliverance, reiterating and adding to God's law for them.

DEUTERO-PAULINE ("second-Pauline"), descriptor of letters that claim to have been written by Paul, but were probably written by someone else who identified with the Pauline tradition.

DEVIL, English translation of the Greek *diabolos,* "accuser," equivalent to the Hebrew *satan.* In Christian tradition, it eventually becomes another name for evil personified as God's cosmic opponent, Satan.

DIASPORA, "Dispersion," Jewish people who remained outside Palestine after the Babylonian exile.

DISCIPLE, a student and follower of a religious leader. In the gospels, Jesus and John the Baptist both have disciples.

ECCLESIASTES (Hebrew Bible), known in Hebrew as Qohelet ("teacher" or "preacher"), a book that is a collection of teachings and insights from an unknown Jewish philosopher. His perspective is more stoic than that of Proverbs, concluding that there is no point in trying to influence God or the world. All human labor, even when aimed at seeking knowledge and wisdom, is vanity. The best you can do is enjoy life while you still can.

EDEN, the mythical homeland of Adam and Eve, from which they are banished after eating from the Tree of Knowledge.

EGYPT, the ancient Near Eastern superpower to the southeast of ancient Israel, centered along the Nile River. According to biblical tradition, the descendants of Joseph and his eleven brothers live there for 430 years, becoming a great multitude but falling into slavery under a Pharaoh who "did not know Joseph," before God liberates them in the Exodus.

EL SHADDAI, a name for the biblical God usually translated "God on High" or "God of the Mountains"; literally, it translates as "God of Breasts."

ELIJAH, the prophet and harsh critic of the Northern Kingdom during the reign of Ahab and Jezebel (1 Kings 17). Because he did not die but was taken up in a chariot of fire (2 Kings 2), Jewish tradition has sometimes expected his eventual return. In the gospels, Jesus was sometimes believed to be Elijah. At Passover seders, an empty seat and glass of wine are often kept for Elijah.

ELISHA, Elijah's disciple who asks for a "double portion" of his spirit. He dons Elijah's prophetic mantle after Elijah is taken up in a chariot of fire.

ELIZABETH, Mary's relative and mother of John the Baptist. Her story is in the beginning of Luke.

ELOHIM, although literally the Hebrew plural for "gods," a term more commonly used as a name for the God of Israel.

ENOCH, the father of Methuselah; his end is described ambiguously: "God took him" (Genesis 5:24). Jewish and Christian traditions have sometimes asserted that he, along with Elijah, did not die, but became immortal.

EPHESIANS (New Testament), Paul's letter to the community at Ephesus, emphasizing the unity of Jewish and gentile believers. This theme is developed through three different analogies for the church: as Christ's body, as Christ's temple, and as Christ's bride. Based on textual evidence, some scholars argue that Paul was not its author.

EPHRAIM, son of Joseph and brother of Manasseh. In the land allotment the tribe of Joseph was divided into two half-tribes named after these two sons. During the time of the Divided Kingdom, Ephraim was an especially prominent region. The prophets sometimes use the name to refer to the whole Northern Kingdom.

EPIPHANY, a revelation or sudden manifestation of the divine. In Western Christian tradition, Epiphany is a holiday commemorating the visit of the Magi to the baby Jesus. In Eastern Orthodox tradition, it commemorates the revelation of Jesus at the moment of his baptism by John.

EPISTLE (Greek *epistole*), letter.

ESAU, Jacob's twin brother and the legendary progenitor of the Edomites.

ESCHATOLOGY (from Greek *eschaton,* "end"), a branch of theology concerned with end times—when, how, and why. Paul's already-but-not-yet theology is sometimes described as "realized eschatology."

ESTHER (Hebrew Bible), a biblical story of Jewish deliverance from genocide in a foreign land. Its heroine is Esther, a Jewish woman who becomes queen of Persia, the very empire that has called for the annihilation of all Jews. The story is celebrated with much carnival wildness every year in the Jewish holiday of Purim (Hebrew "lots," referring to the lots that were cast for the fate of the Jews).

EUCHARIST, "Thanksgiving," another name for the Christian ritual of Communion or the Lord's Supper, a shared meal in which bread and wine are consecrated as Christ's body and blood, commemorating the Last Supper, that is, the Passover seder that Jesus hosted before his arrest and crucifixion (e.g., Matthew 26). In some Christian traditions, it is understood in terms of sacrifice: by partaking of the elements, one partakes of Christ's sacrifice for the forgiveness of sin. In other traditions, it is understood in terms of community: those who share the meal signify their oneness in Christ.

EVE, in the creation story in Genesis, the first to eat from the Tree of Knowledge. *See also* Adam and Eve.

EXEGESIS, the practice of close, analytical reading of a text in order to draw out as many levels of meaning as possible.

EXODUS (Hebrew Bible), the second book of the Bible, recounting the story of the emancipation of the Hebrew people from bondage in Egypt. Memory of this event forms the core of biblical theology, the belief that the God of Israel is a God of liberation, who hears the cries of the oppressed and acts on their behalf. The Exodus story itself is the focus of the first half of the book. The second half is about the Israelites' subsequent sojourn in the wilderness of Sinai—between Egypt and the Promised Land. This time of wilderness wandering continues through the rest of the Torah.

EZEKIEL (Hebrew Bible), the book of visions and stories of Ezekiel, a priest who prophesied during the Babylonian exile. Like the other large prophetic collections, the dominant theme of the early chapters is judgment against God's people, and the dominant theme of the latter chapters is hope for an imminent restoration. The book concludes with an extended vision of a new creation, New Jerusalem, and new Temple.

EZRA AND NEHEMIAH (Hebrew Bible), two biblical books recounting the return of the Jewish people to Jerusalem after the Babylonian exile. Ezra was a priest who sought to rebuild the religious life of the community and instituted a policy of ethnic cleansing that dissolved all marriages of Jews to non-Jews. Nehemiah's leadership was more directly governmental and was remembered above all for rebuilding the wall of Jerusalem. The authors and editors responsible for 1–2 Chronicles may also have compiled these books.

FALL, THE, the traditional Christian interpretation of the story of Adam and Eve's expulsion from Eden after partaking of the Tree of the Knowledge of Good and Evil. It asserts that human beings are inherently "fallen" from perfection, bound to sin and alienation from God. Atonement through Christ is the means by which people are redeemed by God from their fallen state.

FLOOD, THE, the mythical near destruction of the world by God as told in Genesis 6–9.

GABRIEL, the archangel who explains Daniel's dreams to him in the book of Daniel and the angel who announces the births of Jesus and John the Baptist in the Gospel of Luke.

GALATIANS (New Testament), Paul's letter to the community at Galatia. It is his side in an argument about how and in what sense gentile Christians are "Jewish." Do gentile converts need to follow the laws of the Torah? Keep kosher? Do the men need to be circumcised? Paul says no. In Christ, he argues, such categories of identity (along with gender and class) are irrelevant.

GALILEE, the northern region of Palestine, south of the Sea of Galilee and west of the Jordan River, where Jesus grew up and began his ministry.

GEHENNA, the New Testament name for a place south of Jerusalem where garbage was burned. In ancient times it was purportedly a site of human sacrifice. Jesus uses it as a metaphor for damnation after death. Later it was associated with hell as a place of eternal damnation.

GENESIS (Hebrew Bible), the first book of the Bible (and of the Torah). Known in Hebrew by its first word, *Bereshit* ("In the beginning" or "When began"), it has two main parts: the primeval history, which gives mythological beginnings (chaps. 1–11), and the ancestral history (chaps. 12–50), which focuses on Abraham and Sarah (and Hagar) and their descendants. By the end, Joseph and his twelve brothers have moved from Canaan, the land promised to Abraham, to Egypt. Many of the stories in Genesis began as independent oral traditions before being incorporated into the overarching narrative.

GENTILE, a non-Jew (Hebrew *goy*).

GETHSEMANE, a grove area on the Mount of Olives to which Jesus takes his disciples after the Last Supper on the night before he is killed.

GNOSTICISM, an early Christian movement that emphasized salvation from the material world through special knowledge (Greek *gnosis*), as in the apocryphal *Gospel of Thomas.* Later Christian leaders declared it a heresy.

GOG AND MAGOG, in Ezekiel 38–39, rulers of a nation that will attack Israel and arouse God to action. In Revelation (influenced by Ezekiel), they are forces that Satan will rouse against God in the final battle.

GOLDEN CALF, the idol that Aaron makes from melted-down jewelry when the people clamor for gods to lead them while Moses is on the mountain with God.

GOLGOTHA. *See* Calvary.

GOLIATH, the Philistine giant whom David kills with a slingshot.

GOSPEL (Old English *godspel,* "good story" or "good news"; from Greek *euangelion,* "good news" or "happy message"). (1) The good news proclaimed by and about Jesus, as in the opening of the Gospel of Mark: "The beginning of the good news [*euangelion*] of Jesus Christ, the Son of God." (2) A literary work that proclaims this message, e.g., the Gospel of Matthew.

GOSPEL OF THOMAS, a Coptic translation of an apocryphal (noncanonical) Greek gospel comprised of 114 sayings of Jesus (many of which are similar to those found in the canonical gospels). It was discovered in Egypt in 1945 along with many other Gnostic Christian texts. The original from which it was translated may date to the first century CE.

GREEK, the dominant language of the Greek and Roman empires (until Latin took hold in the West during the third century CE). All of the New Testament literature was written in Greek.

HABAKKUK (Hebrew Bible), one of the twelve Minor Prophets, a book built around a dialogue between a Southern prophet named Habakkuk and God concerning the problem of theodicy: if God is just and powerful, why does God "look on the treacherous" and remain "silent when the wicked swallow those more righteous than they" (1:13)?

HAGAR, the slave girl of Sarah and mother (by Abraham) of Ishmael.

HAGGAI (Hebrew Bible), one of the twelve Minor Prophets, a book concerning the rebuilding of the Temple in Jerusalem after the Babylonian exile. The prophet scolds the people for focusing on building their own new homes instead of God's and envisions a future for Jerusalem that will be even greater than its past.

HAM, the son of Noah and father of Canaan. After he saw Noah drunk and naked, Noah cursed him.

HAMAN, the Persian villain in the story of Esther who convinces King Ahasuerus to send out an edict calling for the annihilation of all Jews.

HANNAH, the mother of the judge and prophet Samuel. In response to her fervent prayer, God grants her the child, whom she dedicates to priestly service.

HANUKKAH (Hebrew, "dedication"), a Jewish holiday commemorating the rededication of the Jerusalem Temple after its desecration by Antiochus IV Epiphanes. The story is told in 1–2 Maccabees, in the Apocrypha.

HEBREW, the original language of most of the Hebrew Bible (some portions were written in the closely related language of Aramaic). It is one of the earliest known alphabetic languages.

HEBREWS (New Testament), a New Testament "letter" that reads more like a sermon. Based on interpretations of Jewish Scriptures, it argues for the superior status of Christ over the prophets, priests, and even Moses. The anonymous author was probably a Jewish Christian.

HEROD, the name of seven different rulers appointed by Rome in the region of Judea before and during the first century CE. The most important ones in the Bible are: (1) Herod the Great (40–4 BCE), who rebuilt the Temple and was ruling all of Judea when Jesus was born; (2) Herod Antipas (4 BCE–39 CE), his son, who was responsible for the execution of John the Baptist; and (3) Herod Agrippa II, before whom Paul appeared in Caesarea (Acts 25–26).

HERODIAS, great-granddaughter of Herod the Great. John the Baptist criticized her and her husband/relative Herod Antipas, leading to John's beheading.

HOLY SPIRIT, in Christian theology, the Third Person of the Trinity, God's active presence in the world. The concept is rooted in Hebrew biblical references to God's spirit, the animating force of life (*ruach,* which also means "breath" and "wind"). In Acts 2, after Jesus's ascension, the Holy Spirit descends on his followers at Pentecost.

HOSEA (Hebrew Bible), a book of prophecies by Hosea, who was active in the Northern Kingdom around the middle of the eighth century BCE. Hosea is the first of the twelve Minor Prophets of the Hebrew Bible.

HOSHEA, the last king of the Northern Kingdom (Israel) before its destruction by the Assyrians.

HULDAH, a prophet in King Josiah's court in Jerusalem. When a "book of law" (probably some form of Deuteronomy) is discovered, she declares it to be from God, thereby inaugurating a massive reform (2 Kings 22). Thus Huldah is not only an early female religious authority, but the first canonical authority.

IMMANUEL (Hebrew *'immanu-'el,* "God with us"), the name of a child born to a young woman (the Septuagint has "virgin") that Isaiah proclaims as a sign of hope to the Israelites (7:14). In the Gospel of Matthew, the birth of Jesus is understood to be a fulfillment of that proclamation.

INCARNATION (literally "in-fleshing," i.e., embodiment), in Christian tradition, the embodiment of God in the human form of Jesus.

ISAAC, the son of Abraham and Sarah who marries Rebekah and fathers Jacob and Esau.

ISAIAH (Hebrew Bible), the first and the longest of the prophetic books. It actually includes sayings from two or three different prophets. The earliest, Isaiah of Jerusalem, was active in the Southern Kingdom (Judah) during the second half of the eighth century BCE (chaps. 1–39). The prophetic sayings in the latter portions of the book (chaps. 40–55; 56–66) date to more than a century later, during the exilic and postexilic periods.

ISHMAEL, the son of Abraham and Hagar, from whom the Ishmaelites are descended. Muslim tradition traces its biblical origins to him.

ISRAEL (from Hebrew *sarah*, "fight" or "contend," plus *'el*, "God"; hence "God fights," but also "contends with God"). (1) The name that God gives Jacob, because he has "striven with God and with humans, and [has] prevailed" (Genesis 32:28). (2) The name of the Israelite people descended from Jacob/Israel's twelve sons/tribes. (3) The name of the ten tribes of the Northern Kingdom after they secede from the Southern Kingdom (Judah).

JACOB, the son of Isaac and Rebekah and twin brother of Esau. God names him Israel, and the twelve tribes are descended from his twelve sons.

JAMES. (1) James the son of Zebedee and brother of John, who was one of the twelve disciples. (2) James the son of Alphaeus and Mary, another of the twelve disciples. (3) James the brother (or perhaps other close relative) of Jesus, who became a prominent leader of the early Jesus movement in Jerusalem and was martyred around 60 CE.

JAMES (New Testament), a brief letter from James, who may have been Jesus's brother, mentioned in Galatians as a leader in the Jerusalem church. It focuses on ethical teachings drawn primarily from the Jewish Scriptures. Contrary to Paul's teaching, it emphasizes living out one's faith through good works. Faith without works, James insists, is dead.

JEHOVAH, a name for God that was erroneously derived from adding the consonants of the Hebrew tetragrammaton to the vowels inserted by Masoretic scribes for the word *'adonai,* which was to be said or read instead of the divine name. *See also* tetragrammaton.

JEREMIAH (Hebrew Bible), the book of sayings and stories of the prophet Jeremiah, who was active in the Southern Kingdom (Judah) during the latter part of the seventh century until around the time of the exile in 587 BCE. Jeremiah's harsh judgment against Judah did not make him very popular. He suffered greatly on account of his calling and sometimes complained bitterly about it.

JERICHO, the walled city that Joshua and his armies purportedly destroyed by marching around it and blowing trumpets. The archaeological site of this very ancient city shows no evidence of such massive destruction.

JEROBOAM I, the first king of the Northern Kingdom (Israel); Shechem was his capital (ca. 922–901 BCE).

JEROME (d. 420), the patron saint of librarians and translators; editor and translator of the Latin Vulgate version of the Christian Bible (Old and New Testaments), which eventually became the standard Bible for all of Western Christendom until the Protestant Reformation.

JERUSALEM, also known as Zion, the capital city of the United Kingdom and then of the Southern Kingdom, Judah. It was first captured from the Jebusites by King David. David's son and successor, Solomon, built the Temple there.

JESSE, the father of King David.

JESUS (Hebrew *Yeshua,* i.e., Joshua, "God delivers"), Jesus of Nazareth, central figure proclaimed as Messiah and Son of God in the New Testament. *See also* Christ.

JETHRO, Moses's Midianite father-in-law.

JEW (Hebrew *yehudi*), one from *Yehudah,* that is, Judah; in the ancient world, as today, a term referring to both an ethnic/cultural and a religious identity.

JEZEBEL, the powerful wife of King Ahab in the Northern Kingdom who promoted worship of the Canaanite deity Baal along with the God of Israel. Although popular culture has often associated her with sexual power and promiscuity, the biblical narrative does not.

JOB (Hebrew Bible), the story of a perfectly righteous and godly man who becomes the subject of a divine test: whether he will remain faithful to God if everything is taken from him. The story begins and ends with brief, straightforward narrative. Between these prose bookends is some of the most fascinating, theologically provocative poetry in the Hebrew Bible, in which Job contends with his friends over the meaning, or meaninglessness, of his suffering.

JOEL (Hebrew Bible), one of the twelve Minor Prophets; Joel was probably a postexilic prophet from Judah. His vision begins with a plague of locusts brought on by God as judgment against the people and their rulers for unfaithfulness.

JOHN, 1, 2, AND 3 (New Testament), three letters traditionally attributed to an elder named John (also associated with the Gospel of John). The first, which is anonymous, encourages its addressees to remain steadfast to their new identity and to love one another, as God is love. Its metaphorical use of light and darkness is reminiscent of the Gospel of John. The second, which is from "the elder," warns against false teachers and urges its addressees to live in truth and love. The third is from the same "elder" and is addressed to an otherwise unknown man named Gaius, whom the author thanks for showing hospitality to some of his friends.

JOHN, GOSPEL OF (New Testament), the fourth gospel, sometimes called the "spiritual gospel." John stands apart from the other three gospels in many respects, emphasizing what one needs to know and believe more than what one needs to do. It emphasizes Jesus's divine identity as "the way, and the truth, and the life," the good shepherd, the vine, the light, and the one mediator between God and humankind.

JOHN OF PATMOS, the self-named author of Revelation, or the Apocalypse of John, who is writing while in exile on the island of Patmos in the Aegean Sea.

JOHN THE BAPTIST, the prophetic forebear and baptizer of Jesus Christ in all four gospels. In Luke, he is the son of Elizabeth and Zechariah, and therefore Jesus's relative. He is beheaded by Herod Antipas and Herodias, because he criticized their marriage (they were relatives).

JONAH (Hebrew Bible), one of the Minor Prophets that is the story of a reluctant prophet, Jonah, who tries to escape his calling to prophesy against Nineveh, only to be swallowed by a big fish. Three days later the fish spits him out and he goes to Nineveh. When the people hear his prophecies, they repent and God relents. Knowing this would happen in the end, Jonah is indignant.

JONATHAN, the son of King Saul and best friend of David. He and David conspire against Saul. Ultimately both he and Saul are killed in battle, and David becomes king.

JORDAN, the river that runs through the middle of Palestine, from the Sea of Galilee in the north to the Dead Sea in the south. The Israelites cross it to enter the land of Canaan, and Jesus is baptized in it by John the Baptist.

JOSEPH. (1) The son of Rachel and Jacob who was sold by his brothers into slavery in Egypt, where he eventually rose to prominence and reconciled with his family (Genesis 36–50). (2) The husband of Mary, mother of Jesus. (3) Joseph of Arimathea, a prominent figure in the Jewish Sanhedrin who was a secret follower of Jesus and who arranged to have Jesus's body buried in his garden tomb.

JOSHUA (Hebrew Bible), a book recounting Israel's invasion, led by Joshua after Moses's death, of the land Canaan, claimed as the Promised Land given to Abraham and his descendants by God. For many, Joshua is the most difficult of biblical books, as it tends to glorify "holy war" against the land's indigenous populations. It represents a theology and nationalism that few today can embrace.

JUDAH. (1) The fourth son of Leah and Jacob, the progenitor of one of the twelve tribes. (2) Another name for the Southern Kingdom, formed when the Northern Kingdom seceded from the United Monarchy in 922 BCE. Judea is the name used for the same region under the Greek and Roman empires. *See also* Jew.

JUDAS ISCARIOT, one of Jesus's twelve disciples. He betrays Jesus to the authorities for money. There are two different traditions concerning his ultimate demise: in Matthew, he returns the money and hangs himself; in Acts, he buys a field and then falls on a rock and disembowels himself.

JUDE (New Testament), a brief letter from Jude, who calls himself "a servant of Christ and brother of James" (traditionally identified with Jesus's brother). He writes to a community that has undergone division on account of "intruders" who are spreading false teachings and acting immorally. He tells them to "hate even the tunic defiled by their bodies" (v. 23).

JUDEA. *See* Judah.

JUDGES (Hebrew Bible), a continuation of the story, begun in Joshua, of the Israelites' early years in the land of Canaan, before the establishment of a monarchy. Various tribes came together under "judges" who were raised up by God to deliver them from enemies. The basic cycle for the story of each judge is as follows: the people abandon God; God abandons them; they are oppressed by others in the land; they cry out for deliverance; God raises up a judge who delivers them; the judge eventually dies; and the cycle begins again.

JUNIA, an influential female leader in early Christianity whom Paul commends as "prominent among the apostles" (Romans 16:7).

KINGS, 1 AND 2 (Hebrew Bible), books beginning with the death of David and the enthronement of his son, Solomon, and continuing with the history of the Divided Kingdom, after the split into the Northern Kingdom (Israel) and the Southern Kingdom (Judah, with Jerusalem as its capital), synchronizing the respective chronologies as they go. The ending is grim: the Assyrians obliterate the Northern Kingdom in 722 BCE, and the Babylonians conquer Jerusalem in 587 BCE and take the people into exile.

LAMENTATIONS (Hebrew Bible), a collection of five poems that describe, in painfully graphic detail, the destruction of Jerusalem and the exile of its people by the Babylonians. Although later tradition attributed these poems to the prophet Jeremiah, they are anonymous. The dominant voice is Zion, personified as a mother lamenting over the loss of her children.

LAZARUS, a friend of Jesus and brother of Mary and Martha in the Gospel of John. Jesus raises him from the dead.

LEAH, the first wife of Jacob and mother of Reuben, Simeon, Levi, Judah, Issachar, and Zebulun.

LEVIATHAN, a monstrous figure associated with the sea and primordial chaos in several different texts of the Hebrew Bible. In some, Leviathan appears as an enemy of God and a threat to the order of creation (e.g., Isaiah 27). In others, God identifies with Leviathan (e.g., Job 41).

LEVITICUS (Hebrew Bible), the third book of the Bible, following Exodus. Named for its focus on the priestly tribe of Levi, it contains regulations for conducting sacrifices; consecrating and ordaining priests; distinguishing between "clean" and "unclean" things (including the kosher food laws); Yom Kippur; and various matters of sexuality, business, farming that set the Israelites apart as God's holy people. "Be holy, for I am holy" is the refrain.

LOGOS, Greek for "word," but also "reason" (or "logic") as well as, in Jewish philosophy, "wisdom" and "law" (or "Torah"). In the prologue to the Gospel of John ("In the beginning was the Word . . ."), it has all these potential connotations.

LOT, Abraham's nephew and the supposed ancestor of the Moabites and Ammonites.

LOT'S DAUGHTERS, the mothers, through an incestuous relationship with their father, Lot, of Moab and Ammon, the biblical progenitors of the Moabites and Ammonites (obviously a slanderous story of the incestuous origins of rival peoples).

LOT'S WIFE, one who, when Lot's family was allowed to escape Sodom before it was destroyed by fire and brimstone, stopped to look back at their former home and was turned into a pillar of salt.

LUKE, a physician who traveled with Paul. Later tradition identified him as the writer of the third gospel and Acts (both were originally anonymous).

LUKE, GOSPEL OF (New Testament), the third gospel, often called the "social gospel" because it emphasizes Jesus's special concern for the poor and the oppressed and proclaims God's liberation as a social-political revolution. Written around 80–85 CE, this is the only gospel with a second volume, the Acts of the Apostles.

LXX. *See* Septuagint.

LYDIA, a prominent businesswoman ("dealer in purple cloth") who converted to Christianity (Acts 16) and supported Paul's ministries.

MACCABEES, 1 AND 2, books in the Apocrypha telling the story of Jewish deliverance from oppression under the infamous Seleucid ruler Antiochus IV Epiphanes. A priest named Mattathius leads the first rebellion, but the hero of the story is his son and successor, Judas, also known as "Maccabeus," or "hammer." The story of his purification and rededication of the Temple is the basis of the Jewish holiday of Hanuk-kah ("dedication").

MAGI (Latin; Greek *magoi*), the "wise men" from the East who follow a star to the baby Jesus in Matthew.

MALACHI (Hebrew Bible), the last of the twelve Minor Prophets. Mala-chi consists of eleven brief oracles addressed to the people of Jerusalem after they had returned from exile and finished rebuilding the Temple. The oracles criticize their complacency and the corruption of their leader-ship, while again envisioning a future purification and redemption.

MANASSEH. (1) The son of Joseph and the Egyptian Asenath; brother of Ephraim. The Josephite tribe was divided into two half-tribes, Ephraim and Manasseh; their land allotment was divided by the Jordan River. (2) A king of the Northern Kingdom (Israel) who was criticized for religious syncretism (2 Kings 21).

MANNA, often called "bread from heaven," a flaky food that fell from the skies to feed the Israelites during the wilderness wanderings. A portion of it was kept in the Ark of the Covenant.

MARK, known in Acts as John Mark, the son of a prominent Jew named Mary; he was a travel companion of Barnabas and Paul on a mission de-scribed in Acts. Later tradition identified him as the writer of the second gospel (originally anonymous).

MARK, GOSPEL OF (New Testament), the shortest and earliest of the four gospels. Written around 70 CE, it has a condensed, terse style that is often compared with that of Hebrew biblical narrative. It includes no infancy narratives, but begins with Jesus's baptism by John the Baptist. The story ends as abruptly as it begins, with the women who witnessed the empty tomb running away in fear and silence.

MARY (New Testament). (1) The mother of Jesus. (2) The sister of Martha and Lazarus. (3) The mother of James and Joseph and witness to the empty tomb in Mark and Luke. (4) The mother of John Mark and host of disciples' meetings. (5) Mary Magdalene, a prominent follower of Jesus (later erroneously identified with the woman caught in adultery in John) and witness to the empty tomb in all four gospels.

MATTHEW, GOSPEL OF (New Testament), the first of the four gospels. Probably written around 80–85 CE, it presents Jesus as a rabbi and interpreter of Torah as well as a fulfillment of it. His teachings, especially through parables, focus on the illusive "kingdom of heaven," and he continually points away from himself and toward God.

MESSIAH (Hebrew, "anointed one"), originally a king or priest ritually anointed with oil; also one "anointed" by God to carry out a divine plan. In Isaiah, for example, Cyrus of Persia is called God's messiah because he overcomes the Babylonians and helps restore Jerusalem. In the gospels, of course, Jesus is called Messiah. "Christ," from *christos,* is the Greek equivalent.

METHUSELAH, the oldest person in the Bible. According to Genesis 5, he lived 969 years.

MICAH (Hebrew Bible), one of the twelve Minor Prophets. Micah was active in Jerusalem and in the Northern Kingdom (Israel) during the eighth century BCE. The opening three chapters are indictments against both kingdoms. The remainder of the book appears to be a collection of several separate prophetic sayings that may have been added later.

MICHAEL, an archangel associated with apocalyptic visions of divine judgment in Daniel and Revelation.

MIDIANITES, according to biblical legend, the people descended from Midian, the son of Abraham and his wife Keturah. Moses takes refuge with the Midianite Jethro and marries his daughter Zipporah. In Judges, Gideon defeats the huge Midianite army with his small troupe.

MIDRASH (from Hebrew *darash,* "pursue"), a Hebrew word referring to biblical interpretation. The Jewish tradition of midrash places a premium on creative, generative meaning-making in relation to the particular details of the text.

MINOR PROPHETS, the twelve smaller prophetic texts of the Hebrew Bible: Hosea, Joel, Amos, Obadiah, Jonah, Micah, Nahum, Habakkuk, Zephaniah, Hagai, Zechariah, and Malachi.

MIRIAM, the older sister of Moses and Aaron who watches over baby Moses and later leads the victory celebration after crossing the Reed Sea.

In Numbers, she is stricken with leprosy for seven days after questioning Moses's authority to speak for God.

MOABITES, the enemies of Israel east of the Dead Sea and north of Edom. Biblical legend demeans them as descendants of Lot resulting from his incestuous relationship with his elder daughter.

MONOTHEISM, the doctrine that there is only one God.

MORDECAI, the cousin and adoptive father of Esther. His refusal to bow before Haman leads Haman to convince King Ahasuerus to kill all Jews in Persia. When that plot is reversed, Mordecai is exalted by Esther, while Haman is humiliated and ultimately executed.

MOSES, the heroic leader of the Exodus from Egypt and the mediator between God and the Israelites in the wilderness, delivering the law and judging them according to it. Early tradition believed that he also wrote the Torah.

MOUNT HOREB, in Deuteronomy, the name of the mountain where the Israelites receive the law; also the place where Elijah meets God after slaying the prophets of Baal.

MOUNT OF OLIVES, also known as Olivet, a long ridge of mountains east of Jerusalem. David flees from his son Absalom to this area, Jesus delivers his lament over Jerusalem from one of its summits, and Jesus and his disciples go there (Gethsemane) after the Last Supper, the night before he is killed. It is also traditionally believed to be the site of Jesus's ascension (Acts 2:1).

MOUNT SINAI, in Exodus, the name of the mountain where the Israelites receive the law. In Deuteronomy, however, it is called Mount Horeb.

NAAMAH, according to postbiblical Jewish tradition, the name of Noah's wife. While Noah gathers the animals, she gathers seeds from all the plants.

NAHUM (Hebrew Bible), one of the twelve Minor Prophets; this very brief book celebrates the fall of Nineveh, the capital of the Assyrian Empire, which was destroyed by the Babylonians in 612 BCE.

NAOMI, the Israelite mother-in-law of the Moabite Ruth.

NAZARETH, the small town just southwest of the Sea of Galilee where Jesus grew up and began his ministry.

NEBUCHADNEZZAR II, the ruler of the Neo-Babylonian Empire (605–562 BCE) who brought about the destruction of the first Jerusalem Temple and the exile of the Jewish people.

NEHEMIAH (Hebrew Bible). *See* Ezra and Nehemiah.

NEPHILIM, the legendary antediluvian giant offspring of "sons of God and daughters of men" in Genesis 6.

NERO, emperor of Rome (54–69 CE). Paul was probably executed during his persecutions in the mid-60s.

NINEVEH, the last capital of the Assyrian Empire.

NOAH, the man who "walked with God" and was therefore spared from the flood. He, his family, and the animals rode it out in an ark.

NORTHERN KINGDOM, the coalition of ten northern Israelite tribes, under Jeroboam I, that did not accept Rehoboam, Solomon's son, as king after Solomon's death (922 BCE) and seceded from the United Monarchy. It is called Israel; the Southern Kingdom is called Judah.

NUMBERS (Hebrew Bible), the fourth book of the Bible, after Leviticus. Named for its opening scene, in which the Israelites are counted, it continues the story of the wilderness wanderings, as the people depart from Sinai for the oasis of Kadesh-barnea, whence they attempt to invade Canaan. Many of its stories depict the Israelite people as faithless complainers who are oblivious to God's devoted care and direction.

OBADIAH (Hebrew Bible), one of the Minor Prophets; a brief pronouncement of judgment on the Edomites, because they served as auxiliary forces in the army of Babylon when it sacked Jerusalem in 587 BCE. It is the shortest book in the Hebrew Bible.

PALESTINE, the band of land along the eastern coast of the Mediterranean Sea between the Sinai Peninsula to the south and Syria to the north. The Greek historian Herodotus (fifth century BCE) was the first to call the region by this name, which derives from the people who occupied its coastland, the Philistines.

PARABLE, Jesus's signature mode of teaching. A parable is a kind of extended metaphor, in which a difficult concept, such as the "kingdom of heaven," is compared with a more familiar one, usually in a brief story. Like other metaphorical thinking, parables are not reducible to a single, "this equals that" interpretation.

PASTORAL LETTERS (New Testament), 1–2 Timothy and Titus. Traditionally attributed to Paul, these three letters are addressed to individual church leaders and are concerned with pastoral responsibilities and structures of authority. Such concerns reflect a time after Paul, probably around 100 CE.

PAUL, the Pharisee and former opponent of the early Jesus movement (then called Saul) who experienced a vision of the risen Christ and then became crucial to the spread of Christianity throughout the Greco-Roman world, especially among Gentiles. His letters, which are the earliest writings in the New Testament, develop many key theological concepts that have shaped Christian doctrine. Indeed, some argue that Christianity is at least as much "Paul" as it is "Jesus."

PENTATEUCH, the Greek name ("five books") for the Torah in the Septuagint.

PENTECOST, the Greek name for the Jewish harvest festival of Shavuot, or Feast of Weeks, which commemorates the giving of the Ten Commandments. In Acts, the disciples are observing Pentecost in Jerusalem when the Holy Spirit descends on them. Thus Pentecost became a Christian celebration commemorating the coming of the Holy Spirit to the church.

PERSIA, the ancient Indo-European empire that, under Cyrus the Great, defeated Babylon, restored the Jews to Jerusalem, and supported the rebuilding of the Temple.

PETER (Greek *Petros*, Aramaic *Cephas*, "rock"), one of Jesus's disciples and a key leader in the early Jesus movement based in Jerusalem. His original name was Simon, but Jesus renamed him after he was the first to declare him the Messiah. Based in part on Jesus's proclamation in Matthew 16:8 ("on this rock I will build my church"), Catholic tradition considers him the first pope.

PETER, 1 AND 2 (New Testament), two letters attributed to Jesus's disciple Peter. The first is an exhortation to believers to live out their faith as witnesses to the transformation they have experienced, even and especially when facing severe persecution. The second, which argues against those who question why the Second Coming of Christ seems to be taking so long, seems to have been written much later. Although it is possible that Peter wrote the first letter, most scholars consider the second to be pseudonymous.

PHARISEES, a pious Jewish sect that was concerned with applying the Torah to every aspect of life. Paul was a Pharisee, and it is likely that Jesus's own Jewish background was closely related.

PHILEMON (New Testament), a personal letter from Paul, in prison, to a wealthy friend and fellow Christian named Philemon. Paul has met and converted Philemon's runaway slave, Onesimus, and is sending him back. He says to Philemon, "Welcome him as you would welcome me" (v. 17).

PHILIPPIANS (New Testament), Paul's letter, probably written during his first imprisonment in Rome in the early 60s CE, to the community at Philippi, in Macedonia, which was the first that Paul had helped found. A major theme of this letter concerns one's unity with Christ in and through suffering.

PHILISTINES, enemies of biblical Israel during the time of the judges (e.g., Samson) and the early monarchical period (under Saul and David) located along the southern coast of Palestine. In Western culture, the term often refers to uneducated enemies of high culture.

POLYTHEISM, the belief in many gods.

PONTIUS PILATE, the Roman procurator of Judea who presided over the trial of Jesus and sentenced him to death by crucifixion.

POTIPHAR, the Egyptian high official under whom Joseph served. His wife tries to seduce Joseph and later accuses him of trying to rape her.

PRISCA AND AQUILA, according to Paul (Romans 16), prominent leaders in the early Jesus movement who risked their lives for Paul, who had a great influence on the spread of Christianity to Gentiles, and who hosted a church in their house. Perhaps they were the original married co-pastors.

PRODIGAL SON, in Jesus's parable (Luke 15), the younger son who squanders his entire inheritance and is then welcomed home by his father with open arms.

PROMISED LAND, another name for the land of Canaan, that is, Palestine, the region west of the Jordan River, from Egypt in the south to Syria in the north. In Genesis 12, God promises it to Abraham's offspring.

PROPHET, one who is called to speak on behalf of God. Biblical prophets do not so much predict the future as offer alternative ways of seeing and understanding past, present, and future.

PROVERB, a saying that succinctly (often metaphorically) expresses simple wisdom, e.g., "Better is a dry morsel with quiet than a house full of feasting with strife" (Proverbs 17:1).

PROVERBS (Hebrew Bible), a collection of ancient Israelite wisdom literature framed as a patriarchal discourse. It emphasizes practical advice drawn from observations of society and the natural world, which are believed to testify to the meaningful order of creation. The book also includes a poem to Wisdom (Hebrew *Hokmah*), personified as a female divine cohort.

PSALMS (Hebrew Bible), the hymnal or songbook of ancient Israel. Written over many centuries, this collection of 150 songs embraces a diverse range of emotions and experiences, both personal and collective.

PSEUDONYMOUS (literally, "falsely named"), a term referring to any text that falsely claims to be written by someone else.

PURIM, the carnivalesque Jewish holiday celebrating the deliverance of the Jewish people in the story of Esther. The word means "lots" and refers to the lots cast by Haman before he and Ahasuerus decide to kill all the Jews of Persia.

Q (abbreviation for German *Quelle*, "source"), the hypothesized source for the sayings of Jesus that are found in Matthew and Luke, but not in Mark or John.

RABBI, Hebrew term for a religious teacher and scholar.

RACHEL, Jacob's second, but favorite, wife and younger sister of Leah. Her sons are Joseph and Benjamin.

RAHAB, the prostitute from Jericho who hosts the Israelite spies. When Jericho is destroyed, she is saved. She was the mother of Boaz, the great-grandfather of David.

REBEKAH, the niece of Abraham, wife of Isaac, and mother of Jacob and Esau.

REED SEA, the swampy waters near the Red Sea that the Israelites cross during the Exodus from Egypt.

REHOBOAM, the son of Solomon and last king of the United Monarchy of Israel (922–915 BCE). His oppressive policies pushed the ten northern tribes to secede.

RESURRECTION, the revival of a dead person. Some Jewish movements, such as the Pharisees, believed in the resurrection of the dead. Jesus resurrected people from the dead (e.g., Lazarus). Following Jesus's own resurrection, however, he ascended into the heavens. The bodily resurrection of the dead is a key concept in Paul's theology and subsequent Christian doctrine.

REVELATION (New Testament), also known as the Apocalypse, a book of visions revealed to an otherwise unknown Christian named John while exiled on the island of Patmos. The book concludes with a cosmic battle between the forces of God and the monstrous forces of evil identified with the Roman Empire. Derived from the experiences of marginalization and persecution, the book draws heavily from Jewish Scripture and a dense network of symbolism to offer a radically alternative way of seeing what was happening and would soon happen in the world.

ROMAN EMPIRE, the vast multiethnic empire that ruled the entire region around the Mediterranean Sea (from modern-day southern Germany in the north to Egypt in the south) from 63 BCE. Its capital was Rome. Judea was a province within this empire until 135 CE, when the Romans put down the second Jewish revolt and destroyed Jerusalem.

ROMANS (New Testament), the first of Paul's thirteen letters in the New Testament. Written while imprisoned in Rome, shortly before he was killed, it is seen by many as a last will and testament, his best attempt to present his theology in full. Its central argument is that people are justified and saved not by good works or obedience to the law, but by grace through faith. Luther considered it the purest expression of the gospel in the New Testament.

RUTH (Hebrew Bible), the story of King David's Moabite great-grandmother. When Ruth's husband dies, Ruth accompanies her mother-in-law, Naomi, back to Israel. There she and Naomi succeed in finding a way to survive and thrive in a patriarchal world.

SABBATH (Hebrew *Shabbat,* "seventh"), the seventh day of the week, from sundown Friday to sundown Saturday. God commanded the Israelites to observe the Sabbath by resting and doing no work during that day, just as God rested on the seventh day after creating the world.

SADDUCEES, an elite, aristocratic Jewish sect that accepted only the Torah as Scripture and therefore rejected concepts such as the resurrection of the dead. This group had close ties with Roman authorities and strong influence over the Temple priesthood.

SALOME. (1) According to the Jewish historian Josephus, the name of the daughter of Herodias by her first husband (Herod, son of Herod the Great). Although her name is not given in the gospels, this is the young woman who dances before her uncle Herod Antipas (Herodias's second husband) and then asks for John the Baptist's head on a platter. (2) An otherwise unknown witness to the crucifixion (Matthew 27; Mark 15) and the empty tomb (Mark 16).

SAMARIA, the capital of the Northern Kingdom (Israel).

SAMARITANS, in the time of Jesus, a marginalized Jewish sect based in central Palestine. Believed to have descended from the survivors of the Assyrian destruction of the Northern Kingdom in Samaria (722 BCE), they had their own version of the Torah. Jesus's story of the "good Samaritan," who was more righteous than others, thus challenged common prejudice against them.

SAMSON, a Nazirite and judge in Israel who was legendary for his strength, cleverness, and complicated love interests (Judges 13–16). His story concludes with his destruction of the Philistine temple by pulling it down on top of himself.

SAMUEL, the last judge of Israel. His mother, Hannah, dedicated him as a baby to priestly service under the high priest Eli at Shiloh, where the Ark of the Covenant was held.

SAMUEL, 1 AND 2 (Hebrew Bible), named for Israel's last judge, Samuel, two books telling the story of the rise of the United Monarchy. Giving in to the pleas of the people for a king to govern them "like the other nations," God has Samuel appoint Saul the first king of Israel. Soon, however, Saul appears destined to fail, at which point Samuel anoints young David (while Saul is still king). David's story is the main focus of the narrative from 1 Samuel 16 to the beginning of 1 Kings.

SANHEDRIN, the Jewish supreme court in Jerusalem, presided over by the high priest of the Temple.

SARAH, Abraham's wife and the mother of Isaac, whom she bears in her old age. Her name is changed from Sarai to Sarah after God promises to give her a child.

SATAN (Hebrew *satan,* "accuser" or "opponent"), in later Jewish and Christian tradition, the proper name for God's cosmic opponent (e.g., in Revelation). That later idea of Satan should not be retrojected into the story of Job, where the character of *ha-satan,* "*the* accuser" (with a definite article) serves God as something like a prosecuting attorney in the divine court.

SAUL, the first king of Israel. Not long after Samuel anoints him king, he appears doomed to failure. David is his successor.

SCAPEGOAT, someone on whom the wrongs of others have been blamed. The term originates in the ritual of Yom Kippur in Leviticus 16, where Aaron places all the sins of the people onto a goat and then sends it into the wilderness.

SCROLL, a roll of parchment (made from cured animal skin) or paper (made from papyrus reeds). In the Greco-Roman world, the scroll was the dominant medium for literature well into the third century CE, although Christian usage appears to have begun moving from the scroll to the codex as early as the second century. Within Judaism, the parchment scroll remains the privileged medium for the Torah and other Scriptures.

SECOND TEMPLE, the Jerusalem Temple that was rebuilt after the Babylonian exile.

SEPTUAGINT, the traditional name for the early Greek translation of Hebrew Scriptures. It is sometimes abbreviated LXX, referring to the legend that seventy rabbis independently produced the exact same translation.

SERAPHIM, six-winged creatures that Isaiah sees attending the throne of God (Isaiah 6). One touches Isaiah's mouth with a hot coal to purify him and prepare him to prophesy.

SETH, the third son of Adam and Eve, born after Cain kills Abel and is then banished by God.

SHABBAT. *See* Sabbath.

SHEMA, the Hebrew imperative "Hear" and the name of the traditional Jewish declaration of faith: *Shema yisra'el,* "Hear, O Israel . . ." (Deuteronomy 6:4).

SHEOL (Hebrew, "the pit"), the underground place of the dead. In later Christian and Jewish tradition, it was associated with the Greek concept of Hades and was conceived as the place from which the dead would be resurrected. Neither concept should be confused with Gehenna, or "hell."

SILAS, the Aramaic name of Silvanus, a companion of the apostle Paul and Barnabas, also mentioned as co-sender of two Pauline letters (1 and 2 Thessalonians).

SIMEON, according to Luke, a righteous man in Jerusalem who had been told by the Holy Spirit that he would not die before seeing the Messiah— which he does when Mary and Joseph bring the baby Jesus into the Temple.

SODOM AND GOMORRAH, the two cities that God destroyed on account of their injustices. When two angels visit Lot and his family in Sodom in order to warn them of the coming annihilation, the men of the city try to rape them. Although this story illustrates the depravity of the city, the association of God's judgment on Sodom and Gomorrah with homosexuality is a false one.

SOLOMON, the second son of David by Bathsheba and David's successor to the throne. Although Solomon is famous for his legendary wisdom and for building the Jerusalem Temple, his policies also contributed to the breakup of the United Monarchy under his son, Rehoboam.

SONG OF SONGS (Hebrew Bible), also known as the Song of Solomon (based on the first line, "The song of songs, which is Solomon's . . ."), a collection of erotic love poetry involving a young woman and young man. God is never mentioned in the book, but many read it as a religious allegory.

SOUTHERN KINGDOM. *See* Judah.

STEPHEN, a Hellenistic Jewish follower of Jesus who, according to Acts 7, was stoned to death for blasphemy. Thus he was the first Christian martyr.

SUKKOTH (Hebrew, "booths"), the Festival of Tabernacles (or Booths), a fall agricultural festival in which participants stay in temporary shelters reminiscent of the tents in which the Israelites lived during their wilderness wanderings.

SYNAGOGUE, a gathering of Jewish people for worship and prayer. Later the term refers to specific buildings set aside for such congregations. Although the origins of synagogue culture are obscure, it clearly grew and developed quickly after the destruction of the Jerusalem Temple in 70 CE. The origins of early Christian house-churches are closely related to those of the synagogue.

SYNOPTIC GOSPELS, the gospels of Matthew, Mark, and Luke, which clearly share much of the same material. The "Synoptic Problem" concerns how to explain the similarities and differences between them. Almost all of Mark, the shortest, appears in Matthew and Luke, and most scholars believe that it must have come first.

TABERNACLE, the portable shrine used by the Israelites until Solomon built the permanent Temple. Its construction is described in detail in the second half of Exodus. Home to the Ark of the Covenant, it represented divine presence.

TALMUD, the massive collection of rabbinic commentary on the Torah. It is organized into two main parts: the Mishnah, or "oral Torah," which comments and expands on passages from the Torah, and the Gemara, which comments and elaborates on the Mishnah. Talmudic literature reads like a dialogue involving many different voices, which rarely end up agreeing. There are two different editions: the Jerusalem Talmud (*Talmud Yerushalmi*), which was produced in the middle of the fifth century CE, and the much longer Babylonian Talmud (*Talmud Bavli*), which was produced somewhat later. Each contains oral traditions that date centuries earlier.

TANAK, a common acronym for the tripartite canon of Hebrew Scriptures: Torah, Nevi'im ("prophets"), and Ketuvim ("writings").

TARSUS, the home of the apostle Paul. It was the capital of the Roman province of Cilicia.

TEMPLE, the center of Israelite cultic and national life in Jerusalem in the biblical period. It was built by King Solomon, destroyed by the Babylonians, and then rebuilt by the Judeans, with the support of Cyrus of Persia, after the Babylonian exile. It was then destroyed again by the Romans in 70 CE.

TEN COMMANDMENTS, the ten laws given to the Israelites through Moses after the Exodus. They are given in Exodus 20 and reiterated in Deuteronomy 5.

TETRAGRAMMATON (Greek, "four letters"), a designation for the primary Hebrew name for God, given as four consonants without vowels: *Y-H-W-H.* Most scholars concur that it was originally pronounced *Yahweh.* From an early period in Jewish history, however, it was considered too sacred to pronounce. Readers therefore orally replaced it with another name, usually *'adonai* ("my Lord"). Later scribes (the Maso-retes) apparently added the vowel sounds from *'adonai* (or in some cases *'elohim*) to the consonants of the tetragrammaton to remind readers not to pronounce it. Later Christian translators, unaware of this practice, put the vowels and consonants together, yielding the hybrid YeHoWaH, or Jehovah. In most modern English Bibles, including the New Revised Standard Version, the tetragrammaton is translated "LORD" in small capi-tals (to distinguish it from the Hebrew *'adonai* and Greek *kyrios*, "lord" or "Lord"). When it appears in combination with *'adonai* (*'adonai yhwh*, in which case the scribes used the vowels from *'elohim*, "God"), it is trans-lated "LORD GOD." *See also* Adonai and Jehovah.

THEODICY, the field of questions concerning the justice of God in a seemingly unjust world: why, if God is all-powerful and just, the wicked prosper and the good suffer; why there is meaningless or unjustifiable suf-fering in the world; and so forth. Questions of theodicy pervade biblical literature, but Job is the biblical epicenter.

THEOPHILUS, the addressee of the Gospel of Luke and its sequel, Acts. The name means "lover of God." It may have referred to an actual person (Jew or Gentile) or been a fictional addressee (i.e., anyone who loves God and wants to know more).

THESSALONIANS, 1 AND 2 (New Testament), two letters of Paul to the community at Thessalonica. The first is the earliest surviving Pauline letter (about 50 CE) and therefore the earliest text in the entire New Testament. Apparently the community was concerned that some of them had already died, before the Second Coming. The letter assures the com-munity that Christ will come very soon, and that, when he does, he will raise the dead first, and then the living. The second letter reflects a dif-ferent understanding of the Second Coming, leading many scholars to conclude that it is pseudonymous.

THOMAS, one of Jesus's twelve disciples, remembered in the Gospel of John for doubting the resurrection until he was able to touch Jesus's wounds with his own hands.

TIBERIUS, Caesar Augustus's stepson and the second Roman emperor (14–37 CE) who reigned during the time of Jesus.

TIMOTHY, 1 AND 2 (New Testament). *See* Pastoral Letters.

TITUS (New Testament). *See* Pastoral Letters.

TORAH (Hebrew, "teaching" or "law"), the name of the first five books of Hebrew Scriptures.

TOWER OF BABEL, a high tower that, according to Genesis 11:1–9, the earth's people, speaking one language and working together, plan to build to "make a name for themselves" and avoid being scattered throughout the land. Concerned (as at the end of Genesis 3) that they will become like gods, God confuses their language. No longer able to communicate, they abandon the tower and disperse across the face of the earth.

TRANSFIGURATION, the gospel story in which Jesus brings Peter, James, and John to a mountaintop where he is transfigured into an apparition of light clothed in dazzling white and is then joined by Moses (representing the law) and Elijah (representing the prophets). Peter enthusiastically offers to make a dwelling place for each of them.

TRANSJORDAN, the plateau region east of the Jordan River (i.e., "east bank"), now part of the country of Jordan. According to biblical tradition, Joshua gave it to the tribes of Gad, Reuben, and the half-tribe of Manasseh, but they never secured it.

TWELVE DISCIPLES, the twelve members of Jesus's "inner circle" of followers. There is some disagreement, however, about exactly who they were. Mark (3:16–19) and Matthew (10:1–5) list the following: Peter, his brother Andrew, James the son of Zebedee, his brother John, Philip, Bartholomew, Thomas, Matthew, James the son of Alphaeus, Thaddaeus, Simon the Cananaean, and Judas Iscariot. The Gospel of Luke replaces Thaddaeus with Jude. The Gospel of John does not list all twelve by name, but mentions one named Nathaniel and also refers to an unnamed one called the "beloved disciple" (traditionally identified with John).

TWELVE TRIBES, according to biblical legend, the territorial and familial groups descended from Jacob's twelve sons: Leah's sons Rueben, Simeon, Levi, Judah, Issachar, and Zebulun; Rachel's sons Benjamin and Joseph (later split into two half-tribes, Ephraim and Manasseh); Zilpah's sons Gad and Asher; and Bilhah's sons Dan and Naphtali.

VASHTI, the queen of Persia at the beginning of the story of Esther. When she refuses to be displayed as an object of group ogling, King Ahasuerus has her removed.

VIRGIN BIRTH, the biblical account (in Matthew and Luke only) of the birth of Jesus by an unwed virgin, Mary, who conceived by the Holy Spirit. There are other ancient stories of auspicious births by virgins.

VULGATE (Latin, "common"), a Latin Bible that does not refer so much to a specific text as to a biblical tradition. It was first translated from Hebrew, Greek, and Old Latin versions of Scripture by Jerome at the beginning of the fifth century. Jerome did not include the texts of the Apocrypha, because they appeared only in the Greek versions. After his death, however, they were added back into the canon. In the West, it was *the* canon of Scripture until the Reformation, when scholars began to challenge it based on their own translations from Hebrew and Greek.

WORD. *See* Logos.

YAHWEH, YHWH. *See* tetragrammaton.

YOM KIPPUR. *See* Day of Atonement.

ZECHARIAH (Hebrew Bible), one of the twelve Minor Prophets. The first part is similar to Haggai and focuses on rebuilding the Jerusalem Temple after the Babylonian exile. The second part (chaps. 9–14) incorporates sayings from a later period that envision the future reign of God's messiah.

ZEPHANIAH (Hebrew Bible), one of the twelve Minor Prophets. This collection opens with a vision of total annihilation, in which all life will be swept away in a scene of divine wrath. Its sayings date to the reign of Josiah, a reformer in Judah from 640 to 609 BCE.

ZILPAH, the maidservant of Leah with whom Jacob had two sons, Gad and Asher.

ZION, another name for Jerusalem, often used in biblical passages that personify the city as a mother or bride (e.g., Isaiah and Lamentations).

ZIPPORAH, Moses's Midianite wife, the daughter of the Midianite priest Jethro. Moses meets and marries her while on the run after killing an Egyptian slavemaster who was abusing a Hebrew slave.

Suggestions for Further Reading

BIBLES

The HarperCollins Study Bible. Revised Edition. San Francisco: HarperSanFrancisco, 2006.

The Jewish Study Bible. Featuring the Jewish Publication Society TANAKH Translation. New York: Oxford University Press, 2004.

The New Oxford Annotated Bible with Apocrypha. Augmented Third Edition. New York: Oxford University Press, 2007.

BOOKS ABOUT THE BIBLE

Alter, Robert. *The Art of Biblical Narrative*. New York: Basic Books, 1981.

———. *The Art of Biblical Poetry*. New York: Basic Books, 1985.

Beal, Timothy *The End of the Word as We Know It*. New York: Houghton Mifflin Harcourt, forthcoming.

———. *Religion and Its Monsters*. New York: Routledge, 2002.

Borg, Marcus J. *Reading the Bible Again for the First Time: Taking the Bible Seriously but Not Literally*. San Francisco: HarperSanFrancisco, 2001.

Brueggemann, Walter. *The Message of the Psalms*. Philadelphia: Fortress, 1985.

———. *The Prophetic Imagination*. Second Edition. Philadelphia: Fortress, 2001.

———. *Theology of the Old Testament: Testimony, Dispute, Advocacy*. Philadelphia: Fortress, 1997.

Crossan, John Dominic. *God and Empire: Jesus Against Rome, Then and Now*. San Francisco: HarperOne, 2007.

De Hamel, Christopher. *The Book: A History of the Bible*. London: Phaidon, 2006.

Ehrman, Bart D. *Misquoting Jesus: The Story Behind Who Changed the Bible and Why.* San Francisco: HarperOne, 2005.

Evans, Craig A., and Emanuel Tov, eds. *Exploring the Origins of the Bible: Canon Formation in Historical, Literary, and Theological Perspective.* Grand Rapids, MI: Baker, 2008.

Fewell, Danna Nolan, and David M. Gunn. *Gender, Power, and Promise: The Subject of the Bible's First Story.* Nashville, TN: Abingdon, 1992.

Fredriksen, Paula. *From Jesus to Christ: The Origins of the New Testament Images of Jesus.* New Haven, CT: Yale University Press, 1988.

Friedman, Richard Elliott. *Who Wrote the Bible?* San Francisco: HarperSanFrancisco, 1997.

Gunn, David M., and Danna Nolan Fewell. *Narrative in the Hebrew Bible.* New York: Oxford University Press, 1993.

Heschel, Abraham J. *The Prophets: An Introduction.* New York: Harper & Row, 1962.

Keefer, Kyle. *The New Testament as Literature: A Very Short Introduction.* New York: Oxford University Press, 2008.

Linafelt, Tod. *The Hebrew Bible as Literature: A Very Short Introduction.* New York: Oxford University Press, forthcoming.

McKenzie, Steven L., and Stephen R. Haynes, eds. *To Each Its Own Meaning: An Introduction to Biblical Criticisms and Their Application.* Revised Edition. Louisville, KY: Westminster John Knox, 1999.

Miles, Jack. *God: A Biography.* New York: Knopf, 1995.

Newsom, Carol A. *The Book of Job: A Contest of Moral Imaginations.* New York: Oxford University Press, 2009.

Trible, Phyllis. *God and the Rhetoric of Sexuality.* Philadelphia: Fortress, 1986.

BIBLE DICTIONARIES

Freedman, David Noel, ed. *The Anchor Bible Dictionary.* New York: Doubleday, 1992.

Hayes, John H., ed. *The Dictionary of Biblical Interpretation.* Nashville, TN: Abingdon, 1999.

Powell, Mark Allan, ed. *The HarperCollins Bible Dictionary, Condensed Edition.* San Francisco: HarperOne, 2009.

Acknowledgments

This book began in conversation with my editor, Michael Maudlin. That conversation continues, and the book is much better for it. Thanks, Mickey. Thanks also to my literary agent, Gail Ross, for taking care of business and keeping it fun and interesting. I am grateful to HarperOne production editor Lisa Zuniga and copyeditor Ann Moru for their super-smart, patient, efficient attention to every detail of the manuscript; and to Marlene Baer, who first approached me with the idea that soon morphed into the idea for this book; and to my teacher Walter Brueggemann, who recommended me to her. His abiding influence is evident throughout.

I have benefited tremendously from the insights, suggestions, and corrections of many friends and colleagues, especially Ed Gemerchak, Barry Hartz, Geraldine Beal (the most biblically literate person I know), and Tel Mac in Diaspora alumni Tod Linafelt, Kyle Keefer, and Brent Plate. Many thanks as well for the ready support of my department chair Peter Haas and my department administrators Sharon Skowronski and Lauren Gallitto.

I am especially grateful to the hundreds, maybe thousands, of students I've gotten to know in the various introductions to biblical literature I've taught since the inaugural run of "Dead Prophets Society" over fifteen years ago. You have made me believe ever more deeply in the power of these strangely fascinating stories to inspire new ways of seeing and thinking and being in the world. Seeing you come alive in relation to them, and being surprised by your fresh interpretations, is what I live for. Thanks especially to three recent students whose final papers influenced particular selections in this book: Charity McDonald (on Handel and Isaiah), Christine Louise Michalak (on the Byrds and Ecclesiastes 3), and Daniela Rojas (on *East of Eden* and Genesis 4).

I also want to acknowledge all those amazing biblical stories, poems, and other texts that I was not able to include. This book is like a "greatest hits" compilation tape. I hope it leaves you wanting to read more and go deeper.

Finally, and as ever, I am most grateful for the wise advice, critical attention, and steadfast encouragement of my best friend, colleague, and love of my life, Clover Reuter Beal, to whom I dedicate this book.

Index